Trattorias of Rome, Florence, and Venice

ALSO BY MAUREEN B. FANT

Dictionary of Italian Cuisine
(with Howard M. Isaacs)

Women's Life in Greece and Rome
(with Mary R. Lefkowitz)

Eat Like the Romans:
The Visitor's Food Guide

Trattorias of Rome, Florence, and Venice

A GUIDE TO CLASSIC EATING,

DRINKING, AND SNACKING

MAUREEN B. FANT

THE ECCO PRESS

An Imprint of HarperCollins*Publishers*

TRATTORIAS OF ROME, FLORENCE, AND VENICE: A GUIDE TO CLASSIC EATING, DRINKING, AND SNACKING. Copyright © 2001 by Maureen B. Fant. All rights reserved. Printed in the United States of America. No part of this book may be used or reproduced in any manner whatsoever without written permission except in the case of brief quotations embodied in critical articles and review. For information, address HarperCollins Publishers Inc., 10 East 53rd Street, New York, NY 10022.

HarperCollins books may be purchased for educational, business, or sales promotional use. For information please write: Special Markets Department, HarperCollins Publishers Inc., 10 East 53rd Street, New York, NY 10022.

FIRST EDITION

Designed by Cassandra J. Pappas

Library of Congress Cataloging-in-Publication Data
Fant, Maureen B.
    Trattorias of Rome, Florence, and Venice: A Guide to Classic Eating, Drinking, and Snacking / Maureen B. Fant.
        p. cm.
    ISBN 0-06-095687-9
    1. Restaurants—Italy—Rome—Guidebooks. 2. Restaurants—Italy—Florence—Guidebooks. 3. Restaurants—Italy—Venice—Guidebooks.
    I. Title.
    TX907.5.I8 F36 2000
    647.9545—dc21   00–050344

01 02 03 04 05 RRD 10 9 8 7 6 5 4 3 2 1

For Francesco

As this book goes to press, most European countries are in a swivet over so-called Mad Cow Disease (BSE), known in Italy as *mucca pazza* (mad cow). The European Commission is expected to rule soon on whether certain cuts of meat from animals old enough to have been exposed to infection should be banned from sale. Such a ruling would affect many traditional dishes described in this book, notably the *bistecca alla fiorentina*. It really would just mean we'd be eating more veal than beef for a few years. Stay tuned.

Contents

FLORENCE

VENICE

Acknowledgments and Apologia

LIKE MANY ITALIAN CITY DWELLERS, my companion, Francesco Filippi, and I have formed bonds with a handful of eating places on our usual beat, near the Colosseum. Otherwise, unless we are doing research, when we eat out it is for something new or special rather than seasonal local dishes, which we eat at home or in a couple of local trattorias. It is no longer true, if it ever was, that, if you avoid obvious tourist traps, it is impossible to get a bad meal. Locals, accordingly, choose their eateries conservatively and with care. Thus, when foreign visitors arrive and want to explore the local cuisine—as indeed we do when we travel—we have often found ourselves short of places outside our own neighborhood to which to take or send them. The Rome section of this book provides some. The Florence and Venice sections, on the other hand, are written from the point of view of a nonresident. They contain less inside information, fewer insiders' tips, but in compensation, the point of view is more that of the presumed reader, a food-loving visitor.

For all three cities, the selection is highly personal and reflects the intense research of some months added to the experience of more than twenty years' residence in the center of Rome. This was a commitment in time, money, and digestion that has limited the number I have been able to include. I hope that future editions will contain more. Please e-mail suggestions to me at ristoranti@libero.it. I will post the inevitable corrigenda et addenda on www.mbfant.com.

Some of the restaurants were visited in the context of research for articles I have written for the *New York Times* Travel section, mostly the "Choice Tables" feature. My debt to Nancy Newhouse, the travel editor, and her staff, especially, but not only, Janet Piorko, Marilyn Minden, and Florie Stickney, is great. Over the nearly ten years that they have allowed me to contribute to the section, not only have they encouraged me to believe that I am actually able to describe restaurants in some useful way but they have—through a passion for detail ("What were the chairs covered with?") and a relentless search for truth ("But what did it *taste* like?")—taught me what the reader has a right to ask and know. This book may not live up to their standards, but I hope they will enjoy it anyway.

My precious friend and colleague, Howard M. Isaacs, editor and publisher of *The Italian Traveler,* has taken me along on many of his research meals around Rome over the years. He has also generously not only not objected to my mining our joint *Dictionary of Italian Cuisine* for this book's glossary but even provided many helpful suggestions for handling it.

The books that helped me choose some of the restaurants are listed in the bibliography, but two deserve special mention: Faith Heller Willinger's *Eating in Italy* and the Slow Food Association's *Osterie d'Italia 2000.*

The list of friends who provided help in the form of tips, opinions, and table company began forming decades ago, but a few can be singled out for recent contributions. The incomparable Faith Willinger, with characteristic generosity and attention, suggested many places in her town, Florence, to include or omit. Tips for Venice came from Diane and Cesare Benelli, Christine and Roderick Conway Morris, Liz and Geoffrey Leckie, and Holly Snapp and Geoffrey Humphries. In Rome, the good sports included Judith Harris and David Willey, Joan Geller, Antonio Mallamo and Miriam Maiorino, Susan Adler, and many others.

Extra-special thanks go to friends who live in the United States but who provided tips and allowed themselves to be pressed into service during their all-too-brief visits to Italy in the past year: Gael Greene, Edward Kaim, Jim and Diana Zurer, John Bailey, and Judy Lewis and her family. Jim, who makes sure I miss nothing published in cyberspace on Italian dining, has become my Virgil of the Internet, and while we're out there, my friends in CompuServe's extraordinary Italian Forum are always generous with their tips and spot-on in their observations.

At Ecco I am obliged especially to Daniel Halpern and his kind and patient assistant, Patricia Fernandez. In Rome, during the home stretch in the preparation of the book, Lisa Aronsson provided good-humored and invaluable support in fact-checking, phone research and some table research, and many other tasks. Stefania Valente provided similar valuable assistance in the early stages.

My top table assistant—the one without whom this book could have been neither started nor completed—is Francesco Filippi, to whom it is dedicated.

Trattorias of Rome, Florence, and Venice

Quick Start

IF YOU DO NOT INTEND to read the introduction, here, in brief, is what you can expect to find in this book.

The book contains a personal selection of about one hundred eating and drinking places in central Rome, Florence, and Venice. The emphasis is on traditional food and drink, and the main type of establishment listed is the trattoria, though some wine bars, restaurants, and other types are included for various reasons. The organization is alphabetical within each city.

Each city section begins with a brief introduction to the local food scene and listing of principal classic local menu items. An extensive glossary of food terms at the end of the book provides additional information; most italicized terms are contained therein.

Each entry contains:

- the restaurant's complete address and phone number (don't forget to dial the area code even locally) and, where available, fax, e-mail, and website
- weekly closing day and, where possible, approximate vacation dates

- nearby landmarks and other geographical information
- credit card information
- type of establishment
- type of cuisine
- price range

For more on the listings, see page 17.

Introduction

THE TRATTORIA

As GENERALLY DEFINED, a trattoria is a small, informal, usually family-run establishment serving complete meals, which, until recent years, represented the traditional home cooking of a specific geographical area. The geographical scope may range from neighborhood to region (in the strict sense of one of the twenty political divisions of Italy). The establishment need not be located in the area whose food it serves (you can find Tuscan trattorias all over Italy), but it usually is.

The differences between the Italian trattoria and the Italian *ristorante* are mostly of degree. Both are sit-down eating places. In both groups, with some notable exceptions, the best ones tend to be small, family-run operations; in a trattoria, all hands may be related by blood or marriage, while a *ristorante* will probably have more hired help. Both may serve traditional local or regional cooking; and both may use starched white napkins and tablecloths. The *ristorante* may not always use stemware and porcelain, but it is usually fancier and more expensive. The *ristorante* is more likely to extend the boundaries of its menu beyond the traditional dishes of the immediate geographical area, though some *ristoranti*—such as those in Rome's Jewish quarter—specialize in the traditional dishes of a few city blocks, and the menus of some new trattorias are all over the map. A *ristorante* tends to draw its customers too from a wider geographical base. A trattoria serves primarily its immediate neighborhood, though an exception has to be made for those particularly good trattorias, their cover blown by Italian guidebooks, that draw gastronomic pilgrims from far and wide.

A trattoria is a refuge for hungry neighbors, who go there for their favorite dish and a chat with the owner. The true trattoria adopts a conservative cooking style. It is a repository of local home cooking, in part dishes its customers can just as well cook themselves at home, and in part the foods their grandmothers (actual or hypothetical) used to make but that nobody has the time for today. This makes the trattoria a place where, by partaking of a meal, one can partake of the shared experience of an Italian region, or town, or neighborhood, or family.

If, then, the hero of our story is the trattoria, understood as an informal, traditional place to sit down and be served a full meal whose gastronomic roots are in the local home cooking, here we meet the first of several paradoxes. A guide to trattorias should not by rights exist. If you were to follow the true spirit of the trattoria, you would make friends with the trattoria nearest where you live, or are staying, and always go there. Moving around town looking for a new trattoria is a modern phenomenon.

The true, or at least typical, trattoria exists for its regular customers and treats newcomers with diffidence. The good side of this is that it does not take much to become a regular—two or three meals in close succession should do the trick—and the sense of satisfaction is immense when you get that first confidential tip about what to order, or when the owner remembers what you like. Theoretically, you should look in the Yellow Pages, find a trattoria near you, ascertain that it meets certain minimum standards, and cultivate it. The menu will not differ much from that of the trattoria six blocks away, or across town, but you will eat better in your trattoria because it is yours. To an extent, that is not just theory, but it is truer today in the peripheral areas of the cities, where most people make their homes, than in the *centro storico,* where businesses, tourists, and impossible rents have forced families out.

Many Italians who look back on coming home from school to a hot lunch prepared by their Mamma remember their youthful exasperation at eating the same meal day in, day out. And so it is in the true trattoria. The repertoire is small, the menu finite. You go there for comfort, not for thrills. I probably shouldn't say this, but you might get bored. So, if you are spending several days in Italy and plan to eat out, you have three choices, all equally "authentic." Many Italians use each approach at different times.

The conservative approach consists of developing a relationship with a trattoria by returning repeatedly and letting your gastronomic adventures run the gamut from, say, *spaghetti alla carbonara* to *bucatini all'amatriciana,* or from *ribollita* to *pappa al pomodoro,* or from *fegato alla veneziana* to, well, *fegato alla veneziana.* You will probably save money and enjoy an illusion of the so-called real Italy, assuming it exists. Not all Italians are gourmets; many go out to a trattoria, or pizzeria, *per stare insieme*—"to be together"—with friends or relatives, with absolute quality far less important than a *simpatico* setting and a democratic price.

The more aggressive approach requires comparative analysis of Italian and English-language guidebooks, advice from local friends, and a fair amount of experimentation to choose places that, you hope, offer not just traditional food but the definitive version—that elusive taste somebody's great-grandmother, who never left the kitchen except to go to church, may once have achieved.

The third approach to eating out pretty much shuns tradition altogether and seeks the new. It tends to be the choice of those locals who regard trattorias as providing poor imitations of the food they prepare at home.

Discriminating foreign visitors will probably choose a modified conservative approach and will be happy to settle for the restaurant version of grandmother food. This is why so many good traditional restaurants sometimes seem full of foreigners. But for visiting foreigners, who quite rightly want the true tastes of Italy—grandmother food— the conservative approach has more appeal than it does for local foodies, who undoubtedly make better *carbonara* at home than they can get in a trattoria. Such locals eat out when they want something different, maybe even international or at least interregional—not grandmother food.

TYPES OF EATING PLACES AND FOOD SERVICE

Here follows a brief summary of the many kinds of eating and drinking places in Italy. Bear in mind that the categories can overlap, and the definitions are not hard and fast.

Ristorante Generically, a restaurant; the term is usually used for places aiming, with varying degrees of success, at a certain tone, but a *ristorante* can still be quite casual. Everyday speech draws a distinction between *ristorante* and *trattoria* ("How did you like that new place?" "It's pretty good for a trattoria"). In this book, the English word *restaurant* is used generically for any sort of eating place, while the Italian *ristorante* refers to the Italian concept of something a little fancier than what prevailing community standards recognize as a trattoria. The *ristorante* may be large, with a varied menu and professional staff. It can also be tiny and family-run, but elegant. *Ristoranti* may specialize in local cooking, or classic Italian cooking, or highly innovative Italian cooking, or anything they want in any combination.

Trattoria An informal restaurant specializing in home-style cooking, ideally of the labor-intensive sort that nobody has made at home for decades. In reality, the term

covers a wide range of price and quality and is sometimes allowed to remain part of an establishment's name
long after said establishment has evolved into a very
upmarket *ristorante*. Although most specialize in the local
food, homely establishments sometimes offer the food of
another area or region without losing their trattoria status. I would concede the name "trattoria" less willingly
to the large and growing category of casual restaurants
operated by enterprising young people who attempt to
reinvent the wheel, fix the unbroken, and generally forget
the lessons of their grandmothers. When they do this
expensively, their places can be called *ristoranti*. These
tend sometimes—through a preponderance of flans and
puddings—to give the impression that they just unpacked
their food processors. They often ape the top creative
restaurants but have neither the experience nor the money
to match their ambition. Many very modern trattorias,
especially in Florence, use rustic décor to affect an air of
venerability.

Osteria Etymologically, this is any place with an *oste*,
host, meaning landlord, innkeeper, publican, or the like.
Traditionally, this was the place where the neighborhood
men would gather for conversation, card games, and wine
poured into carafes from a barrel. Food was of secondary
importance; often the customers brought their own (this
is the origin of the "bread and cover" charge still in use
today). *Osterie* still exist in nearly their original form, but
most have evolved into trattorias (where you have wine
with your food rather than food with your wine) or wine
bars, where you order from an extensive list of boutique
producers. The Slow Food Association, dedicated to the
discovery and preservation of traditional food and wine,
calls its guidebook to traditional regional eating and drinking places *Osterie d'Italia*. Within the book, it distinguishes
between *trattoria* and *osteria,* and between *osteria tradizionale,* for places that have been in business for generations, and *osteria di fondazione recente,* for new ones. In any

case, the word *osteria* in a restaurant name, or its variant spellings, such as *hostaria,* cannot alone convey what the establishment is like.

Trattoria-pizzeria A normal trattoria that also serves pizza in addition to the regular menu (usually only in the evening, though this is changing).

Pizzeria A restaurant serving primarily made-to-order pizza (either thick-crust Neapolitan or thin-crust Roman) and its standard accompaniments—*supplì, filetti di baccalà, bruschetta,* and a few others. The best *pizzerie* have wood-burning ovens. The pizzeria is open only in the evening, while the *pizza al taglio* (q.v.) is usually open from mid-morning to mid-afternoon.

Tavola calda Literally, hot (i.e., steam) table. It is an eating place offering prepared dishes—pastas, meat or fish, and vegetables—cafeteria-style or to take out, or both. If roasted meats, such as chicken on a spit, are also available, the designation *rosticceria* is added.

Pizza al taglio Usually a storefront where pizza made in rectangular pans, or, without a pan, in long ellipses, is kept at a counter to be sliced and sold (by weight). These shops tend to be open from mid-morning to late afternoon.

Wine bar The English term is used in Italian to indicate a modern-style *osteria* (q.v.). Typically there is a long and wide-ranging wine list, including a number of wines available by the glass. Food options range from a choice of expensive salamis, cheeses, and salads to a few hot dishes and desserts. The menu almost always looks as though the ingredients have been ordered from a catalogue of fashionable gourmet items.

Bar Typically the term refers to a coffee bar. In its minimum configuration, espresso and all its variations, as well as soft and alcoholic drinks, are served at a counter where clients stand. There is always something available to chew as well, such as a sandwich or a pastry. To these bare bones may be added tables (with higher prices than counter service) and a wider variety of food, including hot meals from a steam table (*tavola calda*, q.v.). The bar is an essential part of every neighborhood.

Hostaria This and other variations on the word *osteria* (q.v.) are virtually meaningless in Italian. They are archaic holdovers used in the names of restaurants at all points in the scale of elegance.

Gastronomia The word means gastronomy, but it is also used for the entire category of what might roughly be considered elaborate bar food—that is, more than nibbles but less than meals. A good assortment of ready-made sandwiches, pizzas, and fried items is usually meant.

Mescita The verb *mescere* means to pour wine, and it is used today for the service of wine by the glass as well as by carafe and bottle.

Bottiglieria A wine bar before the term was invented. Until the explosion on the scene of the expression and concept of the modern wine bar, upmarket urban dwellers used to go out in the evening to places serving good wines and light meals, and they called them *bottiglierie* (bottleries). Now that there is an English term to describe the place, the Italian word has reverted to its original meaning—a wine shop where house wine can be drunk by the glass or carafe.

Vineria In Florence, essentially a *bottiglieria* (q.v.).

Bacaro A Venetian *bottiglieria* (q.v.). These are one of the delights of the Venetian scene—old wood-paneled wine shops where a variety of wines are available by the glass (the glass has a special shape and name, *ombra* or *ombreta*) and delightful snacks, known collectively as *cicheti,* are sold by the piece or small portion.

Gelateria   Ice cream shop. It may be part of a bar or stand alone. The units of ice cream are *coppette* (or *bicchierini*), cups, and *coni,* cones; each comes in two or three sizes and holds up to three flavors. You are always offered whipped cream (*panna*) on top.

ETIQUETTE AND RULES:
EATING LIKE THE ROMANS

You think you've been eating Italian food all your life, and now you find out that not only have you not been eating Italian food, you have been eating it wrong. Here are some prohibitions and some suggestions.

Make It Black   Never ask for a cappuccino after a meal. Restaurants are by now so used to foreigners and their cappuccino obsession that many even list it on the menu. You may be sure they do not expect serious eaters actually to order it. Do, however, ask for a cappuccino for breakfast in your hotel. There is sometimes an extra charge, since it comes from the bar rather than the kitchen, but it's usually worth it to avoid hotel breakfast coffee. The best breakfast—cappuccino's moment of glory—is first thing in the morning in a bar accompanied by a *cornetto,* croissant. After meals, you ask for *un caffè* or *un espresso* (not "expresso"), and expect it to arrive *after* dessert.

Block That Cheese   Never ask for Parmigiano with fish-based sauce or those that contain garlic or hot pepper. If you are not served cheese when you think you ought to have it, don't demand it, but ask whether cheese goes with the dish (*"Scusi, ma il parmigiano sta bene con questo piatto o no?"*).

Put Down That Spoon The only utensil you should touch pasta with is a fork, never a knife (except in large formats, such as *lasagne al forno*), and, contrary to a widespread belief, not even a spoon, unless, of course, the pasta is in soup. The table is set with spoons in expectation of soup. And by the way, you never have soup and pasta in the same meal except in a *menù degustazione*.

Watch the Water Water is not mixed with wine except if the wine is *vino sfuso* (served in a carafe) and is awful. Rather than dilute a wine you can't stand, it is more usual to ask for a bottle instead. *Acqua minerale* comes in three basic styles of fizz: completely flat (*liscia*, or *non gassata*, such as Fiuggi and Panna); heavily fizzy (*gassata* or *gasata*, such as San Pellegrino); and slightly fizzy (*effervescente naturale*, such as Ferrarelle or Nepi). The heavy fizzers have usually had gas added. If you ask for *naturale*, which many people do, don't expect every brand of water to be perfectly still; there may be a very, very slight completely natural fizz. I have seen tourists get very exercised over this barely perceptible effervescence to the point where the exasperated waiter, who didn't have another brand to offer, just filled a bottle with tap water. Which reminds me: Italians drink *acqua minerale* because they like it; the tap water is fine.

Bibs Are for Bambini But to avoid tomato splatters, gentlemen without neckties (if that is not an oxymoron) may tuck their napkins into their shirts. Those who would like to act more refined but do not feel refined enough to eat without making a mess may press their napkin against their bosom with the palm of their left hand (if right-handed) when they lift their fork. Everyone would be well advised to do this when eating *spaghetti alle vongole* (insidious tiny oil splatters) or *bucatini all'amatriciana* (globs of tomato sauce catapulted by the spring action of the long, thick pasta). Do lean over the plate, though keeping the face a decent distance away from it and making a show of interest in the conversation without staring at your companions as they shovel it in. If you are wearing a white silk blouse, or tend to be slow or awkward with spaghetti, the better part of valor is to order a *pasta corta* (a short pasta such as penne or rigatoni), a stuffed pasta (e.g., *ravioli*), or, easiest of all, *risotto*. Should you splatter after all, ask the waiter for the Borotalco, a brand of talcum powder. This is considered the best first aid for shirts and ties, and you need have no embarrassment whatsoever about asking for it.

Don't Play with Your Food Eat one food at a time. You can have a meal of just pasta and salad, but the salad is the second course. If you are served several foods simultaneously—such as tasting portions of two or three pastas—do not skip back and forth. Eat the most delicately flavored item first, then move on to the next most delicate item, ending with the strongest flavors. The same holds for cheese plates. A good restaurant will place cheese on your plate in order; work clockwise from twelve o'clock.

THE GASTRONOMIC DAY

Convinced that skipping breakfast at home is a good way to save calories, or that *caffelatte* and *biscotti* make a nutritious way to start the day—you wanted to know about the Mediterranean diet?—starving workers throng the cities' bars at mid-morning for cappuccino and *cornetti* or, a little later, for *pizzette* or various sorts of sandwiches.

The fortunate ones who can still go home for lunch may join the whole family for pasta, a *secondo piatto,* and fresh fruit at about 2 P.M. And although today many working people settle for sandwiches or a single course in a *tavola calda* or trattoria near the office, a number of trattorias are open only at lunchtime, reflecting their traditional role of providing a substitute for home cooking. If the three- or four-course meal was not consumed at lunch, then dinner can be a full-blown evening-long affair.

For a light evening meal, the traditional choice is a pizza, while modern times have brought wine bars and various other alternative restaurants, which offer plates of cheeses or salamis, and where you can order just one thing, be it savory or sweet.

In Florence and Venice, where the influence of mass tourism is even greater than in Rome, this structure is more elastic.

COOKING STYLES

Here follows a gross oversimplification of some of the major generic culinary tags used in the listings.

Cucina casareccia or *casalinga* Home cooking—what a reasonably competent home cook might, if so inclined, make today in the same locality.

Cucina regionale The traditional cooking and ingredients of a particular region, including foods that might be ambitious for a home cook. Region here refers to the twenty *regioni* (e.g., Lazio, Toscana, Veneto) into which Italy is divided.

Cucina tradizionale More or less the same as *cucina regionale,* though the catchment area might be narrower than regional.

Cucina creativa Modern cooking, often of a high level, that invents new dishes and combines ingredients in new ways. There is usually no regional orientation (or only a slight one deriving from the use of local ingredients), but the traditional structure of the Italian meal is respected.

Gourmet Traditional or innovative high-level cooking with ambience and wine list to match.

A WORD TO THE WISE

Here is a miscellany of advice for trattoria self-defense.

Sunday Evening When you fear you hear only English, French, and German, relax. Although many restaurants perform a public service by remaining open on Sunday evening, you should not expect to see many Italians dining. Because most of them have had a huge lunch with the family, on Sunday evening they eat lightly; this means pizza, which is why pizzerias are crowded on Sunday evening and *ristoranti* contain a disproportionate number of foreigners.

Wandering Minstrels, Vendors, and Other Intrusions And a rose by any other name is a pain in the neck. Trattorias are particularly subject to invasion by vendors of roses or Oriental baubles. It is customary to shoo them gently away. Wandering "musicians" are customarily suffered, then tipped (L. 1,000 or more, but there is no obligation) in such a way as not to encourage an encore.

Smoking By the time you read this, there may be a law against smoking in restaurants in Italy. It is fairly certain not to be enforced or even enforceable. At present, many restaurants with multiple dining rooms, one of which could easily be dedicated to nonsmokers, do not create a nonsmoking section, though many Italians would choose it. You may just have to lump it.

Order Conservatively It should become apparent from the descriptions of the restaurants listed in this book what are the traditional, classic dishes of the three cities. Even in the trattorias listed here, you will do best ordering only the local cuisine no matter what else is offered (and you will be rewarded for a little preliminary reading on the subject). If you have to eat in a place not recommended by any reliable authority, there is even more reason to order conservatively. And be suspicious of extra-long menus. Many establishments—*horribile dictu*—use so-called *precotti*, precooked foods. Pasta with tomato sauce (*pomodoro*) or butter and Parmesan (*burro e parmigiano*) and grilled meats are usually safe.

Fish   Italians like fish, and even parts of Italy that never used to see fresh seafood are now regularly supplied. The usual preparation is simply grilled or baked, with potatoes and sometimes some tomatoes. Waiters are all expert at stripping a fish from the bone and will usually do the job for you, but in a very modest place, you might be expected to fillet a small (one-person) fish yourself, and in fact Italians don't bat an eyelash at heads and tails. It's a useful skill to acquire. Another issue is that for some years, Britain and the United States have been crazy for half-cooked fish, a state which they call by a number of names, such as "seared" or "rare." The same people are appalled to find that Italians eat their fish "overcooked." Well, there are two things to say about that: (1) when in Rome, do as the Romans do; (2) do not confuse "cooking" with "overcooking." Properly cooked Italian fish is cooked through. That is not overcooked, and it is the culture. If the fish is dry or burned, you can blame the cook, but not the culture. In general, Italians feel fish should be either uncooked, which includes really raw (*carpaccio* or sushi), smoked (*affumicato*), or marinated (*marinato*), or else cooked through. Note that elaborate fish dishes with sauces are almost exclusively the province of fancy restaurants. Everywhere else the choice is baked, boiled, or grilled and the flavorings lemon and olive oil. And that's plenty.

Vegetarians, Picky Eaters, and Other Problems   It can happen that you're recovering from a stomachache, you are following a special diet, you have allergies, you don't trust a place, or you just don't like anything on the menu. Any trattoria or restaurant should be able to serve you some plain boiled rice (the Italian cure-all for whatever ails you), *spaghetti aglio e olio, spaghetti con pomodoro,* some boiled greens (*verdura lessa*), or a grilled steak or chop.

Reservations, telephones, and *telefonini*   With a few exceptions (noted in the text), Italian restaurants do not require reservations more than a day or two in advance. This is mostly because Italians do not like to commit themselves too early to spending an evening one way or another, with the exception of First Communions and weddings—to which, unless you are a guest, you will want to give a wide berth on grounds that other people's conviviality is fine for them. Please don't upset the equilibrium by sending faxes three months ahead.

The world laughs at the Italian use of *telefonini* (cellular phones) as though (in the eyes of the world) it were a fashion item. Nothing of the sort: it is a necessity of urban life owing to the dearth and unreliability of public telephones. If you are staying in Italy for more than a few days, you should consider procuring one, and program it immediately with the numbers of the restaurants you think you might like to try, as well as several radio taxi numbers. You can thus call ahead to make sure there is a table, and call again when you find it takes you twice as long to get there as you expected.

Wine Service   The restaurants in this book marked with a ➤ symbol can be trusted to make an effort at serving wines properly, but in the average trattoria, don't expect cork sniffing, tasting, or even stemmed glasses. Wine is generally not available by the glass, except in wine bars, the smallest unit being instead the *quartino,* or quarterliter carafe, considered the correct amount for one person. Long or short, the wine list is unlikely to have anything but Italian wines, except in places marked with the ➤.

Italian Dressing   Salads are dressed with olive oil and salt and usually vinegar, though sometimes lemon, or sometimes just with oil. Salads may be brought to the table dressed, but sometimes arrive nude for the diner to dress. There is no other kind of salad dressing. Salads containing tomatoes do not usually have vinegar because the tomatoes are considered sufficiently acidic on their own.

Dining al **Fresco** It seems very Italian to eat outdoors, people-watching or gazing at a monument. But look again. Many restaurants offer outdoor tables only on the sidewalk, or even in the street itself, with inadequate protection from sun, traffic fumes, noise, and bag snatchers. Don't automatically choose to sit outside—you'll notice the Italians don't.

Your Bag Don't hang it on the back of your chair.

Language Not all Italians, even in the restaurant business in major cities, speak English, though Florence and Venice are better than Rome in this respect. Most English translations of menus are incomprehensible or incomplete. Leave your dignity at home and be ready to try whatever it takes to understand and be understood. And take heart that people in Italy—including restaurateurs, waiters, and other customers—are always willing to help.

WHAT THE LISTINGS CONTAIN

This book was conceived as a guide to the trattorias and wine bars of the historic centers of Rome, Florence, and Venice, three major cities and favorite tourist destinations. (Rome, with a population of more than three million, has the largest representation. It is also where I live.) The geographic parameters have been respected, but during the course of research, my criteria for inclusion of eateries expanded to include some elegant restaurants that in one way or another have a trattoria at heart or in their past and some lesser places, such as ice cream bars, that are too good not to point out. I have left out super-elegant restaurants of international or highly creative orientation, including the great hotel restaurants, and more modest establishments that aim at a creative cuisine rather than at a traditional one.

In addition to trattorias, I've included a few elegant restaurants or modern casual restaurants that are particularly respectful of the local food and/or wine, as well as some establishments offering primarily drinks or snacks rather than full meals. I omitted many excellent establishments either because they are more innovative than traditional or because I've not managed to go there yet. Some trattorias included specialize in the food of regions other than the one in which they are located. There are, of course, no foreign restaurants.

The geographic limitations are the city centers: Rome and Florence inside or within walking distance of the city walls (even where the walls no longer exist); Venice, the city itself, not including the islands of the lagoon (except one on Giudecca) or the Lido. With a very few exceptions, every establishment listed offers the visitor a portal into the shared gastronomic experience, and with it the social history, of the historical center of its city.

The listing for each establishment is as comprehensive as I could make it. The name of the restaurant is, in most cases, given as it is printed on the restaurant's business card; the telephone directory, your receipt, and the door may show other names. The ratings are an overall assessment of the total experience: food, service, and ambience. Ratings are relative only within the establishment's own category (for example, a top wine bar and top restaurant would have the same score). The rating symbols are: 🏛 for Rome, ⚜ for Florence, and 🦁 for Venice.

🏛🏛🏛🏛🏛 The establishment aims high and hits the mark.

🏛🏛🏛🏛 An excellent place of its kind, but less (often much less) ambitious than 🏛🏛🏛🏛🏛.

🏛🏛🏛 A modest place that does a great job as far as it goes.

🏛🏛 Go there if you're hungry and in the neighborhood, but don't go out of your way. In some cases this is a negative judgment; in some cases it just reflects the reality that every neighborhood has similar places just as good as this one.

🏛 As for 🏛🏛, only more so.

The symbol ✎ indicates that the establishment deserves mention for the special attention it pays to wine, which is not a normal trattoria trait. Other information includes:

- what the establishment is (e.g., trattoria, wine bar)
- the type of cuisine it serves; if this is in quotation marks, it is the establishment's own claim; otherwise, the words are mine
- the street address
- additional information to help pinpoint the location, such as you might show to a taxi driver or someone of whom you are asking directions
- the postal code, which places the street at a glance in a given part of the city
- ☎ the telephone number and 📠 fax (if any). Dial the area code even locally, and use the zero for international calls. If you lose the number, you may never find it again except in another guidebook, since many restaurants are listed in the local phone book under a name other than the one by which they are known.
- the E-mail and website, if any
- Ⓜ 🚤 the nearest metro or *vaporetto* stop, if any
- 📷 the nearest landmark or monument of tourist interest, the place you might visit in connection with the restaurant
- ∅ the day of weekly closing (*riposo settimanale*) and, if consistent from year to year, approximate vacation dates, though these may vary and should be double-checked
- ⏱ the hours the restaurant claims to be open, if they differ greatly from the norm, though be warned: nothing

obliges a restaurant to stay open late if all the customers have left
- whether there are outdoor tables, and whether these are in the middle of the street or in a nice garden (see page 17)
- ♿ whether there is wheelchair access
- whether reservations are suggested, advised, or a must (reservations are irrelevant to bars and similar places)
- approximate price of a meal according to the scale below
- [VISA] [MasterCard] [Diners Club] [▬] the credit cards the restaurant claims to accept, if any, as of July 2000; here too you had best ask when you phone for a reservation

The review itself contains my completely subjective remarks about the place and some menu specialties.

Prices are indicated with the euro symbol and may be converted to lire with the help of the table below. They are intended only as a guide and are per person for a full meal with house or low-end wine. Establishments that do not serve full meals, or where you will probably drink or snack rather than dine, are automatically given the lowest price rating. Be aware that the choice of fish or an expensive wine or even the addition of an extra *contorno* (vegetable) can boost the cost from one category to another. Also, the more elegant the restaurant, the more courses you will probably eat. For example, in Rome, antipasto and dessert are usually the least interesting course in a trattoria and are often skipped, but they may well be the most interesting in a restaurant with a skilled creative chef.

€€€€	more than L. 100,000	(€52)
€€€	L. 70,000 to 100,000	(€37–51)
€€	L. 40,000 to 70,000	(€21–36)
€	under L. 40,000	(€20)

L. 1,000 = €0.52; €1.00 = L. 1936.27. These exchange rates are permanent and do not fluctuate. The euro will definitely replace the lira in January 2002.

Rome

Eating in Rome

THE GASTRONOMIC PILLARS of Rome are deep-frying and the *quinto quarto* (literally, "fifth quarter," as variety meats are known in Rome). The Eternal City can also claim a native pizza tradition (thin-crusted) and superb locally grown vegetables—led by the artichoke, except in summer, when eggplants, peppers, green beans, and zucchini reign about equally. Roman food can be very, very delicious, but that is not widely recognized in the rest of Italy, or in English-speaking countries, where Tuscany is taken as the measure of all things cultural and gastronomic. Eat a properly cooked *carciofo alla romana* with its melding of four flavors—artichoke, *mentuccia* (pennyroyal, a mint-like herb), garlic, and olive oil—or *saltimbocca alla romana,* flavorful scallops of veal, to which thinly sliced prosciutto and fresh sage leaves have been attached, cooked in white wine. For dessert, try a slice of *torta di ricotta*—a smooth purée of ricotta cheese in a tender piecrust. Accept no nonsense: Roman food is wonderful.

Unfortunately, the Roman trattoria cannot often be counted on to do justice to the city's culinary heritage. Most trattoria food is cooked quickly and simply. The fact itself of taking the trouble to prepare a labor-intensive slow-cooked traditional specialty like *coda alla vaccinara* (oxtail braised in tomato sauce) raises an establishment's status to above average.

Also, with notable exceptions, the restaurant scene, like Rome itself, lacks polish. You will do well to be suspicious of too much attention to décor and nice manners. In fact, there is absolutely no way to tell by a restaurant's appearance what its food will be like. But do not count on receiving a warm welcome, friendly service, or comfortable surroundings at a Roman trattoria.

Most of the restaurants listed are upscale trattorias, in the middle socioeconomic range. Nowadays, cheap neighborhood places tend to be outside the center, where more families live, and in any case, they are best for their own neighbors. Today the pizzeria is the place where Romans gather to make noise and *stare insieme,* pass the time together, but even pizzerias are disappearing, or rather being converted to Chinese restaurants, most of dubious quality. The collection offered here also includes a handful of top restaurants, those that have a trattoria in their past or in their spirit somewhere. A few gelaterias and *pizza al taglio* places are listed too, since they are also part of the local scene.

PRACTICAL MATTERS

Lunch usually begins at about 1:30 P.M., often later, though, increasingly, also earlier for foreigners and working people. Dinner begins between 8:30 and 9:30 P.M., though it is almost always possible to start at 8, and sometimes even 7:30—if you don't mind eating with mostly foreigners. Despite the late start, however, don't expect to be welcomed much after 10 P.M. Sit-down restaurants, plain or fancy, expect you to eat a full meal, though not necessarily a large one, and will voice their displeasure if you don't order at least two courses. Go to a bar, *tavola calda,* or wine bar if you need a meal outside regular mealtimes or want to eat just a salad or a plate of pasta.

Most of the establishments listed are well within the Aurelian walls, or at least within walking distance of major monuments. I have not given bus numbers, as they are subject to change. Rome has two subway (Metropolitana) lines, A and B, which intersect at Termini, the main railroad station. In the few cases where a Metropolitana stop is useful, it is given with the restaurant's address. Get a detailed map (I love the Falk series with its nifty cuts and folds) and keep it handy, and plan to do a good deal of walking. Taxis can be flagged down or telephoned (063570, 064994, 066645, and numerous others); there are also taxi stands throughout the city, including those at Piazza di Spagna, Largo Argentina, and the Colosseum, and two on Viale Trastevere (at Piazza Belli and Piazza Mastai).

The Rome Menu

THE LIST THAT FOLLOWS contains common items on Rome menus. They are defined in the Glossary, where additional dishes and terms are also listed. In Rome's trattorias, the antipasto course is often skipped; the most important course is unofficially the pasta, at which Rome excels, including hearty pasta-and-legume soups. If you don't want meat or fish, you can have a vegetable as your main course, such as a *carciofo alla romana* (or two); another meatless main dish is *scamorza,* a pear-shaped fresh cheese that is melted on the grill. Salads or vegetable side dishes are usually served with the meat but often eaten afterward. They can also be ordered after the meat course.

Dessert is not highly evolved in Rome. Despite a number of traditional caloric favorites, such as *zuppa inglese,* fresh fruit remains popular, and pineapple has inexplicably replaced native species in trattorias. Ice cream served in trattorias and pizzerias tends to be commercial, and you can be sure all that crème brûlée is not homemade. Cakes, however, may be, as may crème caramel, a standard.

ANTIPASTO

gratin of zucchini, eggplant, and sweet peppers
(a rudimentary plate of grilled vegetables adorned
with bread crumbs, parsley, and possibly garlic)
marinated eggplant and zucchini (oily, tasty chunks of eggplant and slices of zucchini, fried first, then marinated)
antipasto all'italiana (prosciutto and salami with an
artichoke heart and a few olives)
prosciutto e melone or *fichi* (prosciutto with melon slices or
peeled fresh figs, both in summer)
alici marinate (fresh anchovies marinated in vinegar or
lemon juice and not to be confused with what comes
out of a jar)
bresaola (thin-sliced air-cured beef, really a northern
specialty but used on Roman Jewish tables as a
prosciutto substitute; served with lemon and olive oil
and often *rughetta*)
deep-fried *fiori di zucca* (squash blossoms usually filled
with mozzarella and anchovies), *filetti di baccalà* (fillets
of salt cod), *crocchette* (potato croquettes), *supplì al
telefono* (rice croquettes)
insalata di mare (boiled mixed seafood, including a large
proportion of squid, dressed with olive oil and lemon
or vinegar; it is likely to be made on the premises only
in good restaurants, not modest trattorias or pizzerias)
bruschetta (toasted chewy bread rubbed with garlic and
drizzled with olive oil, possibly with additional
toppings, principally raw tomatoes)
frittata (a type of unfolded omelet usually filled with
vegetables)
fave con pecorino (in spring, raw fava beans are served in
their pods with chunks of *pecorino romano* cheese)

PRIMO

agnolotti (meat-filled ravioli)
brodo (meat broth with something in it, usually a small pasta)

cannelloni (pasta tubes filled with either ground meat or
ricotta and spinach; they usually come with béchamel
and tomato sauce)

fettuccine al ragù, al pomodoro or *ai funghi porcini* (egg
noodles with tomatoey meat sauce or meatless tomato
sauce or with olive oil and *porcini* mushrooms,
probably frozen except at good places in season)

gnocchi (potato flour dumplings served, traditionally, on
Thursday, with meat or tomato sauce)

lasagne al forno

minestrone or *zuppa di verdura* (vegetable soup)

pasta al burro e parmigiano (plain pasta, best if an egg pasta,
with only butter and Parmesan; this is one of the
dishes you can always ask for in a trattoria, whether or
not it is on the menu)

pasta con broccoli in brodo di arzilla (tomatoey skate broth
with pieces of broccoflower and broken spaghetti)

pasta e ceci, lenticchie, or *fagioli* (very hearty pasta and
legume soups)

penne all'arrabbiata (short pasta with tomato sauce
flavored only with garlic, hot pepper, and parsley;
this is actually one of the lighter pastas, if you're
planning a substantial main course)

pomodoro e riso (a large tomato filled with cooked rice,
served in summer; the portion can be one tomato
or two)

ravioli (filled with ricotta and spinach, sauced with either
pomodoro or *burro e salvia,* butter and fresh sage leaves)

rigatoni con la paiata (pasta with the intestine of milk-fed
calves. Order it only in one of the places where it is recommended in this book; when it's bad it's disgusting)

spaghetti con aglio, olio, e peperoncino (with olive oil, garlic,
and hot pepper; this is one of the dishes you can always
ask for in a trattoria, whether or not it is on the menu)

spaghetti con pomodoro e basilico (light, fresh tomato sauce
with garlic and fresh basil, in summer)

spaghetti or *bucatini* (occasionally *rigatoni*) *all'amatriciana,
alla carbonara, alla gricia* (made with the *guanciale,* cured

pork jowl, three ways: with tomatoes, with egg, with
just pecorino cheese)
stracciatella alla romana (egg-drop soup)
tonnarelli cacio e pepe (square-cut spaghetti with lots of
pecorino and black pepper)

SECONDO

abbacchio a scottadito (grilled baby lamb chops)
abbacchio arrosto (roast lamb. Order this and other roasts
with caution—ask whether they're fresh from the
oven; your concern will earn you respect)
coda alla vaccinara (oxtail cooked for hours in a rich
tomato and celery sauce)
coratella coi carciofi (organ meats with artichokes)
fagioli con le cotiche (beans, usually *cannellini,* cooked with
tomatoes and pork rinds)
fave al guanciale (fresh fava beans cooked with cured pork
jowl; in spring)
fritto misto (Always ask what it contains. If it's not
called *vegetariano,* it probably contains brains; if it is
vegetariano, it probably contains mozzarella)
garofolato (beef pot roast with strong clove flavor)
grigliata mista di pesce (mixed grill of fish, but smart eaters
usually choose a single item)
insalata caprese (sliced mozzarella and tomatoes with olive
oil and basil, a summer favorite, but don't expect the
finest *mozzarella di bufala* in a modest place)
involtini (usually, rolled slices of beef stewed in tomato
sauce)
lombata, braciola, bistecca alla brace (grilled steaks and chops)
lumache alla romana (land snails cooked in tomato sauce
with mint)
melanzane alla parmigiana (eggplant baked in layers with
cheese and tomato sauce; available year-round, but
summer is its season)
mozzarella in carrozza (mozzarella sandwiches egg-dipped
and fried)

pesce or *baccalà in guazzetto* (fresh fish or salt cod baked with a light tomato sauce)

pesce, all'acquapazza, al forno con patate, alla griglia (fresh fish baked with a light tomato sauce, or with potatoes, or grilled)

pollo alla romana con i peperoni (cut-up chicken pot-roasted with sweet peppers and flavored with marjoram)

pollo, abbacchio, or *coniglio alla cacciatora* (chicken, lamb, or rabbit stewed with vinegar and rosemary)

polpette or *polpettine, fritte* or *in sugo* (meatballs served fried and sauceless or in tomato sauce; if the latter, be sure to ask for *purè*, mashed potatoes)

polpettone (meat loaf)

porchetta (herb-roasted pork; usually more picnic or snack food than table food)

saltimbocca alla romana (veal scallops with prosciutto and sage)

scallopine in vino bianco (veal scallops cooked in white wine)

scamorza alla griglia (a grilled white cheese)

scampi or *mazzancolle alla griglia* (grilled prawns or shrimp)

seppie con i piselli (cuttlefish stewed with peas)

spezzatino, bocconcini di vitello (veal stew)

stufato, stufatino (stew)

trippa alla romana (tripe in tomato sauce with mint)

vitello arrosto (roast veal, usually served with roast potatoes)

vitello tonnato, vitel tonné (cold roast veal with a tuna-caper sauce)

CONTORNO

agretti (a peculiar green vegetable served with lemon and olive oil, in spring)

broccoletti or *cicoria, all'agro* or *in padella* (broccoli rabe or chicory, boiled and served with lemon and olive oil or sautéed with garlic and hot pepper)

carciofi alla romana, alla giudia (whole artichokes either
   braised or deep-fried)
fagiolini (green beans, in summer, served with lemon and
   olive oil)
insalata verde, mista (green salad, mixed salad, the latter
   with tomatoes and possibly fennel and carrots;
   dressing is rigorously oil and vinegar; don't embarrass
   yourself by asking for anything else)
misticanza romana (wild salad greens; rare in restaurants,
   where the designation usually means mesclun or
   any mixed salad, but don't miss it if you find the real
   thing)
puntarelle con la salsa (a bitter crunchy salad with an
   anchovy-garlic dressing; in winter)
rughetta (rocket or arugula, called *rucola* elsewhere; in
   salad alone or with other ingredients)
spinaci al burro or *all'agro* (spinach, especially in winter;
   served with butter or lemon and olive oil)

DESSERT

charlotte (ice cream cake)
crème caramel
crostata di visciole (tart with sour cherries, or their jam,
   and custard)
crostate (various fruit tarts, usually made with jam)
frutta fresca (fresh fruit, which Italians are skilled at
   peeling and eating without a mess)
frutti di bosco, fragole, fragoline di bosco, with *crema gelato* or
   limone e zucchero (wild, or off-season, hothouse berries
   or strawberries served with *crema*-flavor ice cream or
   lemon juice and sugar)
montebianco (a chestnut and meringue dessert)
palle del nonno (fried ricotta balls)
panna cotta (bland, caloric white custard often served with
   berry, caramel, or chocolate sauce)
pera cotta (a pear cooked in wine, often with prunes too)
tiramisù

torta della nonna (yellow cake filled with custard and
   topped with pine nuts)
torta di ricotta (ricotta-filled pie)
tozzetti (hazelnut *biscotti* to be dunked in sweet wine)
zabaglione (egg yolk whipped with sugar and Marsala)
zuppa inglese (variable, but always elaborate and messy,
   concoction of liqueur-soaked cake with custard)

LOCAL WINES

Roman table wines have traditionally come from the
Castelli Romani, the volcanic hill towns lying southeast of
the city, the best known of which is Frascati, followed by
Marino and others, each of which is a DOC zone in its
own right. Another nearby DOC zone is the Colli Albani,
with similar wines. These wines are mostly light, fresh,
dry whites, and many trattorias do not even have a house
red wine. While it is rare to find a really good Castelli
wine in a trattoria carafe, don't spurn the fine ones on wine
lists. The red of Olevano (pronounced o-LAY-vano), in the
mountains east of Rome, is locally considered a very good
table wine. Cerveteri (cer-VAY-teri), north of Rome and
best known for its Etruscan necropolis, also produces a
widely consumed white. The province of Viterbo has given
us Est!Est!!Est!!!, which has both awful and good versions.
But most trattoria wine lists, often rudimentary, will sooner
carry a few southern, Tuscan, and Piedmontese labels than
seek out the better producers from nearer home.

Rome Listings

RISTORANTE AGATA E ROMEO

AGUSTARELLO A TESTACCIO

OSTERIA DELL'ANGELO

RISTORANTE VEGETARIANO ARANCIA BLU

TRATTORIA ARMANDO AL PANTHEON

AUGUSTO

FIASCHETTERIA BELTRAME-CESARETTI

LA BOTTEGA DEL VINO DI ANACLETO BLEVE

RISTORANTE LA BUCA DI RIPETTA

DA BUCATINO

RISTORANTE PIZZERIA AL CALLARELLO

RISTORANTE LA CAMPANA

CANTINA CANTARINI

ENOTECA CAVOUR 313

DA CESARE

CHECCHINO DAL 1887

OSTERIA CHECCO ER CARETTIERE

RISTORANTE IL CIAK

LE COLLINE EMILIANE

ENOTECA CORSI

CUL DE SAC 1

DITIRAMBO

OSTERIA IL DITO E LA LUNA

LA DOLCE VITA

ENOTECA AL PARLAMENTO (ACHILLI)

ANTICA ENOTECA DI VIA DELLA CROCE

PALAZZO DEL FREDDO FASSI

FERRARA

DAR FILETTARO SANTA BARBARA

FRONTONI

IL GELATO DI SAN CRISPINO

OSTERIA LA GENSOLA

GIGGETTO AL PORTICO D'OTTAVIA

GIOLITTI

HOSTARIA ROMANESCA

PIZZERIA LEONINA

TRATTORIA LILLI

TRATTORIA DA LUCIA

PIZZERIA AI MARMI (EX-PANATTONI,
"L'OBITORIO")

TRATTORIA MONTI

ANTICA TRATTORIA AL MORO

HOSTARIA DA NERONE

NINO

TRATTORIA OTELLO ALLA CONCORDIA

RISTORANTE PARIS

RISTORANTE LA PIAZZETTA

RISTORANTE LA PIGNA

AL PONTE DELLA RANOCCHIA

IL QUADRIFOGLIO

RICCI (EST! EST! EST!)

IL SANPIETRINO

RISTORANTE SETTIMIO

SORA LELLA

SORA MARGHERITA

TRATTORIA ST. TEODORO

OSTERIA DELLA SUBURRA (DA SILVIO)

TAVERNA DEI QUARANTA

TRAM TRAM

TRIMANI IL WINE BAR

RISTORANTE VECCHIA LOCANDA

VOLPETTI PIÙ

ZI' FENIZIA

Ristorante Agata e Romeo

🏛🏛🏛🏛🏛 | ELEGANT RESTAURANT | GOURMET
(MICHELIN STAR) | ✎

Via Carlo Alberto 45, 00185 Roma
☎ 06/4466115 | 📠 06/4465842 |
agataeromeo@tiscalinet.it
Ⓜ A: Vittorio Emanuele
📷 Santa Maria Maggiore, Santa Prassede,
Piazza Vittorio Emanuele
∅ Saturday and Sunday
Reserve well in advance
€€€€

*O*n a broad street running between the basilica of
Santa Maria Maggiore and Piazza Vittorio Emanuele, you will see a brightly lit glass-paneled door and a
large excrescence of tufa and brick. The latter is a frag-
ment of Rome's fourth century B.C. Servian walls. The
former leads to one of Rome's most respected restaurants.

The sign outside still says "hostaria," recalling the days
of the Parisella family's trattoria. It is now part of Roman
restaurant lore how a medical student from Benevento
named Romeo Caraccio married the Parisellas' daughter
Agata and how together they turned the old place into
an elegant, intimate restaurant of international repute,
Romeo as *patron* and sommelier and Agata as chef. Today
their elder daughter, Maria Antonietta, who speaks English, backs up her father in the dining room. The kitchen
is full of aspiring chefs from around the world who have
come to study with Agata. Celebrities, tourists, and splurg-
ing locals dine side by side (though the tables are comfortably spaced), and all receive the same treatment. There is
nothing noisy, nothing showy here. The tone is just right
for Rome: a gracious refuge without airs.

Be sure to come with an appetite, because you don't want to miss a thing. Even the breadsticks are outstanding. Agata is a conservatively creative chef. Although the trattoria is far behind her, her refined menu, which changes almost completely four times a year, always has an allusion to Roman or Latian tradition, which might be *spaghetti alla carbonara, alla gricia,* or *all'amatriciana*—not refined beyond recognition but superb specimens of their genre. An elegant treatment of a traditional Roman soup, *pasta e broccoli in brodo di arzilla,* is always on the menu and earns whoever orders it a *Piatto del Buon Ricordo.* She also has a superb vegetarian *fritto misto* in her repertoire.

We recently enjoyed the antipasto of thin, thin green beans topped with a pile of tender rings of cuttlefish and dressed simply with oil and balsamic vinegar, and the flan of *pecorino di fossa* (aged in tufa caves near Romeo's hometown) with a little pear sauce, and a salad of smoked salt cod. The ravioli filled with *branzino* is superb, and so is the *risotto* with herbs and goat cheese. Second courses include both meat and fish. The rack of lamb has just a scattering of herbs, and there is usually a duck-breast dish and something rich and beefy, such as the *stracotto* (pot roast) garnished with vegetables deep-fried but light as a feather.

Instead of ordering à la carte, you can try one of the two tasting menus, both with wines to match. The briefer Menù del Buon Ricordo is more traditional and includes the *Piatto del Buon Ricordo, brodo di arzilla con pasta e broccoli* (skate broth with broken spaghetti, broccoflower, and tomatoes). The fabulous gourmet Menù Agata e Romeo goes on forever and includes three wines, a *spumante,* a white, and a red. If you order à la carte, you can choose from Romeo's renowned list (with extremely reasonable markups) or accept his interesting suggestions.

Save some room for cheese and dessert. Maria Antonietta will serve you some of Italy's finest cheeses from a prize-winning selection with a taste of honey or *mostarda* and a half bottle of dessert wine from one of Rome's best cellars.

Agata's desserts always incude her famous *millefoglie*, with crumbled pastry over crème chantilly, or some sherbets (don't miss prickly pear in the fall), and plenty of chocolate.

Agustarello a Testaccio

🏛 🏛 🏛 | TYPICAL TRATTORIA | *CUCINA ROMANA*

Via Giovanni Branca, 98 (Piazza S. Maria Liberatrice),
00153 Roma
☎ 06/5746585
📷 Testaccio
∅ Sunday
Reservations advised
€€ | 🔲 none

*E*xperts—such as vendors in the Testaccio market, a few minutes' walk away, and any number of Roman foodies—consider this homely trattoria, founded in 1957 and still managed by Agustarello's family, one of the truly authentic sources of the real Testaccio cuisine (see Checchino, page 56, for what that means).

The menu includes the usual Testaccio classics, such as *spaghetti all'amatriciana, coda alla vaccinara, pagliata,* and *trippa. Involtini* (rolls of beef cooked in tomato sauce) are a good choice if you don't want innards. A wine list offers some twenty labels, and desserts are *artigianali,* meaning homemade but not on the premises.

Osteria dell' Angelo

♔ ♔ | IDIOSYNCRATIC TRATTORIA |
CUCINA ROMANA

Via Giovanni Bettolo, 24–26 (Circonvallazione Clodia),
00195 Roma
☎ 06/3729470
📷 Sort of near Vatican
∅ Saturday lunch and Sunday | Sidewalk tables
Reservations essential
€ | ▭ none

*P*roximity to the Vatican has nothing to do with
the name. The angel in question is Angelo Croce,
former athlete and, since 1986, restaurateur (though the
place has been there since 1922). He runs a well-oiled
operation in two pokey rooms adorned with boxing and
football memorabilia, plus additional sidewalk tables in
warm weather.

The Angel himself, with the air of a football coach,
recites the day's menu, which varies from day to day
within a fairly circumscribed repertoire of Roman specialties, some the product of research, not trattoria standards.
Orders are taken one course at a time. A recent dinner
with friends was typical. The antipasto arrived automatically: excellent plain *bruschetta,* white pea beans, a wild
boar sausage each, and a tasty concoction of tuna and
mashed potatoes. *Primi* were *tonnarelli cacio e pepe* (oily
sauce and heavy pasta, but we cleaned our plates) and
excellent *fettuccine* with a meat sauce (tomato and roast
pork). The *secondi* were interesting as well as good: meatballs studded with raisins, sturdy *involtini* in tomato sauce
(one to a customer), and fresh ham *in porchetta*—i.e., pot-
roasted with the herbs used for the roast whole hog that is

a fixture of the countryside of Lazio. *Contorni* were *cicoria ripassata* or *rughetta* salad.

The prix fixe dinner (L. 35,000) covers *antipasto, primo, secondo, contorno,* and dessert, as well as mineral water and the house white wine from Lanuvio, south of Rome, including bread and service. Dessert is likely to be home-made anise cookies (*ciambelline*) to be dunked in sweet red wine from Olevano, in the mountains east of Rome. Coffee and grappa are extra, or, as the brown-paper place mat menu says, *"se pagheno a parte."* Lunch is à la carte.

Ristorante vegetariano Arancia Blu

🏛 | VEGETARIAN RESTAURANT | 🥄

Via dei Latini, 55/65 (Via dei Sabelli), 00185 Roma
☎ 06/4454105
Ⓜ Metro B: Tiburtina
📷 San Lorenzo
🕐 dinner only (after about 8:15) | ♿
Reservations suggested
€€ | 💳 none

*A*nybody who has ever been to an Italian open-air market understands that Italy is vegetable heaven. Here you'll find the most voluptuous sweet peppers—red, yellow, green, marbled; sleek eggplants in all sizes, shapes, and shades of purple and white; zucchini as tiny as your little finger—to say nothing of the salad greens. You'll never badmouth broccoli, spinach, and cauliflower again after tasting them in Italy. And can you imagine a surfeit of artichokes? As for grains and legumes in the diet, well, the

New Year begins with a plate of lentils, and how about *pasta e fagioli*? Even *farro* (emmer) is mainstream. Who doesn't like spaghetti with tomato and basil? And *insalata caprese*? *Melanzane alla parmigiana*? In fact, many people are *de facto* near-vegetarians—it's not a political statement, it's just that the Mediterranean diet draws more from the plant kingdom than from the animal.

But even though there is no actual need for vegetarian restaurants, many *de iure* vegetarians enjoy the assurance that no *cotiche* (pork rinds) will find their way into their beans, no meat broth into their *minestrone*. The Eternal City accommodates even them with a handful of macrobiotic and vegetarian restaurants.

Arancia Blu is the vegetarian restaurant that has captured the heart of the Italian guidebooks. My yoga teacher, a nonfanatical vegetarian and good cook, and I went to check it out.

It's interesting sociology, sort of a throwback to the 1970s, the days when waiters and waitresses might have taken orders and brought food to the table but actually providing service would have been politically incorrect. Music and warm lighting and walls of neatly arrayed wine bottles create an air of pre–dot-com but post–baby-boom affluence; hippie meets yuppie, Italian-style. The annoying paper napkins and paper place mats are presumably reverse snobbery. The premises are huge (also used for courses and events) but articulated into manageable-size dining rooms, of which the smallest by far is reserved for nonsmokers with special uncomfortable chairs.

Fabio Bassan's cooking style is Italian-cum-exotica, with some fine moments, such as an antipasto of green beans and boiled potatoes with a deconstructed *pesto* sauce—some whole pine nuts, basil leaves, and shavings of pecorino represented the ingredients of the *pesto* unprocessed. Presentation is attractive—a heap of ravioli arranged so that their points formed a snowflake, or star, or what-have-you—or (presumably) whimsical—a legume terrine sliced and sauced like school meat loaf with gravy. The whimsy, however, didn't help the taste of what was mostly pressed beans and bread crumbs, left mostly un-eaten. On a hot summer evening, there was not a single cold dish or salad. Spices and nuts are used in un-Italian ways, and there is a tendency toward the highly piquant. But whether or not you agree with Mr. Bassan's choices, the food is conceived and prepared with care; this is not your fifty-different-rice-salads vegetarian menu. There is also a good choice of cheeses, including two tasting plates, one of *formaggi erborinati,* including Stilton.

The wine list, appended to the menu, is extensive, with a few foreign labels as well as a great many Italian.

Trattoria Armando al Pantheon

🏛 🏛 🏛 | TRATTORIA PLUS *CUCINA ROMANA* AND MORE

Salita de' Crescenzi, 31 (Piazza della Rotonda), 00186 Roma
☎ 06 / 68803034
📷 Pantheon, Piazza Navona
∅ Saturday evening and Sunday
€ € |

*T*his is a rather amusing, friendly little place just spitting distance from the Pantheon, run by the two Gargioli brothers, Claudio (in the kitchen) and Fab-rizio (in the dining room). It consists of one small room, with cork-faced walls and pine wainscoting, ceiling fans, and vintage prints and photos. The menu offers the usual favorites, such as *carbonara, matriciana, gnocchi* (on Thurs-day), *saltimbocca,* tripe (on Saturday), as well as some very individual dishes, supposedly based on ancient, or at least old, Roman recipes.

Spaghetti alla Claudio is a house specialty consisting of nicely *al dente* spaghetti with olive oil, saffron, *peperoncino,* and sliced mushrooms, which I thought was rather tasty but Franco thought was awful. The name is both a play on the name of the chef and a reference to the demise by mushroom of the emperor Claudius, but the banal button mushrooms used are less than imperial. The emperor was fed a poisonous species of *Amanita,* famously like the prized *Amanita caesaris,* still available at a price today in the fall in Italy and called *ovolo.*

Polpettine di farro in *salsa di Gorgonzola* or *tartufo* are faux meatballs made from emmer, and in texture they reminded me of falafel with tahini. Though this dish is listed as a main course (evidently a meat substitute), *farro* is usually served instead of pasta, and we found the *polpet-tine* worked better as a *primo piatto.* The *ossobuco* is good, tomato-less and served with peas. *Faraona* (guinea hen) cut up and stewed in dark beer with dried *funghi porcini* and black olives is the tasty house specialty.

The handwritten wine list is brief but sufficient, and there's a good house white from the Castelli. The home-made desserts are really excellent; the *torta di ricotta* with a crumbly crust and strawberry jam was stunning.

Augusto

🏛 | TYPICAL TRATTORIA | *CUCINA ROMANA*

Piazza dei Renzi, 15 (Via della Pelliccia), 00153 Roma
☎ 06/5803798
📷 Trastevere
∅ Saturday evening and Sunday
Reservations not accepted
€ | ▭ none

*O*ffering traditional cooking, a genuine trattoria atmosphere (but without the Fellini characters), and low, low prices, this Trastevere eatery has been packing in the customers since 1954. It's located in a single spartan room (but look for the old marble sink) opening right onto the street, very near the English-language Cinema Pasquino, and makes a change from the customary postmovie pizza. In warm weather, tightly packed picnic tables are set up outside in the piazza.

Don't expect to see a menu or get a receipt (unless you want to put the paper tablecloth in your bag). The day's offerings will come from the *casalinga* repertoire: say, *rigatoni all'amatriciana*, homemade *fettuccine, pollo alla romana, involtini, trippa,* or roast pork. Desserts, including *tiramisù* and *crostate,* are homemade.

Fiaschetteria Beltrame-Cesaretti

🏛 🏛 | ARCHETYPAL TRATTORIA |
CUCINA ROMANA

Via della Croce, 39 (Via del Corso), 00187 Rome
☎ No phone
📷 Piazza di Spagna, Mausoleum of Augustus, Ara Pacis
∅ Sunday
Reservations impossible
€€ | 💳 none

*T*his is like the fashionable alternative to Sora Margherita (page 105), where well-dressed patrons drop in for comfort food at shared tables in the single closely packed room, which holds about thirty. The word *fiaschetteria* comes from *fiasco,* the straw-covered wine bottle, and indeed *fiaschi* ranged on a long, high shelf are a prominent décor item, but so is the interesting (and important-looking) collection of small paintings and drawings. The absence of a telephone should not make us forget that we are in the elegant Piazza di Spagna neighborhood, where glitzy boutiques and badly dressed tourists have not entirely canceled out the local memory of charm and intellectual life.

The menu, which is based on old favorites (for example, *tonnarelli cacio e pepe* or *baccalà alla romana*) also offers some cold dishes, in huge portions, though they are less successful.

Across the street is Vertecchi, favorite haunt of stationery junkies. It's open all day and sells art and party supplies as well as paper, pens, expensive diaries, and fashionable schoolbags and pencil cases.

La Bottega del Vino di Anacleto Bleve

🏛🏛🏛🏛 | SHOP-LUNCH | GOURMET | ➤

Via Santa Maria del Pianto, 9/11 (Via Arenula, Via del Portico d'Ottavia), 00186 Roma

☎ 06/6865970

📷 Jewish quarter

∅ Sunday

🕐 Shop open 9:30 A.M. to 1:00 P.M., 4:30 to 8 P.M.; lunch served 12:30 to 3:30 P.M.

Reservations advised but not always needed

€ | [card] [VISA]

*S*ince 1970, Anacleto Bleve has run one of the most respected wine and liquor (and oil and vinegar) shops in Rome. And one of the most amusing light lunches in Rome is served right there in the shop. The doors close and tables are set amid the single-malt whiskeys and balsamic vinegars as well as in an adjoining room. The day's offerings are set out in a glass case; the drill is to get up and choose, then return to your table and wait to be served. Wines are served by the bottle or glass, and the foods always include an assortment of salamis, cheeses, smoked fish (such as swordfish), and salads, as well as something warm from the oven, such as a potato timbale, and some desserts. Miscellaneous gourmet treats include irresistible smoked salmon rolls filled with crabmeat (charged by the piece) and *parmigiano* with *aceto balsamico tradizionale*. A complimentary glass of sweet, fizzy, and delicious Moscato d'Asti usually concludes the meal.

Ristorante La Buca di Ripella

🏛🏛🏛 | TRATTORIA PLUS |
CUCINA ROMANA AND MORE

Via di Ripetta, 36, 00186 Roma
☎ 06/3219391
📷 Via del Corso, Piazza del Popolo, shopping
Ø Sunday evening and Monday; August
Reservations suggested
€€ | MasterCard D DINERS CLUB 🔲 VISA

*V*ia di Ripetta is the western tine of the so-called trident, the three streets radiating out from the bottom of the magnificent Piazza del Popolo (the other two are Via del Corso and Via del Babuino). At the other end of the street are the Ara Pacis and Mausoleum of Augustus, with a Fascist-era piazza laying claim to both monuments. It's a funny old street, with a public hospital, the arts high school, a residential hotel, offices and apartments, and lots of shops, including specialty food shops, art supplies stores, bookshops, and fashionable boutiques. There is also a good handful of casual eating places. One of the most venerable of these, founded in 1956, is this pleasant sort of neighborhood trattoria. Its rustic décor, featuring two ox yokes and a gigantic bellows suspended near the ceiling, contrasts endearingly with the chi-chi neighborhood. Service is provided by competent smart-mouthed waiters ("What do you have for dessert?" "We'll find something.").

Along with some tourists, habitués traditionally include professionals and show people. On a Saturday evening, we saw families and some women alone or in pairs, still a relatively unusual sight.

The menu contains absolutely nothing fashionable— what a relief! You can choose *lasagne al forno, penne all'arrabbiata,* or *rigatoni all'amatriciana.* The *pasta e fagioli,* a hearty soup made with borlotti beans, tomatoes, and *ditalini* pasta (very short tubes), is served in a snappy tureen, with a jar of flaked *peperoncino* and a bottle of extra virgin olive oil on the side. The excellent *melanzane alla parmigiana* comes on the plate, not in an incandescent metal baking dish as it often does, and the portion is small enough to permit eating something else at the meal.

Secondi include various grilled meats, *saltimbocca alla romana, involtini* of beef (tender rolls of meat filled with prosciutto, celery, and carrots) with mashed potatoes to soak up the tomato sauce, and a nice vegetarian *fritto misto.* No fish.

The choice of homemade desserts changes daily. We can recommend the *zabaglione* with chocolate sauce. The same cannot, however, be said for the house white wine (there's no house red). Choose instead something from the brief wine list, which offers a few reasonably priced young reds and whites and some six-figure big Tuscans.

Da Bucatino

🏛 🏛 | CLASSIC TRATTORIA | *CUCINA ROMANA*

Via Luca della Robbia, 84 (Piazza Testaccio), 00153 Roma
☎ 06/5746886
📷 Testaccio
∅ Monday; mid-July to mid-August | Sidewalk tables
Reservations advised in the evening
€€ | ▭ none

*T*he only time I've ever seen this old favorite in a guidebook, it was roundly trounced, and indeed a gourmet haven it's not. It is a traditional trattoria in rustic style a block from the Testaccio market, with some hearty, tasty food and competent service. The main dining room is informal and cozy; the smaller dining room off it is extremely cozy. Sidewalk tables in warm weather are acceptably tranquil.

A sort of wagon is fitted out as an antipasto buffet in one corner of the main dining room, with a full range of marinated and grilled vegetables, *frittata* slices, marinated anchovies, *insalata di mare,* and so forth.

The title role is played by *bucatini all'amatriciana,* of course, in a huge portion and very robust. The *fettuccine con funghi porcini,* sauced with cream, is another heavyweight. The daily menu, written on a blackboard on the back wall, usually proposes a range of the traditional meat dishes, such as something *alla cacciatora,* but they've been featuring fish here since before the fish fad, and it is cooked rather well. A perennial is *merluzzo alla diavola,* a small cod, boned, opened, and grilled.

Dessert will probably be industrially made ice cream, but it is very popular and widely enjoyed.

Ristorante Pizzeria al Callarello

🏛 | TRATTORIA-PIZZERIA | FISH (BUT NOT ONLY); PIZZA

Via Salvator Rosa, 8 (San Saba), 00153 Roma
☎ 06/5747575
📷 Aventine Hill, Church of San Saba, Pyramid of Gaius
Cestius, Protestant Cemetery, Baths of Caracalla, UN FAO
∅ Sunday | Nice outdoor tables
Reservations a must
€€ | [MasterCard] [VISA]

*T*he so-called Piccolo Aventino, or small Aventine
Hill, is one of Rome's most attractive neighborhoods. Without the snob appeal of the main Aventino
(from which it is separated by the broad, unlovely Viale
Aventino), it gives an impression of greater vivacity. The
church of San Saba, its focal point, is a singularly preserved example of Romanesque architecture without
Baroque overlay, and in the quarter's central piazza, every
morning there is a characteristic open market. The only
thing really wrong with the area is the shortage of good
places to eat. In the 1980s, when I lived in the vicinity, Al
Callarello was a simple, friendly trattoria-pizzeria known
only to its neighbors and employees of the nearby United
Nations Food and Agriculture Organization. As an alternative to pizza, *spaghetti alle vongole* and grilled *scampi*
were a worthy splurge. When I left the neighborhood, I
forgot about it until a friend from Perugia dragged us
there to try his "discovery," and soon after I was surprised
to find it listed in the Gambero Rosso guide.

We returned in the summer of 2000 with our Umbrian

friend. The tables beneath green umbrellas on the spacious piazza were still one of the most delightful places inside the walls of Rome to spend a summer evening, and the seafood was still good and reasonably priced. But the service was so unfriendly and inefficient as to ruin the whole experience.

Cheap fish (to call a spade a spade) is box office in Rome, and this restaurant is always full. Thus, when I phoned to book a table for 9 P.M., I was told to come at 8:30—and we'd better be on time, or they'd give the table away (such may be common practice in New York, London, or possibly even Milan, but Rome usually takes a more flexible approach to the clock). It never got any friendlier than that, plus long waits, orders—such as for more wine—unfilled, food running out.

Our first courses consisted of good *spaghetti alle vongole veraci* (creamy sauce, juicy clams), *tagliolini alla mediterraneo* (a misnomer, in that the sauce was made of cream and smoked salmon), and *cecamariti* (thick homemade spaghetti) with zucchini and shrimp (judged good but full of shrimp heads). We'd wanted a *rombo* (turbot) baked with potatoes, the house specialty, but about half an hour after ordering, we were told the *rombi* were finished. Since *orata* and *spigola*, the other two fish offered, are usually farmed, we chose a mixed grill of *scampi, mazzancolle,* and *calamari*, which was mostly good, though the squid was like charred shoe leather. We couldn't bear to stay around for dessert, though I saw some nice *fragoline* (wild strawberries) circulating.

The wine list is limited but equal to the task. The menu also offers various options for ichthyophobes, such as grilled *scamorza*, roast veal, and *filetto al pepe verde*.

You needn't let the staff's total indifference to your happiness keep you away from this otherwise pleasant place, but do plan to go early. In winter, the scene is indoors, of course, below ground level in stuffy though not unattractive rooms.

Ristorante la Campana

🏛🏛 | TRATTORIA PLUS | *CUCINA ROMANA*

Vicolo della Campana, 18 (Via della Scrofa), 00186 Roma

☎ 06/6867820, 06/6875273

📷 Near the Tiber

∅ Monday; August

€€ | [MasterCard] [Diners Club] [card] [VISA]

*I*l locale più antico di Roma (the oldest place in Rome)," boasts the menu. The establishment is attested as early as 1518 and is mentioned in seventeenth- and eighteenth-century sources as well. No wonder it seems tired. In fairness, my last visit was on a Sunday evening (see page 14). When I first began coming to Rome in the late 1960s, La Campana was respected as typical but upmarket, a convenient middle ground between a dive and a splurge. It still represents something genuine in a neighborhood where few old Romans can afford an apartment, but in the context of today's restaurant scene, it has gone from being a restaurant masquerading as a trattoria to a trattoria that thinks it's a restaurant. Never mind. It's a good old place when you want genuine atmosphere with an air of civility. There are three dining rooms in a spare classic-rustic style.

Characteristically, *antipasti* are not the strong suit, except for some sliced cold cuts, or maybe prosciutto, with melon in season. Pastas include *spaghetti all'amatriciana* and *penne con i carciofi*, with a generous quantity of sliced fresh artichokes in a pink cream-based sauce.

Fish is available, but better is the standard repertoire of meat dishes: *scallopine* in various ways, such as *saltimbocca alla romana, coda alla vaccinara, trippa alla romana,* or (what I always wind up ordering) tasty chicken croquettes.

Desserts, which include such caloric standards as *monte-bianco* and *tiramisù,* are homemade. The wine list is rudimentary.

Cantina Cantarini

🏛️ 🏛️ | TRATTORIA | *CUCINA ROMANA;*
FISH ON TUESDAY AND FRIDAY

Piazza Sallustio (Via XX Settembre) 12, 00187 Roma
☎ 06/485528
📷 Horti Sallustiani, Villa Borghese
∅ Sunday; August | Outdoor tables
Reservations a must
€ on meat days; € € on fish days | 💳 💳 💳 💳

*T*here is something anomalous about a hole in the wall like this, with wooden tables and chairs outside the door in the piazza, existing in such a ritzy neighborhood—but that's Rome. It's all very down-home, with a freezer as a doorstop and old photos from 1922, when the place was founded. Customers include families, the fashionable, and intellectuals (to judge only from appearances). Service, provided mostly by the owner, is friendly but hurried.

The tone is raised somewhat, however, by the owner's *marchigiano* origins; this is not for snob value but because the house wine is Verdicchio dei Castelli di Iesi Classico rather than Castelli Romani. (There is also a list of a dozen Marche labels.)

A written menu floats around but is regarded by all with suspicion—"for the foreigners." On our last visit, we ascertained that *antipasti* were available only by overhearing the proposals being made to a competing table. Our protest resulted in an offering of potato *frittata,* good hand-sliced prosciutto, and salami. The *spaghetti alla car-bonara* was good, as was a *pasta fredda. Fettuccine con funghi porcini,* however, was tasteless.

Tuesday and Friday, the menu is all fish. The rest of the week the offerings are the standards; our party tried *pollo con peperoni* (with the peppers left unpeeled), *coniglio alla cacciatora* (really rabbit stew), *scamorza* grilled with sliced prosciutto, and good roast veal with potatoes.

Panna cotta with either cooked *frutti di bosco* or caramel sauce was not thrilling, but a little carafe of *amaro* with fruit was a nice concluding touch.

Enoteca Cavour 313

🏛🏛 | CASUAL WINE BAR | WINE, SNACKS, LIGHT MEALS | 🗝

Via Cavour 313, 00184 Roma
☎ 06/6785496
📷 Roman Forum, Colosseum, Imperial Fora
∅ Sunday; August
€ (very variable) | VISA MasterCard ■

*T*his venerable charmer near the bottom of Via Cavour dates in its present incarnation to 1978 (overhauled in 1984), when innovative young Italians were discovering fine wines and canned corn. Along with Cul de Sac 1 (page 65), it essentially launched the wine bar concept in Rome, though at the time they were still called *bottiglierie.* Its formula of a wide choice of wines by the glass, light meals (at least one salad with canned corn always on the menu), and uncomfortable wooden benches behind an irresistible old shopfront façade was a winner, and for decades it seemed impossible to get in the door. Today couscous and tabbouleh have replaced the corn, and *car-*

paccio outranks salami. The service is friendly, spaced out, and inefficient in the great tradition of the late 1970s, and the funny old place still has its magic, albeit at a higher price.

Go for a light lunch, a predinner *aperitivo* (maybe a Prosecco or an aromatic white wine from Trentino or Alto Adige), or a light supper. There is always a *piatto del giorno* (such as couscous, or a rice timbale), a wide selection of cheeses, cold meats, smoked fish, salads (such as couscous), and some desserts.

Da Cesare

🍷🍷🍷🍷 | CLASSIC RESTAURANT |
CUCINA ROMANA, TOSCANA; PIZZA IN THE EVENING;
GOOD FISH | 🥄

Via Crescenzio 13 (Piazza Cavour), 00193 Roma
☎ 06/6861227
📷 Prati quarter, Vatican
∅ Monday
Reservations not always needed
€€€ (less if pizza) | MasterCard Diners Club AmEx VISA

*W*hen they called Rome the Eternal City, this is the sort of restaurant they were thinking of. It's an institution in the Prati quarter, near the Vatican, on the left bank of the Tiber. The large menu of Roman and Tuscan specialties is divided into meat and fish (carried over into the tastefully painted marine motifs in the long half-paneled dining room). The culinary style is home cooking with very good ingredients.

At a recent dinner, we were impressed by the freshness of the *insalata di mare* (shrimp, mussels, squid, cuttlefish, and celery strips dressed with oil, lemon, and parsley) and the tenderness of the *saltimbocca alla romana* (veal scallops topped with prosciutto and fresh sage, sautéed in white wine). There is a wide choice of classic pastas, with and without seafood, and such Tuscan soups as bean and *farro* served with a bottle of good green olive oil. The vegetables too are superb, such as *carciofi alla romana* and *cicoria ripassata*.

Desserts are homemade. There is a very good wine list emphasizing Tuscan labels, and, a welcome rarity, the house wines are also offered by the glass.

Checchino dal 1887

🏛🏛🏛🏛🏛 | SERIOUS RESTAURANT | GOURMET
CUCINA ROMANA | 🥄

Via Monte Testaccio, 30 (Mattatoio), 00153 Roma
📞 | 📠 06/5743816 | http:www.checchino-dal-1887.com
📷 Testaccio, Protestant cemetery, Pyramid of Cestius
∅ Sunday and Monday; August; one week at Christmas |
Some outdoor tables
Reservations a must
€€€€ | MasterCard DinersClub AmEx VISA

*T*he Mariani family—signora Ninetta and her two soft-spoken, suave, knowledgeable sons, Elio and Francesco—are third- and fourth-generation guardians of a family, Roman, and neighborhood tradition far older than this venerable restaurant. It's still called "Trattoria" on the side of its funny little two-story building, whose rear abuts Monte Testaccio—about which more in a moment—and whose façade looks at the old slaughterhouse, the *mattatoio*.

Various uses have been found for the *mattatoio* complex since it gave up its original function, but it still dominates the gastronomic spirit of the Testaccio quarter. Its workers received part of their wages in kind—in cowhides (which led to a neighborhood cottage tanning industry) and, logically, in meat, the innards, tail, and other leftovers. The Mariani trattoria developed interesting ways of cooking what was nicknamed the "fifth quarter" of the animal, and the rest is gastronomic history.

Today Checchino is the benchmark against which all attempts at traditional urban Roman cooking must be measured. It is an odd hybrid, offering the food of the urban poor of more than a hundred years ago alongside world-class cheese trolleys (yes, plural) and one of the top wine cellars in Italy. Many Romans don't get the point, and some of this excellent restaurant's biggest fans are unprejudiced foreigners—despite a menu that at times sounds like a prop list for a horror film. But if you have a hankering to try *paiata, schienale,* or *coratella* (all in the glossary), this is the place where you can be sure of getting top-quality raw materials as well as superb preparation. If you can't choose, *padellotto alla macellara* has the full assortment.

But the squeamish can do very well here too. The *abbacchio alla cacciatora,* succulent pieces of lamb stewed with rosemary and vinegar, is the best of its kind (and earns a souvenir *Piatto del Buon Ricordo*). *Involtini* are filled with artichoke stems instead of the usual celery. Baby lamb chops are superb. (Note that to be tender, Roman lamb needs to be cooked through; don't ask for it rare.) *Garofolato* (literally, cloved) is a simple beef pot roast with just three pronounced flavors, meat, tomatoes, and cloves, a traditional dish almost never seen on menus. If you can't face an oxtail—though Checchino's is superb—have *tonnarelli in sugo di coda,* pasta dressed with the sauce from the main dish.

Even vegetarians can dine here. The *carciofo alla romana,* a whole artichoke braised with garlic and *mentuccia* (pennyroyal) is the glory of Rome and nowhere better than here. *Tonnarelli cacio e pepe* is long square-cut pasta with pecorino

and freshly ground pepper. Thanks to the extreme econ-
omy and simplicity of this dish, it's a great favorite with
lazy or cheeseparing cooks, with predictable results. Checchino shows how good it can be.

Desserts are in the trattoria spirit—we recently had a
superb moist homemade cake laden with chunks of fresh
peaches, apricots, and medlars, elegant in its simplicity.
But the selection of some thirty-five cheeses—including
Castelmagno, pecorino di fossa, and the original *pecorino
romano* from Lazio, as well as some specimens from
France, Spain, England, and Switzerland—is renowned for
its quality and breadth.

With forty thousand bottles, and more than six hundred different kinds of wine, Checchino's wine cellar is
considered one of the best in Italy, including Château
d'Yquem and a wide selection of 1937 vintage port. A too-
brief digest version of the wine list is appended to the
menu (the tome is rarely offered unless requested), but
Elio or Francesco will make suggestions.

Ask to see the cellar, and through one of its walls you
can see the remains of the peculiar archaeological site
popularly known as Monte Testaccio, meaning Crockery
Mountain. The area of Rome enclosed by the Tiber, Via
Marmorata, and the Aurelian Wall, with Porta San Paolo
(the ancient Porta Ostiensis) and the Pyramid of Gaius
Cestius at the apex of the rough triangle, is known today
as Testaccio. It takes its modern character, as we have seen,
from the *mattatoio,* but in antiquity, it was known as the
emporium and was a busy river port, as remains of ware-
houses along the Tiber there attest. Monte Testaccio covers a surface of 20,000 square meters and today is 35
meters high. What lies below the surface is still largely
conjecture, but to the extent that its composition is
known, it appears to be constructed almost entirely of
carefully stacked broken olive oil amphoras from Spain
and North Africa, dating from the mid-second century to
the mid-third. Apparently, the olive oil residue made these
large, heavy containers unrecyclable, so once their con-

tents were transferred into containers for shipping to other parts of the Empire, the only thing to do was to dispose neatly of the bulky, useless amphoras.

Osteria Checco er Carettiere

🏛🏛🏛🏛 | RUSTIC RESTAURANT |
CUCINA ROMANA; FISH | 🥄

Via Benedetta 10-11-12 (Piazza Trilussa), 00153 Roma
☎ 06/5817018, 06/5800985 | 📠 06/5584282
📷 Trastevere
∅ Sunday evening and Monday | Courtyard tables
Reservations suggested
€€€ | [MasterCard] [Diners] [AmEx] [VISA]

*C*heccho is an old-fashioned Roman nickname for Francesco; *er carettiere* is *romanesco* for "the cart driver." And Checco's cart itself is right inside the door, large as life, shouting "Folklore!"—Eurospeak for "oh, so quaint." This is why many sophisticated Romans take so long to discover what is actually an excellent, if expensive, restaurant offering a large menu of genuine Roman foods, not interpreted but faithfully reproduced. "Hearty" would be an understatement to describe the cooking, which is quite wonderful but makes you wonder whether they ever had to use the cart to wheel out a customer. Checco's last name was Porcelli, if that tells you anything about what to expect, and this fine establishment is the direct descendant of the cart from which he sold first wine and then food. The restaurant was founded in 1935 on the site of an old *osteria*. Signor Porcelli died in 1961, and his granddaughter is in charge today.

Linguistic aside: the restaurant spells the epithet with one r, *carettiere,* though proper Italian uses two. Foreigners learning Italian usually find that the double consonants are the most difficult oral/aural hurdle, since speakers of proper Italian are careful to make a distinction between single and double consonants. You can imagine what fun it is to learn Italian in Rome, where the local speech tends to reverse what is written.

This is one of those places where you learn to distinguish between the tired version of trattoria food and the active, truly committed version. The antipasto course may include a so-called potato *frittata,* consisting of mashed potatoes with tomatoes and onions (no eggs), superb anchovies, marinated zucchini, or *testina* (calf's head), here cut in chunks and presented with pieces of marinated anchovies, and more.

This would be a good place to try *rigatoni con la paiata,* but on our last visit, we had our rigatoni *alla gricia* with, since it was the season, *fave col guanciale,* and a ton of pecorino—very rich, oily, and delicious. *Spaghetti alla carrettiera* is sauced with tomatoes, tuna fish, and mushrooms. *Secondi* might be *involtini nel sugo, saltimbocca alla romana* (enough for two), *coda alla vaccinara, trippa alla romana,* or fresh fish. And don't miss (except in off-season summer) the *carciofi alla romana.*

There is a good wine list. If you want something good but local, which is to say from the Castelli Romani, and is no longer an oxymoron, you might try the Frascati Superiore DOC from Castel de' Paolis.

If by dessert time you haven't ingested enough calories, never fear. There are plenty of good choices. But if you have, try *fragoline di bosco* with just lemon and sugar.

Ristorante Il Ciak

🏛🏛🏛 | TUSCAN TRATTORIA | MEAT; GAME

Vicolo del Cinque, 21 (Piazza Trilussa), 00153 Roma
☎ 06/5894774
📷 Trastevere
∅ Monday
Dinner only; reservations a must
€€€ | [MasterCard] [Diners Club] [💳] [VISA]

*V*egetarians should not even consider accompa-
nying friends to this popular little spot, whose
name and décor theme refers to the onomatopoeic Italian
name for the slate (or clapper board) of moviemaking.
"Ciak, si gira!" is Italian for "Mark it. This is a take."

The street is one of the most frequented in the densely
populated Trastevere quarter, lined with bars and eateries
aimed at the very young and tourists—the undiscriminat-
ing and agoraphilic, in other words. Il Ciak is different,
however. It has a clear gastronomic definition—Tuscan-
style meat and game—and sticks to it. Indeed, the diner is
greeted inside the door by a display of raw meat, and a
little farther in, by the great grill where it all gets cooked.

Antipasti consist largely of *crostini*—liver pâté, olive
paste, mushrooms. Outstanding among the *primi piatti* is
pappardelle with a rich sauce of *cinghiale* (wild boar). There
is also a duck sauce, another Tuscan standby. There are
soups too: *ribollita, minestra di farro, pappa al pomodoro*.

Main dishes are largely grilled (*alla brace*) meats, with
pride of place given to *la fiorentina* (a thick T-bone steak,
served very very rare—or not at all). There are assorted
chops, birds, and sausages, including a *misto* "for the
tourists," as well as some dishes from the kitchen, such as
faraona su crostone, guinea fowl in its sauce resting on

bread. There are also grilled pork livers wrapped in caul fat (*fegatelli di malale nella rete*), once a trattoria standby, practically impossible to find nowadays.

Desserts are the weak point. If you don't feel like venturing out to grab an ice cream elswhere, try a *panna cotta*.

The house wine is Chianti in carafe, and the wine list is heavily regional.

Le Colline Emiliane

🏛🏛🏛🏛　|　REGIONAL TRATTORIA　|
CUCINA EMILIANA

Via degli Avignonesi 22 (Via del Tritone), 00187 Roma
☎　06/4817538
📷　Piazza Barberini, Fontana di Trevi
∅　Friday
Reservations advised
€€　|　MasterCard　VISA

*T*his is a superb small family-run restaurant with a low profile and a very devoted following. It's located on a side street near too-too-bustling Piazza Barberini, from which it provides both spiritual and temporal refuge. It may be one of the greatest bargains in Rome.

The setting is two wood-paneled rooms, just bright enough to see your food. A case with desserts inside the door gets the juices flowing. The terse menu is tightly focused, as the trattoria's name suggests, on the Emilia side of the Emilia-Romagna region. Its spartan typestyle is belied by its voluptuary contents, including many items offered at only a few places in Rome.

Antipasti are *salumi: culatello di Zibello,* the specially cured heart of the prosciutto, or *mortadella,* the original bologna (and bearing no comparison), or *salame di Felino,* a robust medium-grained salami from near Parma, having nothing to do with cats. At a recent lunch, we saw some unlisted, unoffered roasted peppers and sliced grilled eggplant sitting next to the cakes and asked a plate to be brought us. They were of unusual delicacy, superb.

Serious pasta in Emilia-Romagna means fresh egg pasta rolled to transparency and so tender it melts in the mouth. *"Al dente"* does not apply. The most classic of all Emilian pastas is *tagliatelle al ragù,* and what is served here is the genuine article. The plate arrives looking big and mean: a heaping portion of noodles smothered in chopped meat, with only a suggestion of tomatoes, but it's so soft and tender and light you'll have no problem eating the next course, which might be a classic *bollito misto* with green sauce or a hearty *giambonetto* with mashed potatoes. But we haven't finished with the pastas: *tortelli di zucca* are super ravioli filled with a purée of winter squash, shipped down from the north or over from Sardinia, depending on the season (local squash is too watery).

The homemade desserts are exquisite. Crème caramel, *zabaione,* and fresh fruit are staples, while cakes and *crostate* change from day to day. We tasted a superb pear *crostata* embellished with raisins.

The wine list (printed on the menu) is brief, reasonably priced, and largely regional. Sparkling red Lambrusco is de rigueur with *bollito.* For more body, try a Sangiovese di Romagna or Gutturnio. For a white, try Pagàdebit, whose grape is so named because it grows and gives wine, with which to pay the debts, even when all others fail.

Enoteca Corsi

🏛 | TRATTORIA, WINE SHOP | *CUCINA ROMANA* |
🍴

Via del Gesù, 88 (Largo Argentina, Corso Vittorio Emanuele),
   00186 Roma
☎ 06/6790821
📷 Chiesa del Gesù, Pantheon, Chiesa di Sant'Ignazio
Ø Sunday; August | ⏰ Lunch only | No-smoking section
Reservations not essential, but you may have to wait
€ | [MasterCard] [Diners Club] [Amex] [VISA]

I f you don't expect too much from the food, this is
   the *osteria* at its most typical. Corsi is a small wine
shop whose traditional appearance is belied by a collection of boutique wine labels and an impressive selection
of single-malt whiskeys. When I was first taken here for
lunch, in the early 1980s, the eatery was in a room behind
the shop, the *retrobottega*. The blackboard lunch menu
offered a couple of *primi* and *secondi* and some compara-
tively light dishes, such as Tuscan-style tuna fish and *cannellini* beans. In the 1990s, the operation expanded with
the acquisition of a large adjacent space.

The trattoria now has its own front door, with its menu
on a nice easel and a no-smoking section in the window-
less shop, where tables are also set. Try to memorize the
blackboard menu as you enter, as it's the last time you're
going to see the day's potential. A printed menu does cir-
culate, but not widely, and basically you get offered what
it is convenient to bring you. The Italian guidebooks
speak of an excellent wine list, but I've never been offered
it. And indeed some of the big-ticket Piedmontese bottles
I've seen on others' tables would be a little overpowering
for the modest *fettuccine al ragù, gnocchi col pomodoro* (on

Thursdays), roast veal, *polpette,* and other trattoria standards. There are two tiers of house wines, Castelli and, better, Toscana.

Cul de Sac 1

🏛🏛🏛 | WINE BAR WITH FOOD | 🍶

Piazza Pasquino, 73 (Piazza Navona), 00186 Roma
☎ 06/68801094
📷 Piazza Navona, Museo di Roma, Palazzo Altemps
∅ Monday lunch; no vacation
🕐 12:30 to 3 P.M., 6:30 P.M. to 12:30 A.M.
Reservations not accepted
€ | ▭ none

*C*ul de Sac and Cavour 313 (page 54), founded in the late 1970s, are the grandparents of today's wine bars, and Cul de Sac has always struck me as having its act more together than the others. Its only drawbacks are the cramped wooden benches in its constricted, sometimes smoky, space, and lack of reservations. But it has a wine list of fourteen hundred labels and serves excellent soups, pâtés, flans, salads, meats, and cheeses. It is one of the only places in Rome for *pizzocheri* (buckwheat noodles), and in general differs from other wine bars in that it is possible to have a real meal and not still feel hungry when you leave.

Ditirambo

🏛 | CASUAL RESTAURANT | *"CUCINA ITALIANA"*

Piazza della Cancelleria, 74, 00186 Roma
☎ 06/6871626
📷 Palazzo della Cancelleria, Museo Barracco,
   Museo di Roma, Piazza Farnese, Campo de' Fiori
∅ Monday lunch; August | ♿
Reservations needed
€€ | [MasterCard] [Diners Club] [American Express] [VISA]

*T*he name is Italian for dithyramb, which you will,
of course, remember is a Greek choral ode with
something to do with Dionysus, god of wine. (Exactly
what it had to do with Dionysus varied over the centuries.)
It's a cute concept for a wine bar, but this is a restaurant
with a pan-Italian menu and merely serviceable wine list.
The ambience is young and informal (meaning slow),
with place mats and wooden tables for a faux rustic look.
This formula appeals to many people, Italian and foreign.
It's pretty good, with good ingredients, but I'd prefer a
little more focus to the menu.

Our dinner there with a friend began with a "strudel"
of greens and cheese; an *antipasto calabrese* (Calabrian), including marinated artichokes, sun-dried tomatoes (which
actually are Calabrian), and interesting *lampascioni,* a peculiar red bulb resembling a shallot that is so bitter in its natural state that it requires hours upon hours of soaking and
rinsing to be edible; and a nice *antipasto di verdura* consisting of boiled carrots, *piselli con prosciutto,* and leek and fennel au gratin. The pastas were the least interesting course:
testaroli (strips of bread dough cooked like pasta) with
pesto alla genovese (not homemade); rather bland *malfatti*
sauced with *fiori di zucca;* and not entirely successful egg-

plant *gnocchi* with *vongole*. However, *vitella in cartoccio* was a nice juicy veal loin chop cooked with herbs in an aluminum foil packet. *Seppie* with *taccole* (a sort of green bean) was a variation on the traditional *seppie con i piselli*. And *polpette di melanzane* (eggplant patties) was a straightforward, single-flavor vegetarian dish.

Desserts, which run to cakes, ricotta and otherwise, are homemade and quite good. We also tried some delicious chilled figs filled with fig *gelato*.

In the neighborhood, don't miss the small and charming Museo Barracco, where a once-private collection of Greek, Roman, and Egyptian art is housed in the early sixteenth-century *palazzetto* known as the Piccola Farnesina.

Osteria il Dito e la Luna

🏛🏛🏛🏛 | *SUI GENERIS* BISTRO |
CUCINA CREATIVA, SOME SICILIAN | 🥄

Via dei Sabelli, 47 (San Lorenzo), 00185 Rome
☎ 06/4940726
Ⓜ Metro B: Tiburtina
📷 Basilica di San Lorenzo, Campo Verano, University of Rome La Sapienza
∅ Sunday; August
Reservations a must
€€€ | ▭ none

*O*pened in 1986 in the artistic working-class San Lorenzo quarter, this friendly, hard-working bistro-like restaurant broke new ground with its high-quality creative cooking (by the gifted owner-chef and avid researcher, Mino Grassadonia) and extraordinary wine list (100 interesting labels)—both at extraordinarily reasonable prices.

New dishes appear every day on a blackboard, but the menu is basically *cucina creativa* with a Sicilian orientation (for example, superb *caponata* and seafood couscous). However, one of Mino's pièces de résistance is *baccalà mantecato,* baked in a ramekin and served with a lentil sauce. A friend recently grew wistful recalling a main dish of boned stuffed quail she'd had there some ten years ago. The pasta is homemade.

The desserts, which are exquisite, are the equal of any gourmet restaurant costing three times the price. We've tasted a superb pear cake with pistachio sauce and a hazelnut *semifreddo* with hot chocolate sauce.

La Dolce Vita

🌴🌴🌴🌴 | CLASSIC RESTAURANT | FISH; PIZZA

Lungotevere Pietra Papa, 51 (Ponte Marconi), 00146 Roma
☎ 06/5579865
Ⓜ Metro B: San Paolo
◻ Basilica of St. Paul's Outside the Walls
∅ Monday | Outdoor tables
🕐 dinner only, except Sunday
€€€ (less for pizza) | MasterCard Diners Club Amex VISA

*T*he omnipresent owner Giorgio Bodoni is president of the association of Roman restaurateurs, and, as is only fitting, this solidly bourgeois restaurant is one of the best run in Rome. It is located a short taxi ride from the center, near the Tiber across a bridge from the Basilica of Saint Paul's Outside the Walls, which is certainly impressive with its after-dark lighting.

The specialty is fish, and has been since well before the current fish boom. There is a huge antipasto buffet, or you can begin with a delicious, hearty sauté of clams and mussels in a tomato broth, or wimpy and fashionable *carpaccio* (paper-thin slices) of marinated salmon and octopus and smoked tuna and swordfish. The menu is large, and it is safe here to venture into something a little more daring than the standards, such as *linguine* with slivers of *bottarga* dressed with garlic and olive oil, a Sardinian import, or black *fettuccine* (cuttlefish ink is mixed with the dough), sauced with tender pieces of cuttlefish and fresh tomatoes. But Roman tradition is well served. The plain *spaghetti alle vongole* is excellent, as is the *pasta e broccoli in brodo di arzilla*.

For *secondi,* there is a light, crisp *fritto misto* including squid, shrimp, whole small red mullet, cod, and sole. A fresh whole fish, maybe a *rombo* (turbot), baked with potatoes and a touch of tomato is a good choice, or else grilled, or cooked in *acquapazza*.

Typically, the dessert choices are limited, but they are good. There is a fine fruit salad and a delicious concoction (*cucchiaiata,* or spoonful) of cake and custard, cherries, and chocolate.

A serviceable wine list emphasizes Italian whites, north and south.

Enoteca al Parlamento (Achilli)

🏛🏛🏛🏛 | WINE SHOP WITH TASTING AND CANAPÉS |

Via dei Prefetti, 15 (Piazza Montecitorio), 00186 Roma

☎ 06/6873446

📷 Parliament, Via del Corso

∅ Sunday; August 15 to 30 | No tables

🕐 9:30 A.M. to 1:30 P.M., 4:30 to 8:30 P.M.

€ |

A very amusing thing to do to pass the time between shopping or work and dinner is to stop by this charming wine and gourmet shop, which has been here since 1778, just a step from the Parliament, for a glass of wine and as many delicious and imaginative *tartine,* canapés, as your conscience permits. A small bar near the front of the long narrow shop offers fifty wines by the glass in rotation. You could have a Prosecco, a favorite *apéritif,* or take the opportunity to taste an interesting, or even very interesting, white or red.

Antica Enoteca di Via della Croce

🏛🏛🏛 | WINE BAR WITH FOOD |

Via della Croce, 76/b (Via del Corso), 00187 Rome

☎ 06/6790896

📷 Piazza di Spagna

🕐 10:00 A.M. to 1:00 A.M.

€€ (for a meal) |

$\mathscr{F}$ounded in 1726 (though the present management dates only to the mid-1990s), this is one of
Rome's oldest and most beautiful wine bars. With some
one thousand wines, it's also one of the best stocked. It's
frequented by beautiful people—actors and actresses, say—
more than tourists, despite its location in the thick of the
Piazza di Spagna shopping area.

You can have wine by the glass in the front room, either
standing at the bar or seated. In the back room, a menu
offers enough choices to make a light or complete hot or
cold meal, with homemade dessert.

Palazzo del Freddo Fassi

🏛 🏛 🏛 | GELATERIA

Via Principe Eugenio, 65/67 (Piazza Vittorio Emanuele),
  00185 Roma
☎ 06/4464740
📷 Piazza Vittorio
∅ Monday (even if it's a holiday); no vacation. Fassi has a
  complicated schedule that seems to vary every time I ask,
  so double check if you plan to go very early or very late.
  There is a second shop at Via Vespasiano, 56a, in Prati, near
  the Vatican, tel. 06/39725164. The hours are the same at
  both shops.
€ | 💳 none

$\mathscr{T}$he ungentrified Piazza Vittorio quarter is cen-
trally located near Santa Maria Maggiore and the
train station, and were it not fast becoming Rome's Little
Africa, Asia, and Arabia, could claim to be one of the last
traditional neighborhoods of Rome. This is the quarter's
favorite gelateria. The first time I went, I was alone and

had to ask directions from several people, each of whom smiled wistfully at the very mention of the name Fassi. It's more like a boardwalk pavilion than an ice cream parlor, in size as well as style, but there are tables and waiter service. Giovanni Fassi founded the Palazzo del Freddo in 1928, and before that his father, in Sicily, had been running a gelateria since 1880.

My favorite flavor was mint, which seems to have been discontinued, but you might try *cocco* or *riso* (with grains of rice), or even a *caterinetta,* which is a *semifreddo.* Ice cream is available in cones or cups, or to take out.

Ferrara

🏛🏛🏛🏛 | RESTAURANT, WINE BAR, GOURMET SHOP | *CUCINA CREATIVA* | 🔪

Via del Moro, 1A (Piazza Trilussa), 00153 Roma
☎ 06/58333920 | 📠 06/5803769
📷 Trastevere, Ponte Sisto, Cinema Pasquino
∅ Sundays in summer, Tuesdays in winter | ♿
Reservations suggested for restaurant
€€€€ | 💳 💳 💳

*D*uring my first few years living in Rome, in the early 1980s, several different sets of friends introduced me to a wonderful trattoria known as Il Generale, located in Trastevere, near Piazza Trilussa and convenient to the Pasquino, the English-language movie theater. Today on the site of Il Generale, and occupying much of the real estate adjacent to its right, is Ferrara, an extremely stylish multifunction gourmet destination. It's so, well, *designed*—a little faux rusticity here, a lot of sophisticated lighting and shelving there—that I was, frankly, expecting to hate it. But it's good.

The wine bar section offers wines by the glass and light meals or snacks. The restaurant, where a friend and I dined recently, offers a varied and (somewhat precious) creative menu, attractive presentation, and attentive (if not effusive) service. The restaurant's patrons seemed quieter and better dressed than the usual Trastevere crowd. We enjoyed the antipasto of eggplant slices rolled around a filling of chèvre, the *sformato* of rice packaged in eggplant slices, a main dish of exquisitely tender and tasty octopus (*polpetti*), and, for dessert, a sort of fig strudel. The menu offers good vegetarian options, but also a great deal of *carpaccio* of this and that.

The wine list, which is superb, consists of two albums of labels, many with annotation. On the way out, I spotted two bottles behind the counter from which I'd have liked to imbibe—Churchill's White Port (which should actually be served chilled as an apéritif) and *grappa* of Rosso del Conte, a wonderful red wine produced by Tasca d'Almerita in Sicily.

Dar Filettaro Santa Barbara

🏛 🏛 | SPECIALIST HOLE-IN-THE-WALL

Largo dei Librari, 88 (Via dei Giubbonari), Roma
☎ 06/6864018
📷 Campo de' Fiori
∅ Sunday | 🕐 5:30 to 11 P.M.
€ | ▭ none

*Y*ou can eat or take out anything you want here—as long as it's a *filletto di baccalà*. This tiny, plain establishment, which specializes in a single food—batter-fried salt-cod fillets—is a sentimental favorite even of those Romans who have never been there. Located just off Via dei Giubbonari (its tiny piazza is on your right as you walk toward Campo de' Fiori), it is practically invisible when closed.

Filetti di baccalà are a staple of the pizzeria menu, and, as a pillar of the Roman repertoire of *fritti*, often find a place in the *fritto misto* of some very upmarket restaurants. If you don't try the cod at, say, Paris (page 93), do try to have one here. Bland, gummy frozen specimens are invading the city's pizzerias. When it's good, as it is here, the fish is delicate, the batter crisp and golden.

Frontoni

👑👑👑 | *PIZZA AL TAGLIO, TAVOLA CALDA*
WITH TABLES

Viale Trastevere, 52/58 (Via San Francesco a Ripa),
    00153 Roma
☎ 06/5812436 | 📠 06/58345725
📷 Trastevere
🕐 10:30 A.M.–1 A.M., Sunday 5 P.M.–1 A.M.
€ | 💳 none

GELATERIA FRONTONI

Via di S. Francesco a Ripa, 130
☎ 06/5816915

*P*izza bianca may be the secret really favorite food of most Romans. It is a form of *focaccia,* which is a generic term, contrary to the expectations of many American visitors, who have something very specific in mind—probably the softer, thicker *focaccia genovese.* Never mind. *Pizza bianca* is a flatbread. It is baked in the pizza oven in rectangles about a foot wide and three feet long, then brushed with oil and sometimes salted. It is customarily cut into slices just small enough to hold in the hand. The slice is either wolfed down as is, preferably still warm, or split horizontally and filled with something. Ordinary fillings run to mozzarella and tomatoes or prosciutto; tuna fish and tomatoes; mortadella; and maybe grilled eggplant slices.

In early summer, *pizza bianca* enjoys a jump in status from favorite snack or quick lunch to gourmet item. Figs are in season, and you have not lived until you've eaten peeled fresh figs squished whole between the halves of a slice of fresh *pizza bianca* and completed with thin slices of *prosciutto crudo*.

Frontoni, a contender for best *pizza bianca* in Rome, is an institution, albeit recently spruced up, on Viale Trastevere. In season, a pile of peeled figs beckons on top of the counter. All year round, the possible fillings include—in any combination you can dream up—*bresaola,* prosciutto, mortadella, mozzarella, smoked provola, mascarpone, smoked salmon, tomatoes, a mayonnaise-tuna dressing (*salsa tonnata*), sautéed broccoli, diced sautéed eggplant, peppers, zucchini, Brie. Chopped *rughetta* is sprinkled on everything. Try salmon with a little mascarpone; you may decide to forget bagels and cream cheese.

Another counter offers *tavola calda*—ready-made pastas and main dishes—and yet another has regular *pizza a taglio* with, inter alia, tomatoes and Gorgonzola, mozzarella and squash flowers, and chopped tomatoes with a special sauce.

For dessert, go around the corner to the new gourmet gelateria: The yogurt isn't just yogurt, it's Greek yogurt (and Greek yogurt ice cream is delicious); the coffee is *caffè arabica;* the melon is *melone franceschina*—little flavor bombs scarcely bigger than a bocce ball.

Il Gelato di San Crispino

♔ ♔ ♔ ♔ ♔ | GELATERIA

Via Acaia, 56 (Piazza Zama), 00183 Roma
☎ 06/70450412
📷 Near Aurelian Wall, San Giovanni, Baths of Caracalla
Ø Tuesday | No tables
€ | ▭ none

Via dei Panettieri, 42 (Fontana di Trevi), 00187 Roma
☎ 06/6793924
📷 Trevi fountain
Ø Tuesday | Tables
€ | ▭ none

*I*n proper Italian, *gelato,* meaning simply "frozen," is used generically to describe a number of confections. The correct word for ice cream kept in tubs for scooping is *mantecato,* literally, "whipped." *Mantecati,* in fifteen to twenty flavors at a time, are the only items on sale at the two San Crispino shops. The Alongi family, from the Alto Adige region in the far north, founded the first shop in 1993 and added the more central Trevi fountain one, with a few tables, in 1998. Both shops are models of cleanliness, organization (take a number), and patience.

Ingredients are chosen with rigor and fervor, and flavors requiring anything store-bought or preserved are eliminated from consideration. Cones are not used—only cups—because they are considered unhygienic.

The signature flavor, *gelato di San Crispino,* is a form of *crema,* the basic plain Italian ice cream, but with the brilliant addition of bitter *corbezzolo* (arbutus) honey. The *zabaglione* looks like fresh egg yolks and tastes like a fine aged Marsala. The pistachio is mud-colored, not green, and the *nocciola* (hazelnut) is nearly white—artificial colorings are banned.

The fruit flavors are almost as dense and velvety as the creams. The *pera* makes you wonder whether you've ever really tasted a pear before. Pink grapefruit has only the sweetness of the perfect fruit, none of the bite. Banana is wonderful too. *Ribes,* red currant, enjoys a short season and is superb. *Crema di limone* is another favorite.

There are also some liquor-based flavors—Moscato di Pantelleria, Armagnac. Try mixing them with fig or walnut *gelato.*

The original shop is in a residential neighborhood near the third-century Aurelian Wall, a leisurely stroll from the Colosseum area and midway between the Basilica of San Giovanni and the Baths of Caracalla. It is easily spotted by the throng of happy ice cream eaters hanging around outside the door. The Trevi fountain shop has a few tables in a small room at the back.

Osteria la Gensola

🏛 🏛 | TRATTORIA PLUS | SOME SICILIAN DISHES

Piazza della Gensola, 15 (Piazza in Piscinula), 00153 Roma
📞 06/58332758, 06/5816312
📷 Trastevere, Tiber Island
∅ Saturday lunch
Reservations advised
€€ | [MasterCard] [Diners Club] [Amex] [VISA]

Trans Tiberim is Latin for "across the Tiber," and, in the great tradition of left banks, Trastevere (as the name became) has its own identity. The residents—the ones who have been there for at least seven generations, that is—consider themselves the true Romans, a state celebrated annually with a street festival known as La Festa de Noantri, Noantri being *romanesco* for the Italian *noi altri,* "we others," which means, more or less, "we as opposed to the rest of you." Even as late as the 1960s, Trastevere was known as the best quarter for restaurants, and Federico Fellini interviewed Gore Vidal at one of them in his film *Roma.* Today, however, interspersed among evocative corners of heart-wrenching loveliness, and a few good places to eat, is the city's greatest concentration of fast food, tourist traps, and youth hangouts.

During the eighteenth and nineteenth centuries, northern Europeans on the Grand Tour enjoyed slumming in the jolly authentic *osterie* of Trastevere. Scenes of Nordic gentlemen and *trasteverine* barmaids were a favorite subject of Grand Tour painting, and a number of such canvases can be seen in the Thorvaldsen Museum in Copenhagen, devoted to the works and personal collection of the Danish neoclassical sculptor Bertel Thorvaldsen, who died in 1844. One of the best known of these scenes, painted by Ditlev Conrad Blunck in 1837, shows a group of Danish artists, including, prominently, Thorvaldsen himself, in the *osteria* called La Gensola, which at that time had already existed for more than a century.

Fast-forward to the early 1980s, and we find La Gensola a much-loved Sicilian restaurant. It was sold to the present owners in 1985, and the cook is still Sicilian. The menu, which wanders all over the map, highlights the Sicilian dishes, and by all means stick to them: *pasta alla Norma* (with eggplant and *ricotta salata*), *pasta con le sarde,* swordfish *involtini, alici alla beccafico* (fresh anchovies, stuffed and grilled), and for dessert, homemade Sicilian classics, *cannoli* and *cassata.*

Gigqetto al Portico d'Ottavia

🏛🏛🏛 | OLD-STYLE RESTAURANT | *CUCINA*
ROMANA AND ROMAN JEWISH SPECIALTIES

Via del Portico d'Ottavia, 21a (Ghetto), 00186 Roma
☎ 06/6861105 | 📠 06/6832106
📷 Jewish quarter
∅ Monday; two weeks in July or August |
   Outdoor tables | ♿
Reservations suggested, not always needed
€€€ | MasterCard | Diners Club | | VISA

*R*un since 1922 by the Ceccarelli family, this large
traditional restaurant, which specializes in Roman
Jewish favorites, is a reassuring constant.

Because of having been around so long in such a
prominent location, it gets a great many foreign visitors,
and many Romans ignore it, but, while it's not a gourmet
destination, neither is it a tourist trap. It always seems to
be open on days when everything else is closed, and a plate
of deep-fried *filetti di baccalà, carciofi alla giudia, fiori di
zucca,* and maybe a *mozzarella in carrozza* always hits the
spot. The menu also includes plenty of other Roman specialties, such as *coda alla vaccinara*. In late spring, the *fave
con guanciale* here are superb; order them as soon as you
walk in the door, as the supply is always limited.

The sidewalk tables are actually in the remains of the
first-century Portico of Octavia, sister of the first emperor,
Augustus, and a most pleasant place to spend a summer
evening. Indoors, the restaurant is divided into several
rooms and always seems to be bustling.

The house Frascati *bianco* is not quite adequate to the
food, but with a wine list of four hundred labels, there's no
reason not to choose something else.

Giolitti

🏛🏛🏛🏛🏛 | GELATERIA

Via Uffici del Vicario, 40 (Parlamento, Via Campo Marzio),
    00186 Roma
☎ 06/6991243 | www.giolitti.it
📷 Pantheon, Parliament
∅ Monday | ♿ Wheelchair access, but bathroom is small
€ | [MasterCard] [D] [▬] [VISA] (minimum, L. 10,000)

*N*azareno Giolitti's great-great-grandfather used
    to sell milk straight from the cow at the top of
the Salita del Grillo near the Markets of Trajan. Founded
in 1900, the Giolitti *gelateria* has been an institution for
generations, the most characteristic *gelateria* in Rome and
one of the best. The large bar area in classic, elegant style
contains a normal coffee bar, a pastry counter selling
exquisite confections to take away, and, toward the back, a
thronged ice cream counter. A large back room, however,
is a serene classic ice cream parlor, where you can have not
little cups and cones, but proper dishes of ice cream and
elaborate *coppe*. The house specialties (served only at the
tables, not the bar) are the *coppa Giolitti, coppa olimpica,*
and *coppa mondiale,* all based on *torrone*-flavored gelato
with extravagant amounts of whipped cream, chocolate,
and other embellishments.

The fifty flavors are, as always, divided into fruits (seasonal and fresh) and creams, some of which are unconven-
tional. Alongside *ananas, fragola,* and banana (all together)
are green apple, *pinolata* (pine nuts), Mozart and Voglia-
matta (named for the commercial chocolate candies), and
licorice. There are also such imaginative flavors as crème
caramel, *zuppa inglese,* and Grand Marnier (nonalcoholic).
Giolitti invented rice ice cream, which is very difficult to

make well (without any hard uncooked grains), and also solved the problem of how to make "Champagne" (alcoholic) *sorbetto* that would not separate immediately. Date (*datteri*) gelato is one of the most delicious single foods on earth, but I've only managed to find it here once.

Hostaria Romanesca

♔♔ | TYPICAL TRATTORIA

Campo de' Fiori, 40,00186 Roma
☎ 06/6864024
📷 Campo de' Fiori, Museo Barracco, Palazzo Farnese, Palazzo della Cancelleria
∅ Monday
€ | MasterCard DINERS CLUB Cirrus VISA

*T*his is a friendly little survivor with a single small room right on the historic piazza with Rome's most famous market. The décor is all Rosler Franz (the "Roma Sparita" [Vanished Rome] artist whose scenes of the Rome of yesteryear are a favorite theme of trattorias and pizzerias) and Hollywood on the Tiber, with photos of Ben Gazzara, Troy Donahue, Al Pacino, and Francis Ford Coppola.

On a winter Sunday, we tasted *fettuccine romanesca,* a real throwback (to the early 1970s at least), with peas, mushrooms, tomato, and cream. The ravioli with *ricotta e spinaci* were very good. *Polpette* were very large and basic, with a gallon of tomato sauce. *Trippa alla romana* was tasty but lacked mint, an essential ingredient. The *cicoria ripassata* was superb.

In short, it's as authentic and typical an experience as anyone has a right to find in the middle of town.

Pizzeria Leonina

🏛🏛🏛🏛 | *PIZZA AL TAGLIO*

Via Leonina, 84 (Via Cavour, Via dei Serpenti), 00184 Roma
☎ 06/4827744
📷 San Pietro in Vincoli (Michelangelo's Moses), Colosseum, Roman Forum, Imperial Fora
∅ Saturday and Sunday; much of the summer | No tables
🕐 8:30 A.M. to 9:00 P.M.
€ | 💳 none

*I*ce cream and *pizza al taglio* are the only two foods you'll see Romans eating while walking in the street. Both can be treated as a snack or replace a meal, and both, for the duration, make you forget your troubles and feel better about life. It follows that every Roman has a favorite gelateria and a favorite *pizza al taglio,* "the best in Rome." Of course, they can't all be the best in Rome, but this one is a contender.

Narrow, busy Via Leonina runs parallel to Via Cavour, but at a lower level, in the part of the city known as Monti. The shop is invisible when closed, so if you don't see the pizzeria, come back another day. Take a number and try to get close enough to the glass case to see the pizzas and make your choice while you wait. Unlike most *pizza al taglio,* the pizza is thin-crusted and not baked in a pan. Toppings include spicy tomatoes (called *"la burrina"*), potatoes (try it), and vegetables. There are also some dessert pizzas with fruit (such as apples and raisins), Nutella, or ricotta. Your pizza is cut into little squares and either placed on a wooden board, so you can set it on the narrow counter and eat in with a plastic cup of water, or bagged for takeaway.

Trattoria Lilli

🏛 🏛 | LARGE TRATTORIA | *CUCINA CASARECCIA*

Via Tor di Nona, 26 (Lungotevere Tor di Nona), 00186 Roma
☎ 06/6861916
📷 Piazza Navona, Via dei Coronari, Castel Sant'Angelo
∅ Sunday | Outdoor tables | ♿ Wheelchair access but not
to bathroom
Reservations advised (a must on weekends)
€ | 💳 VISA

*F*ounded in 1915, this is one of Rome's classic trattorias, though it is unusually large (it occupies
two floors). The menu, which changes daily, offers very
basic home cooking and is short enough to be convincing.
Rigatoni Lilli has meat sauce (tomato-based) with *scaglie di
Parmigiano* and basil. Or you might have *penne all'arrabbiata* or *bucatini all'amatriciana. Secondi* include fried *polpettine* with *borlotti* beans, *zucchine ripiene,* tripe, *"la fornara"*
(roast veal breast), and rabbit *alla cacciatora.* The restaurant's business card boasts a huge choice of wine, but I
don't know where they keep it.

It's a bargain for its high-rent location, near the Tiber,
within striking distance of the antiques shops of Via dei
Coronari.

Trattoria da Lucia

🍷🍷 | ARCHETYPAL TRATTORIA |
CUCINA CASALINGA

Vicolo del Mattonato, 2b (Via Garibaldi), 00153 Roma
☎ 06/5803601
📷 Trastevere
∅ Monday; three weeks in August | Sidewalk tables
Reservations advised
€€ | 💳 none

*T*his Trastevere trattoria from Central Casting was
founded in 1938 by the original Lucia and contin-
ued by her daughter, Silvana Cestier, and grandson, Renato.
The style of the rather dim but cozy small dining room is
garlic braids and old photographs interspersed among
framed press cuttings—because no trattoria this archetypal is going to be left in obscurity.

The restaurant itself is tiny, but tables are also set up
in the narrow street outside the door. We arrived early for
an early-summer dinner and found all the Italian patrons
indoors and only foreigners outside.

Its admirers consider Da Lucia a major exponent of *la
cucina romana*. I wouldn't go that far, but in a handful of
primi and a few *secondi*, the menu covers the basics with no
useless attempts at being imaginative, and the quality is
certainly better than average. There is a nice vegetable
antipasto and good marinated anchovies to start with, and
the *pane casareccio* is excellent. *Primi* might include *pasta
e ceci, pasta con broccoli e arzilla, spaghetti alla gricia,* and
tortelloni al ragù. We recently had a main course consisting
of a single *involtino in sugo,* which, while good, is usually
served in the plural. It and the *seppie* (cuttlefish) both came
with the same frozen peas.

The homemade desserts are quite wonderful, the crème caramel superb. There is a modest but well-intentioned wine list.

Pizzeria ai Marmi
(ex-Panattoni, "L'obitorio")

🏛🏛 | PIZZERIA

Viale Trastevere, 53, 00153 Roma
☎ 06/5800919
📷 Trastevere
∅ Wednesday; part of August | Sidewalk tables
🕐 6:30 P.M. to 2:30 A.M.
€ | ▭ none

Viale Trastevere is so much a part of popular Rome that one just assumes it has been there since antiquity, when Jews and Christians occupied the quarter beneath the Janiculum hill, on the side of the Tiber opposite the Tiber Island and the Capitoline, Palatine, and Aventine hills. But that broad, congested street, aligned with Via Arenula and Ponte Garibaldi, was created in the nineteenth century when Rome became capital of the united Italy, by demolition of a swath through the middle of a nice medieval neighborhood—remains of which survive south of the *viale* and thanks to which Trastevere is still one of the most characteristic neighborhoods in Rome. Viale Trastevere is lined with cinemas and old-style shops selling hats or bedroom slippers, as well as the latest in video games and telephony. It also has plenty of places to eat, including an international fast food spot that shall remain nameless. Most people's favorite of the many good pizzerias along the viale is ex-Panattoni, but probably not one person in a hundred knows its name.

Founded in 1943 (though the present management goes back only a couple of decades), it is universally known not by its name, which recently changed, but as *l'obitorio* ("the morgue"), for its original 1940s marble tables. Delicious thin-crusted Roman pizza is served to more than a hundred people at a time in winter and more than twice that many with the addition of sidewalk tables in summer. Because service is rapid, you can eat there and not miss the start of the film at the nearby English-language Cinema Pasquino.

Rounding out the menu are *bruschette, supplì, filetti di baccalà,* vegetable *antipasti,* beans, and salads. Most people have beer with pizza, but there are a house white *vino sfuso* and a few bottles.

Trattoria Monti

🏛🏛🏛 | TRATTORIA PLUS | REGIONAL CUISINE, MARCHE | 🍴

Via San Vito, 13/a (Via Carlo Alberto, Via Merulana),
    00185 Roma
☎ 06/4466573
📷 Santa Maria Maggiore, Santa Prassede, Piazza Vittorio
    Emanuele
∅ Tuesday; August
Reservations usually needed
€€€ | MasterCard DINERS CLUB [card] VISA

Ｗith your back to Agata e Romeo (see page 37), turn right and just around the corner, in Via San Vito, you'll find two interesting things. One is a Roman arch, an Augustan reconstruction of one of the original gates of the city walls. It is known as the Arch of Gallienus because a dedication to that third-century emperor was carved in place of the earlier one to Augustus. The other interesting thing is this cozy trattoria (it seats forty-five), run, since 1971, by the Camerucci family from the Marche region. The ambience is rustic and casual, but the house wine is a Verdicchio DOC (backed up by a list that includes some very good labels from the Marche), and the menu is far more refined and varied than similar places usually offer.

Start with a plate of *antipasto marchigiano,* with delicious (and hard to find in Rome) *cremini fritti, olive all'ascolana,* and spreadable *ciauscolo* sausage, as well as *fiori di zucca.* The house pasta war horse is the *tortello al rosso d'uovo,* a single plate-filling *raviolo* filled with ricotta, spinach, and the runny yolk of an egg, with tomato sauce. The same filling minus the egg is also used in ravioli. Other *primi* include homemade pastas and soups. Main courses might be hearty deep-fried lamb chops and artichokes, or an epicene turkey breast with balsamic vinegar, or *baccalà* with raisins and pine nuts in tomato sauce, or *pollo in potacchio,* an herbed stewed chicken typical of the Marche.

Follow Via San Vito to, and across, Via Merulana and find the church of Santa Prassede, where you will see magnificent ninth-century mosaics. The name of the restaurant is that of the district (*rione*) of Rome where it is located, on the Esquiline hill.

Antica Trattoria al Moro

🏛🏛🏛🏛 | SERIOUS RESTAURANT |
CUCINA ROMANA AND MORE | 🥄

Vicolo delle Bollette, 13 (Via delle Muratte), 00187 Roma
☎ 06/6783495, 06/69940736
📷 Trevi Fountain
∅ Sunday; August
Reservations a must
€€€ | VISA

*T*he conceit is that this is an old-style Roman
trattoria—it was founded in 1929 by the great-
grandfather of Franco Romagnoli, the present owner. In
fact, it is an expensive restaurant, and the only restaurant
I know in Rome beneath the top level of glitz where a
majority of male customers wear neckties. Many of them
are politicians and actors.

The food claims to be *cucina romana,* which it is, but it is
so much better and more varied (including variations from
day to day) than most other *cucina romana* that it ought
to have a different name. *Spaghetti alla Moro* is essentially
a lighter than usual *carbonara; rigatoni alla baronessa* has
minced chicken livers and *funghi porcini.*

There is also excellent fresh fish—*scampi alla Moro* are
cooked in the oven with butter and lemon. The *carciofi alla
romana* are among the best in Rome, as is the *abbacchio alla
cacciatora,* made not with stew meat but with whole little
lamb chops in a piquant sauce.

The wine list is very good, and it comes with knowledgeable service (when we asked for advice in choosing a
Dolcetto d'Alba, we were told the characteristics of the
several producers listed).

The bad news is the tightly spaced tables, where about
ninety diners are packed into three rooms. And then there

is the attitude problem. Despite the good food, we'd always found the restaurant so inhospitable that we went rarely, but we made a breakthrough on our last visit, and I will tell you how. As soon as we had shoehorned ourselves into our seats, a hungry Franco asked for a plate of "those *nervetti*" displayed on the table near the door. The waiter said they were *muscolo,* not *nervetti,* but he said it with respect. In a Roman restaurant, anybody salivating over a platter of sliced cartilage gets respect. Of course they were *nervetti,* Franco won the day, and double the respect, and we had solicitous, polite service from both Mr. Romagnoli and the waiter for the rest of the superb meal, which concluded with a most exquisite chestnut mousse.

Unfortunately, we'll probably have to earn our status all over again the next time.

Hostaria da Nerone

🏛🏛🏛🏛 | TRATTORIA PLUS | *CUCINA ROMANA*

Via delle Terme di Tito, 96 (Colle Oppio), 00184 Roma
☎ | 🖨 06/4817952
Ⓜ Metro B: Colosseo
📷 Colosseum, San Pietro in Vincoli (Michelangelo's Moses),
   Domus Aurea
∅ Sunday | Outdoor tables | ♿
Reservations advised
€€ | MasterCard DINERS CLUB AMEX VISA

Since 1965, Eugenio De Santis and his family, from Abruzzo, have run a perfectly wonderful establishment (itself dating to 1929) on the line between *trattoria* and *ristorante,* serving hearty Roman food, and also, especially on Tuesdays and Fridays, very good fish, simply but skillfully prepared.

At lunchtime, the demographics split about evenly between tourists, treated with kindness, and professors from the nearby University of Rome engineering school, treated with deference and the intimacy of long association ("*Professore,* you look as though you need some nice hot soup."). In the evening, the Reeboks and tweeds are replaced by other habitués, some elderly regulars from the neighborhood, some leather jackets and earrings from beyond, but newcomers are always welcomed.

There's a wonderful antipasto buffet, largely vegetable. There's always minestrone and usually a superb legume soup—*pasta e ceci, pasta e lenticchie, pasta e fagioli*—and a meat sauce and a tomato sauce for spaghetti, *rigatoni,* or *fettuccine.* The homemade ravioli, filled with spinach and ricotta and served either with plain tomato sauce or with melted butter and sage leaves, are a house specialty, as is the *spaghetti alle vongole,* among the best in Rome. The *fettuccine* might also have *funghi porcini,* or be served *alla Nerone,* a congeries of ingredients on a *carbonara*-like base. In summer, instead of pasta, try a *pomodoro al riso.*

Grilled *scampi* in their shells (but split and easy to eat) are superb by any standard, as is the grilled swordfish. Sometimes there's a *rombo* (turbot) to grill too. More traditional main dishes can include *coda alla vaccinara; polpettine,* in tomato sauce (with mashed potatoes) or fried and sauceless; and roast veal with roast potatoes.

Desserts are old-fashioned caloric affairs such as *millefoglie* and *zuppa inglese,* and there is also crème caramel and (in an unconvincing and unique bow to fashion) crème brûlée. In summer, have strawberries cut up and served with either a scoop of ice cream or lemon juice and sugar.

Nerone means Nero: the restaurant, and much else in the neighborhood, stands above the ruins of that emperor's Golden House. Eugenio claims to have a wine cellar from which part of the Domus Aurea can be seen, which is certainly possible. One thing is certain: if it's full of fine vintages, he's keeping them to himself.

Nino

🏛️🏛️🏛️ | RISTORANTE | ROMAN AND TUSCAN
SPECIALTIES

Via Borgognona, 11 (Piazza di Spagna), 00187 Roma
☎ | 📠 06/6786752
Ⓜ Metro A: Spagna
📷 Piazza di Spagna
∅ Sunday; August
€€ | 💳 💳 💳 💳

*T*he *fiasco* (flask) of beans cooking in the window
is an irresistible invitation to the cuisine of Tuscany, including bean soup and *la fiorentina*. This fine
restaurant, which seats a hundred, is a classic—sober, reliable, and good—that has had the same management since
its foundation in 1934.

There are also some good old-fashioned Roman dishes,
such as homemade ravioli and *cannelloni*. Old-style meat-
filled, béchamel-drenched *cannelloni* are rather unfashion-
able, which is why it's so nice to come here and have them.
The customers, however, who include actors and journal-
ists, are fashionable enough, as is the Via Borgognona, as
always.

For dessert, try *castagnaccio,* a traditional dense, flat
chestnut-flour cake, which you almost never see served in
a restaurant in Rome. Wines are predominantly Tuscan.

Trattoria Otello alla Concordia

🏛 | TRATTORIA | *CUCINA ROMANA*

Via della Croce, 81 (Piazza di Spagna), 00187 Roma
☎ 06/6781454, 06/6791178
Ⓜ Metro A: Spagna
📷 Piazza di Spagna
∅ Sunday | No-smoking section
Reservations advised, not always needed
€€ | 💳 💳

*I*ts unusual and charming location, in the courtyard of the eighteenth-century palazzo of the
Boncompagni Ludovisi princes, makes this otherwise un-
distinguished trattoria a perennial favorite of tourists,
locals (including a film crowd), and foreign guide writers.
It is not, however, often mentioned by local foodies, except
for its quaint setting. Also, the many food shops on Via
della Croce give the street a blessed air of permanence and
normality in the otherwise superglitzy Piazza di Spagna
quarter.

The setup is a small wood-paneled trattoria (the smoking section) opening onto the courtyard. Built in the courtyard itself is an enclosed air-conditioned greenhouse-thing
with ghastly acoustics and closely packed tables. The
centerpiece in this section is an ancient Roman granite tub
holding an array of fruits and vegetables. The menu is a
large sheet of paper, partly preprinted (before the flood),
partly filled in by hand with specials (though it is not clear
whether these are the day's or the season's). Note that the
English version of the menu is abbreviated.

Having failed to follow my own advice—to order conservatively in conservative-looking places—a friend and I
on a summer evening had some awful pastas that had
promised to be fresh and light. *Orecchiette* with swordfish

was terrible, and so was *fettuccine* with zucchini flowers. You don't want the details. If you want something fresh and summery here, or anywhere, have *spaghetti con pomodoro e basilico.* They also have *lasagne* and *cannelloni,* which are sort of comfort foods.

Chicken croquettes with deep-fried zucchini sticks, which have been on the menu for at least thirty years and probably much longer, are usually pretty good, as are the meat offerings from the standard repertoire, including veal, in chops or as *saltimbocca alla romana* or breaded *alla milanese.*

A ponderous ring binder circulates as a wine list, promising more than it actually contains. Nevertheless, the choice is sufficient to the menu.

The welcome and service are friendly enough, but just because the service seems brisk doesn't mean you get your food any faster.

Ristorante Paris

👑👑👑👑👑 | SERIOUS RESTAURANT | ROMAN AND ROMAN JEWISH CUISINE; FISH | 🥄

Piazza San Calisto, 7a (Piazza Santa Maria in Trastevere),
   00153 Roma
☎ 06/5815378
📷 Trastevere, Basilica of Santa Maria in Trastevere
∅ Sunday evening and Monday; August | Outdoor tables
€€€ | MasterCard DinersClub ☐ VISA

*I*n 1968, at a Trastevere restaurant, I first tasted a *carciofo alla romana.* This important moment in my gastronomic education took place at the Trattoria Silvano Paris, founded in 1890 by Silvano's grandfather, Dario Paris. (Incidentally, the name Paris has nothing to do with France, but is an old Lazio family name.)

Since 1983, another Dario, Dario Cappellanti, and his wife, Iole, have been owner-chefs (their son Giovanni supervises the dining rooms), but they have kept the name Paris for the restaurant out of respect and tradition.

This attractive restaurant, with three inviting dining rooms and outdoor tables in summer, is one of the few places in the city to offer a near-complete picture of the range and possibilities of the traditional Roman repertoire. The menu covers both the deep-frying of the Jewish tradition and the equally typical *quinto quarto* (fifth quarter, or tail and innards), as well as the often-overlooked Roman garden, and superb fish.

Skate (*razza* in Italian, *arzilla* in Roman dialect) is offered as an antipasto, simply boiled and off the bone, dressed with extra virgin olive oil, or as a traditional *primo piatto, minestra di arzilla,* here offered with or without *broccolo romanesco.* Other *antipasti* not to miss are the perfectly marinated fresh anchovies (not to be confused with preserved anchovies in a jar or in salt) and the homemade *bresaola,* cured beef. The Jewish *fritti—carciofo alla giudia, filetto di baccalà, fiori di zucca—*can be ordered at any point in the meal, including as antipasto, or in the *grande fritto misto vegetariano,* in which case you will want to skip the pasta course unless you are very hungry. If you want your fry really, really Roman, try the *fritto di carciofi, cervello, e animelle,* though not in summer; you can't get good brains during the hot months. *Primi* include superb *agnolotti* in meat sauce, delicate but flavorful homemade *tagliolini con scampi e fiori di zucca,* and an excellent tomatoey *pasta e ceci.* Main dishes include, in addition to fresh fish, *straccetti,* a beautifully lean *coda alla vaccinara,* and a rich *stracotto* (beef pot roast cooked in red wine), served with potato croquettes.

Desserts are homemade. If you have room, try the traditional, suprisingly light fried balls of ricotta marbled with chocolate, called (and not only here) *le palle del nonno,* meaning "grandfather's balls." Really.

The extensive wine list (nearly two hundred labels), with French as well as Italian labels, is a good read and invites the diner to visit the cellar and choose directly.

Ristorante la Piazzetta

🏛🏛🏛🏛 | NEW TRATTORIA PLUS |
MOSTLY *CUCINA ROMANA*

Vicolo del Buon Consiglio, 23/a (Via Cavour), 00184 Roma
☎ 06/6991640
Ⓜ Metro B: Colosseo
📷 Colosseum, Roman Forum, Imperial Fora
∅ Sunday | Outdoor tables
Reservations suggested
€€ | VISA MasterCard

*G*ood taste in both senses characterizes one of the newest restaurants in the monumental center of Rome. After twenty-five years as the crack waiter at Hostaria da Nerone (page 89), Franco Bartolini opened his own place in February 2000, located on a tiny street in a very characteristic neighborhood between the Colosseum and Via Cavour. The squarish dining room, which holds about forty, is comfortable and pretty, with spare decoration (just a few pictures) and soft lighting. On a table in the center of the room, marvelous baked goods appear and disappear. Outdoor tables are sheltered from the street.

The menu is simple but enticing. *Spaghetti alle vongole,* ravioli with spinach and ricotta, *fettuccine* with *funghi porcini,* and other classics, but also delicious *rigatoni* with eggplant, Pachino tomatoes, and *ricotta salata,* and sometimes a *risotto.* Main dishes might include *fegato alla veneziana, polpette,* unusually succulent *abbacchio scottadito,* or grilled swordfish. The menu could stop there and be enough, but I expect it will evolve and expand as the restaurant becomes more firmly established.

Exuberance is already evident in the breads and desserts. Enrico La Licata, the pastry chef, punctuates the meal in the evening with exquisite mini-*supplì* to start, followed by different-flavored rolls (onion, poppy seed). Then come the sweets—*brutti ma buoni* cookies, crème brûlée, *millefoglie, torta della nonna,* and a delicious cake made with pears and grappa—all exquisite.

Some decent bottles, offered generically, are available (Greco di Tufo, Müller Thurgau, Pinot Grigio, Chianti, Chardonnay), but we're still waiting for a wine list.

Ristorante la Pigna

🏛🏛🏛 | TRATTORIA PLUS | *CUCINA ROMANA;* FISH

Piazza della Pigna, 54 (Via del Gesù), 00186 Roma
☎ 06/6787993, 06/6785555
📷 Chiesa del Gesù, Largo Argentina, Pantheon
∅ Sunday | Outdoor tables
Reservations advised
€€ | [MasterCard] [Diners Club] [American Express] [VISA]

Several indoor rooms in classic style and an unusually pleasant space outdoors make up this fine family-run restaurant, beloved of neighbors and ignored by guidebooks. You might start with very good fried *fiori di zucca,* and continue with superb *spaghetti alle vongole,* the best of their *primi.* The unusually good house wine comes from the Marche.

For dessert, have the light as a feather *"girasole"* (sunflower), spongecake with creamy frosting.

Al Ponte della Ranocchia

🌳🌳 | CASUAL RESTAURANT | TRADITIONAL
ROMAN AND JEWISH COOKING | 🗝

Circonvallazione Appia, 29 (Via Tola), 00179 Roma
☎ 06/7856712
Ⓜ Metro A: Ponte Lungo
∅ Sunday | Sidewalk tables
Reservations advised
€€ | [MasterCard] [Diners Club] [🔲 Card] [VISA]

T̵he name refers to a neighborhood toponym, Frog
Bridge, not to anything on the menu. The restaurant is a one-room trattoria that offers unusual knowledge
of, and attention to, wine and a menu that derives from
two Roman traditions, Gentile and Jewish, each identified
on the menu with a symbol.

The coexistence of a serious wine list, a Jewish menu,
and a Roman menu is a little artificial, and indeed the
restaurant is relatively new. But the owners have done their
research and come up with recipes that claim a Roman
pedigree but are not found on the menus of more "authentic" trattorias: crisp *guanciale* slices with vinegar, and *ruota
del faraona* ("pharaoh's wheel"), which is *fettuccine* sautéed
with smoked goose, raisins, and pine nuts (for two).

Don't pile onto the subway to make a gastronomic pil-
grimage—it's a modest little place; but the location should
not deter you if you want a change of pace.

Il Quadrifoglio

♔♔♔♔ | INTIMATE REGIONAL RESTAURANT | NEAPOLITAN CUISINE

Via del Boschetto, 19 (Via Nazionale), 00184 Roma
☎ 06/4826096
📷 Palazzo delle Esposizioni
∅ Sunday; August
€€€ | [MasterCard] [Diners Club] [card] [VISA]

*T*his isn't a trattoria, but it's a very nice little niche restaurant to know about when you want something special but easy. The cuisine is genteel, but not over-refined, Neapolitan, and the unusually pretty, precious countrified décor evokes a Campanian rusticity that is idyllic rather than bovine. The ambiance is tranquil and intimate, with service provided by a couple of competent waiters while the owner, Signora Annamaria, buzzes in and out of the dining room, lingering to converse with customers she likes.

The *antipasti,* which are delicious, tend toward starch (puffy light pizzas, *calzoni* filled with cooked chicory and black olives), so be sure to regulate your intake to leave room for the pasta.

The pastas are singularly fabulous and impossible to choose among. *Penne allo scarpariello* is sauced with tomato, then tossed again in the pan; *pasta alla genovese* is made with a sauce derived from roast meat. There is also a worthy *sartù di riso,* the only rice dish in the Neapolitan repertoire. The rice is studded with tiny meatballs and peas and placed in a mold, then turned out and served with tomato sauce.

Secondi include *polpetti* (small octopus) in dense tomato sauce, which is one of our favorites, as are the veal meatballs (*granatine*) flavored with fresh cilantro. The menu usually offers a couple of tasty fish dishes too, such as *cernia* (grouper) fillets with wild fennel, another reason this restaurant makes a nice change.

Desserts are simple: a scrumptious *babà* with custard sauce (a Neapolitan specialty, owing to the long Bourbon influence), or plain *torta caprese,* a simple chocolate cake, or lemon sherbet. A glass of *limoncello* to conclude does not seem out of place.

The brief wine list favors southern labels.

Ricci (Est! Est! Est!)

🏛 🏛 | PIZZERIA

Via Genova, 32 (Via Nazionale), Roma
☎ 06/4881107
📷 Teatro dell'Opera
∅ Monday | 🕐 7 P.M. to midnight
Reservations a good idea for large parties
€ | MasterCard VISA

*T*he sign "Est! Est! Est!" outside the door is the name of a wine from Lake Bolsena, in northern Lazio—according to the traditional *osteria* practice of attracting customers with the name of the house wine. Ricci is the name of the family that has run it since 1905. Art Deco wood paneling and brass give this the most atmosphere of any of Rome's pizzerias.

In addition to superb pizza, there are *fritti,* beans, one or two pastas, and some salads. Frascati and sweet Est! Est!! Est!!! are available in carafe; dry Est! Est!! Est!!! is available only in bottles. There is a brief but worthy wine list, though nowadays most people drink beer with pizza.

Something is going on in Roman pizzadom. Many new pizzerias are opening, and they are serving yeasty

Neapolitan-style pizza rather than thin-crusted Roman-style—and the pizza-crust dichotomy is one of the fault-lines along which Italian society splits. Don't be fooled by pizzerias that seem to offer an ecumenical menu with both styles. Their "Roman" is actually a less-yeasty Neapolitan rather than a true Roman. But in Via Genova, the pizza has always been sui generis and above the fray. The crust is a little softer and thicker than Roman, but not yeasty like Neapolitan. The pizza diameter is a little less than usual, but all pizzas are available in giant format (*gigante*) at twice the price. (The giant is seen more as a single portion for large appetites than to share.)

Il Sanpietrino

🏛🏛🏛🏛🏛 | STYLISH RESTAURANT |
CONSERVATIVELY CREATIVE | 🥄

Piazza Costaguti, 15 (Via del Portico d'Ottavia), 00186 Roma
📞 06/68806471 | 📠 06/68806479 |
http://dimauro-sanpietrino.com;
pdm.dimauro@flashet.it
📷 Ghetto
∅ Sunday and holidays; three weeks in August and first week in January
🕐 evenings only | ♿
€€€ | [MasterCard] [Diners Club] [American Express] [VISA]

*I*n but not of the old Jewish quarter, and scarcely a trattoria, this is a relatively new (founded in 1993), modern restaurant. I include it not so much because the food is wonderful, which it is, but because it offers such a good selection of the wines of the Lazio region—and not just those produced by the partner Armando Di Mauro and his esteemed mother, Paolo Di Mauro, doyenne of Castelli Romani winemakers and a renowned cook. Armando's son Oscar is also a presence in the restaurant, and lest it seem that a slick exterior is incompatible with respect for tradition, one evening Oscar told us, "The chef is practicing *baccalà alla romana,* but I think we're going to send him to my grandmother for a lesson."

This is a very handy place to keep in mind because it covers the difficult ground beneath fancy and above everyday. All the details are taken care of: from the friendly greeting to the elegant candlelit tables, flutes of *spumante,* and impeccable service. The only thing to bear in mind is that dinner can take simply hours.

The restaurant is on the ground floor of the sixteenth-century Palazzo Costaguti in the old Jewish quarter. The discreet street-level entrance leads through a narrow foyer-bar to two intimate dining rooms enlivened with colored tiles. Medieval and Renaissance doorways are embedded in the walls of the farther one. Renaissance paving stones (the basalt *sanpietrini,* still used) give the restaurant its name.

But what about the food? Expect the menu to evolve, but here are some dishes we have enjoyed. The mixed antipasto is slow to arrive but worth the wait. There are baked eggplant with fresh anchovies, a spinach-filled roll of turbot and salmon, delicious marinated salmon, an assertive goose prosciutto (a nod to the Jewish quarter, since goose often replaces pork on Jewish menus), tiny meatballs in orange sauce, and thin-sliced rolled stuffed guinea fowl.

The pastas vary, but the voluptuous *bignolini*—unsweetened choux pastry baked with cheese fondue and *funghi porcini*—seem to have settled in. There's usually a good variety of fish and non. Tender little rolls of veal filled with *provola* cheese and wrapped in thin slices of *guanciale* are a perennial favorite *secondo,* but the *baccalà* is improving, and sometimes there are *cernia* (grouper) fillets cooked with raisins and pine nuts, another old Roman Jewish dish and delicious.

Desserts are superb. Look no further than the gourmet *torta della nonna,* but if you must, try the crème brûlée, the genuine article for once.

Ristorante Settimio

🏛🏛🏛 | TRATTORIA PLUS | *CUCINA ROMANA;* GAME | 🔪

Via delle Colonnelle, 14 (Piazza della Maddalena), 00186 Roma
☎ 06/6789651
📷 Pantheon
∅ Sunday and Monday
Reservations suggested
€€ | 💳 💳 💳

The demographics of the Pantheon area reflect its proximity to the Italian Parliament and its importance as a tourist destination, and its restaurant scene generally reflects its demographics. Settimio, however, apparently caters to neither group, but rather to loyal locals.

The kitchen specializes in game and meat in general, with several offerings of polenta, and the kitchen is better than the eccentric décor suggests, which is very Roman. The tiled walls are covered with graffiti and vintage photos. A large copper pot and a pair of fencing foils are among the wall hangings. We tried a superb roast lamb with potatoes, as well as superb versions of such simple fare as *bruschetta con pomodoro, penne all'arrabbiata* (served with optional pecorino; Parmesan would, of course, be taboo with this spicy dish), *tagliolini con pomodoro,* and a *bistecca alla griglia,* and, for dessert, an excellent chestnut *semifreddo.*

There's a good choice of wines, and service is solicitous and efficient.

Sora Lella

🏛 🏛 🏛 | TRADITIONAL RESTAURANT |
CUCINA ROMANA

Via di Ponte Quattro Capi, 16 (Isola Tiberina), 00186 Roma
📞 06 / 6861601
📷 Tiber Island, Trastevere, Ghetto
∅ Sunday
Reservations advised
€€€ | MasterCard Diners Club [card] VISA

The genealogy of this establishment's owners is important in understanding why it is sort of the sacred cow of the Roman restaurant scene. *Sora* is short for sister (*sorella*). Lella is a woman's name. The actual Sora Lella, whose son Renato Trabalza is still there in the kitchen cooking, founded the restaurant. As popular as she was for her *cucina romana,* her real fame came in fact from being somebody's sister. That somebody was the great Aldo Fabrizi, actor, poet, and embodiment of the popular spirit of Rome.

And so Sora Lella's heirs occupy the only restaurant on the Tiber Island, midway between Trastevere and the Ghetto.

The ambience, in the bottom of a medieval tower, is cozy and rustic—and suggests a lower price tag. Many people, including a number of gourmets I trust, and Italian guidebooks love the restaurant. But others feel that it is too expensive for what it is and that, while the meal is enjoyable while you're eating it, you don't remember anything about it afterward. Fortunately, the last time we ate there I took notes.

We began with an unmemorable "Sora Lella cocktail" made of Prosecco and some sort of *analcolico.* The antipasto was a *carciofo alla giudia* and a slice of a tasty cold *frittata Paesana* containing diced cooked vegetables (including carrots and potatoes). For our *primo piatto*, we had *brodo di arzilla*, which was very hearty, with lots of tomatoes, and very tasty and satisfying *"bombolotti alla ciafruiona"*—half-rigatoni with a sauce of tuna, tomatoes (sort of watery), peas, and artichokes. The *involtini* were enveloped in sweet peppers, according to my notes, and I do remember liking them. *Abbacchio brodettato*, another main course, is an example of the great virtue of this restaurant. It is bony chunks of Roman lamb cooked in an egg sauce. This is an absolute classic of the Roman kitchen that practically nobody makes any more.

But *puntarelle con la salsa* were tired and watery, and a *carciofo alla romana* also seemed watery and overboiled, but Mr. Trabalza assured us his method is authentic, so what do we know? It is very rare for a restaurant to offer artichokes both *alla giudia* and *alla romana;* they usually specialize in one or the other. Possibly the island location is the explanation.

Desserts were pretty good. A *torta di ricotta* came with a glass of sweet Cannellino wine. A *crostata di marmellata di amarene* was served too cold, but it is another too-rare Roman treat; it was matched with a glass of sweet Moscato rosa.

The very impressive wine list includes the region's best labels, but the first three wines we asked for were out of stock. We wanted Paola Di Mauro's Vigna dei Vassalli, her top-line single-vineyard red from Marino in the Castelli Romani. We wound up with Campo Vecchio, a Lazio IGT produced by the worthy Castel De' Paolis, also in the Castelli. My notes say I thought it was too young, which is not surprising considering the inventory problems.

Sora Margherita

🏛 | TRATTORIA | *CUCINA CASARECCIA*

Piazza Cinque Scole, 30 (Ghetto), 00186 Roma
☎ 06 / 6864002
📷 Jewish quarter, Largo Argentina
∅ Saturday and Sunday
Reservations possible but not usual
€ | 🛏 none

*W*hen closed, the unmarked shopfront is not recognizable as a restaurant. When open, it is easily spotted by the collection of press cuttings in the narrow window. This is one of Rome's sentimental-favorite—and most famous—holes-in-the-wall. Some people actually claim to like the food.

I am perhaps unfair: we had very good *agnolotti* not long ago, in a rich, concentrated tomato and meat sauce. *Pasta e ceci,* with tomatoes, was good too, but a plate of *fettuccine* weighed a ton. And the *melanzane alla parmigiana* (listed on the handwritten menu simply as "Parmigiana") tasted of Swiss cheese. That's home cooking, all right: the kind where you cut corners by using packaged cheese slices. Three of us together couldn't be bothered to finish a single slice of the homemade strawberry *crostata*.

The house *vino sfuso* (white) is drinkable (not to be confused with sippable). If you want red, it's Montepulciano d'Abruzzo in a bottle.

Matters of finance: Though prices are low, lunchers who just want just a *primo piatto* (pasta or soup) pay a little extra (L. 13,000 instead of 10,000). Our request for a legally obligatory *ricevuta fiscale* was met with a lot of double-talk and resistance before it was granted.

So what is it about this place that people like so much? It's that it represents a dying breed. A matriarch in the kitchen orders everybody around. There is no décor to speak of except travertine facing halfway up the walls and some miscellaneous old photographs (and, of course, the press cuttings). Tourists, suits, and workers eat elbow to elbow, and solo lunchers seem welcome. A trattoria doesn't get much more typical.

Trattoria St. Teodoro

🏛🏛🏛🏛 | RESTAURANT | *CUCINA CREATIVA;* FISH

Via dei Fienili, 49/50/51 (Piazza della Consolazione,
  Via San Teodoro), 00186 Roma
☎ 06/6780933
📷 Forum Romanum, Capitoline Hill, Theater of Marcellus
∅ Sunday | Outdoor tables
Reservations advisable
€€€ | MasterCard DinersClub Mastercard VISA

*N*ever mind what the name says; it's not a trattoria, and it's pronounced San Teodoro, after a nearby church and street. It is a very pleasant upmarket, and rising, restaurant on the premises of what not so long ago was a real trattoria—*spaghetti alla carbonara* and folding wooden chairs. This is a hidden, magic corner of Rome, an urban island surrounded by the Forum, the Capitoline, and the Via del Teatro di Marcello, and one of the most picturesque spots in which to dine outdoors. Indoors, vaulted ceilings create difficult acoustics, but the dining room is otherwise comfortable. Service is attentive and professional.

A few years ago, the reopening of this restaurant was a gift from heaven. It was open every day, and it was suitably modest for dropping in for lunch after a walk through the Roman Forum, while suitably upscale to take foreign business guests who arrived on Sunday evening for Monday meetings. It is now closed on Sunday and prices have crept up to the level of a serious commitment.

With the exception of the *fritti* offered as an antipasto, which we find a bit stodgy, the food is excellent. A whole fresh fish cooked in the oven with potatoes is a good choice, but for meat eaters there is plenty of lamb and beef, often in innovative, or at least unusual, ways, such as *straccetti* with Gorgonzola. Best of all may be the fresh pastas, made on the premises, sauced with fresh cherry tomatoes, seafood, zucchini flowers, pecorino shavings, and herbs in various delicious combinations.

There is a good list of Italian wines, but our first choice never seems to be available. Dessert could be *sgroppino* or little fruits and nutshells filled with *sorbetti*.

Osteria della Suburra (Da Silvio)

🏛 🏛 | TRATTORIA | *CUCINA ROMANA*

Via Urbana, 67/69 (Via Cavour), 00184 Roma
☎ 06/486531
Ⓜ Metro B: Cavour
📷 Subura, San Pietro in Vincoli
Sidewalk tables
€ |

I've always been afraid to go in there," said a friend who lives nearby. Well, so had I, not that it looks so very awful. It has the sort of nondescript, worn-down look of a place that could go either way. But now I've eaten there twice and would return in a pinch. The first time I followed my own advice, ordered conservatively, and got hearty, tasty Roman fare, typical but not run of the mill. The second time, against my usual precepts, I ordered too adventurously. Let that be a lesson.

On a winter evening, we had a very elemental pasta with *broccolo romanesco* and prosciutto, with those two flavors strong and clear. On a spring visit, I made the mistake of ordering *tagliolini con carciofi,* which I should have guessed would be too much of a challenge. While the pasta itself was chewy and flavorful, the sauce contained little artichoke but much cream and a dash of curry powder to disguise what little artichoke taste might otherwise have survived. My second mistake was not asking for a description before ordering.

Cream and curry (not always together) represent a moment, in the 1960s and 1970s, in the evolution of Roman restaurant food on its march from *Mamma* to *cucina creativa.* The more sophisticated kitchens either rediscovered great-grandmother and began interpreting truly traditional dishes (though a few, bless them, had no need to "rediscover" what they had never lost) or went on to the often excellent interregional Italian-international style best exemplified by any place shooting for a second Michelin star. Today the use of cream as well as such pseudo-sophisticated dishes as *penne alla vodka* (or *wodka*) or *al salmone* are in themselves period pieces. You can never really know when cream will turn up in trattoria pasta sauces, so if you are phobic, ask, *"C'è la panna?"*

However, in general, the menu presents itself with convincing verisimilitude, and the *pane casereccio* is excellent. The selection is broad enough to offer a good choice, including homemade pastas, but not so large as to be suspicious. The *pasta e fagioli,* which contains tomatoes and *pancetta,* is very tasty indeed, and spicy.

There is a brief but decent wine list.

Taverna dei Quaranta

🏛 🏛 | TRATTORIA | *CUCINA CASARECCIA*

Via Claudia, 24 (Via Annia), 00184 Roma
☎ 06/7000550
Ⓜ Metro B: Colosseo
📷 Colosseum
€ | [MasterCard] [DINERS CLUB] [Card] [VISA]

*I*n 1981, a forty-strong cooperative took over a 1930s trattoria. Recent enlargement has not changed the character of this quintessential early 1980s "alternative restaurant." It is the only amusing, economical place to eat near the Colosseum.

A lingering countercultural aura and political correctness (the Egyptian cook is invited to cook Egyptian once in a while) are both part of the place's charm and a source of irritation—for example, to customers who make the mistake of thinking they can have a quick bite before catching a train. While the blue-jeaned service in this ultrademocratic establishment certainly lacks the snap of the professional brigade, it has its dignity and (to its everlasting credit) resembles not at all the enforced cheer rampant in the United States ("Hi, are you guys ready to order?").

Fortunately, the politics do not extend to the menu, and nobody tries to make you eat food that's good for you. The food, which combines traditional Roman and (not overly) imaginative dishes (homemade *fettuccine ai fiori di zucca*), is usually good. The fairly short menu manages to offer something for everyone; there's always some vegetarian main dish, such as baked cauliflower (don't knock it till you've tried it).

In addition to a house white wine from the Castelli Romani, there is a brief list. Desserts are homemade.

Tram Tram

ㅠㅠㅠ | TRATTORIA PLUS | IDIOSYNCRATIC
CUCINA REGIONALE |

Via dei Reti 44/46 (San Lorenzo), 00185 Roma

☎ 06/490416

📷 Basilica di San Lorenzo, Santa Croce in Gerusalemme

∅ Monday

Reservations a must

€€ | [MasterCard] [Diners Club] [credit card] [VISA]

A tram is a European streetcar, and *trantràn* is
an Italian word meaning "the daily grind." This
charming (in its fashion) trattoria in the bohemian (in its
fashion) San Lorenzo quarter is located on the streetcar
tracks; it is decorated (if you can call it that) with tram
parts, including those comfy wooden seats in the smaller
front room. Signora Di Vittorio and her daughters and
various other young women, some in extremely improb-
able clothing, run a loose ship and always seem to be fight-
ing off chaos. But they are sweet and hospitable, and the
food is just yummy.

The regional origins of the menu, which includes both
meat and fish, are in Lazio and in Puglia, strange but not
incompatible bedfellows. *Pappardelle Tram Tram* is broad
noodles in a robust tomato sauce with pieces of lamb and
strips of roasted sweet peppers to be sprinkled with grated
pecorino. *Orecchiette alla Norma* combines the quintessential Sicilian eggplant and tomato sauce with *ricotta salata*
cheese (in place of Parmesan) on Puglia's typical ear-
shaped fresh pasta. The vegetable *lasagne* comes in an
incandescent baking dish bubbling with boiling oil and
molten cheese. It's not what you might call a refined dish,
but it certainly fills the bill on a chilly evening.

Main courses are equally robust. I can't resist the *invol-tini* of Savoy cabbage (*verza*) filled with ground meat in a spicy tomato sauce. We also like the veal *involtini,* rolled *scallopine* stuffed with bread crumbs, prosciutto, and cheese served with unusually delicious roast potatoes.

The wine list, which covers every Italian region, is astonishing and very reasonably priced. If you want to stick with Puglia, you might try a Salice Salentino DOC Riserva 1995 Taurino.

The homemade desserts are worth saving room for, conceivably with a glass of sweet dark, raisiny Moscato di Pantelleria Bukkuram.

Trimani il Wine Bar

🏛 🏛 🏛 🏛 | WINE BAR | 🥄

Via Cernaia, 37b (Porta Pia), Roma
☎ 06/4469630
📷 Termini Station
∅ Sunday | 🕐 11:30 A.M. to 3:30 P.M.; 5:30 P.M. to 12:30 A.M.
€€ (with average wine) | [MasterCard] [Diners Club] [American Express] [VISA]

*M*arco Trimani is the dean of Roman wine retail-ers, and his marvelous old shop is one of the most venerable and best stocked in the city. In 1991, his children, Carla, Paolo, Francesco, and Giovanni, launched Rome's most modern and stylish wine bar. The beautiful bistro-like premises consist of an Art Deco bar and tables on two floors, including an upstairs room where tastings are held.

The wine list features five hundred labels, and wine is served by the glass or bottle. Although it is possible to make a meal from the menu, the aim is to provide light lunches, suppers, or snacks to act as a foil to the wines. This means the food consists mostly of elegant plates of salamis, prosciuttos, cheeses, and smoked fish. There is usually a soup or pasta, and a *sformato* or *torta rustica*. Homemade desserts might be accompanied by a glass of, say, Muffato della Sala, Umbria's superb botrytis wine.

Ristorante Vecchia Locanda

🏛 🏛 🏛 🏛 | CASUAL RESTAURANT |
CUCINA ROMANA, CUCINA CREATIVA | 🖌

Vicolo Sinibaldi, 2 (Via Torre Argentina), 00186 Roma
☎ 06/68802831
📷 Pantheon, Largo Argentina
∅ Sunday | Outdoor tables
Reservations advised but not always necessary
€€ | MasterCard · Diners Club · American Express · VISA

This small friendly restaurant is a gem, noticed but not made much of by the Italian guides. It occupies the premises occuped until seven years ago by Girone VI, beloved of Roman foodies, named for the circle of Dante's Purgatory reserved for gluttons, and indeed after a meal there, many people probably felt they should go to Confession. But though one leaves La Vecchia Locanda (the name means "the old inn") unburdened by the sin of gluttony, one can do very well.

The location near Largo Argentina and the Pantheon draws both tourists and locals, and both receive the same cordial greeting and courteous, efficient service. The menu is very intelligently conceived, with pastas and main dishes of the standard repertoire (such as *saltimbocca alla romana*) and somewhat more daring (such as pasta with artichokes and clams or with zucchini and shrimp), without going over the top. There is also a delicious house veg-etable antipasto, and a choice of meat or fish. The menu, which is bilingual, is organized rationally, with separate sections for dishes using the same main ingredient, such as *tagliata* (sliced rare steak) or *stracci* (very thin-sliced sautéed beef) with various condiments. We recently tried *stracci* with chunks of eggplant and small tomatoes, which was very tasty indeed.

The wine list is quite extensive, covering most of Italy (but vintages are not listed). Desserts are homemade. We tasted a lovely vanilla pudding with *fragoline* (it came with *gianduia* as well), but the coconut chocolate mousse on the menu that had got us all excited was not available.

In winter, there's a cozy upstairs dining room and a larger one downstairs. During the warm months, the whole restaurant moves outdoors into the tiny carless street, and is very romantic (maybe too: the candles are hot on a hot evening, but without them you'd never see your food).

Volpetti Più

🏛🏛🏛 | CAFETERIA-STYLE *TAVOLA CALDA*,
TAKE-OUT | READY-MADE GOURMET;
PIZZA AL TAGLIO

Via Alessandro Volta, 8 (Testaccio, Via Marmorata),
  00153 Roma
☎ 06/5744306 | 🖨 06/5747629 | www.fooditaly.com
  (in the U.S.), www.volpetti.it (in Italy)
Ⓜ Metro B: Piramide
📷 Testaccio, Aventine hill, Pyramid of Cestius, Protestant
  cemetery, train to Ostia Antica
∅ Sunday; no vacation | 🕐 9 A.M. to 3:30 P.M., 6:00 to 10 P.M.
€ | MasterCard DinersClub Card VISA

*N*orcia, the town in Umbria that gave the world
    Benedictine monks, is also the spiritual home of
Italian pork butchers, who are called *norcini,* after the
town. And from Norcia came the brothers Emilio and
Claudio Volpetti, who since 1973 have run one of the most
seductive shops in central Italy, a gourmet *salumeria* in the
Testaccio quarter. Go to the shop for edible souvenirs (rare
cheeses are routinely wrapped for travel here) or for picnic
supplies, say for a trip to Ostia Antica. In season, buy fresh
figs at the Testaccio market, and *prosciutto San Daniele* and
pizza bianca here (ask to have it split). If you go to Ostia,
find an empty Roman house and make your sandwiches.
(Be sure to bring some extra water to rinse your hands after
peeling the figs.) You can buy breads and pizzas, pasta salads, slices of fresh salmon baked in a crust, sliced roasted
meats, olives of every sort, *pomodori al riso, torte rustiche*
(whole or in slices), and every kind of cheese or preserved
meat the Italian peninsula can provide. There are also a few
imports from France and Spain, such as *jamón de Serrano.*

The staff is efficient, friendly, knowledgeable—we learn something new about Italian artisanal food production every time we go. But don't imagine you're going to leave the shop without at least twice as much as you came in to buy.

To sit down and have some of Volpetti's delicacies for a meal or snack, go around the corner to Volpetti Più, at Via Marmorata 47, where an array of the pizzas, pastas, main dishes, and cooked vegetables available for takeout at the shop, and more, are served cafeteria-style to eat in or take away.

Zi' Fenizia

🏛🏛 | *PIZZA AL TAGLIO* | KOSHER, ITALIAN, AND MIDDLE EASTERN

Via S. Maria del Pianto, 65 (Via del Portico d'Ottavia),
   00186 Roma
☎ 06/6896976
📷 Ghetto
∅ Friday afternoon and Saturday (during the day) |
   🕐 7:00 A.M. to 9:00 P.M.
€ | 💳 none

*T*alk about multiculturalism. This tableless shop offers falafel and other Middle Eastern snacks, as well as sandwiches and a very tempting array of cheese-less, porkless *pizza al taglio*—meaning your portion is cut from a large rectangular pizza, weighed, and handed to you wrapped in paper. Cinzia and Michele run a very smooth operation, and when you can have *radicchio* with mushrooms or beef sausage with broccoli, you won't miss the mozzarella.

Florence

Eating in Florence

AN HOUR AND A HALF by Eurostar train from Rome takes us into a completely different gastronomic and, to an extent, climatic zone. Here the winters are colder, and soups and red meat are consumed. But summers are even hotter, and red, ripe tomatoes are exploited too. Delicate white *cannellini* beans and other legumes are found year-round, fresh or dried, alone or in soups. A local breed of cattle, Chianina, provides Italy's finest steaks and roasts. But the real star of what is essentially a highly developed cuisine of poverty is day-old bread. In summer, it is moistened with water and the prized local olive oil and tossed with chopped tomatoes, red onions, and cucumber as a *primo piatto;* it provides the *"pappa"* in *pappa al pomodoro*. In winter, it thickens *ribollita*, the irresistible, nearly solid vegetable soup in which *cannellini* beans and tangy *cavolo nero* predominate. Where Rome favors quick grilling, Florence cooks slowly—stews, game, roasts. The exception is *la fiorentina*, the Florentine *secondo piatto* par excellence, which takes its name from that of the city. It is a thick T-bone steak, usually weighing more than two pounds (and usually shared by two people), ideally of the prized Chianina breed. It is grilled quickly and served *very* rare. Don't even dream of asking for it any other way; spare yourself a rebuke from the waiter and just choose something else. Close the meal with *cantucci,* almond *biscotti,* to dunk in the quintessential Tuscan sweet wine, Vin Santo.

Florence has fewer elegant restaurants than either Milan, which has industry, or Rome, which has government. Its forte is the trattoria, of which there are two basic kinds, old-style and faux old-style. Old-style trattorias use tablecloths and cloth napkins and have probably been managed by the same family for some generations, or at least aim to give that impression. The others tend to be old places taken over by enthusiastic young people. They use heavy wooden or marble-topped tables set with paper place mats and, usually, paper napkins too. They love background music and stay open far into the afternoon and evening.

Florence lies at the heart of the Chianti zone, so it is natural that the wine bar has caught on and developed, meaning that wine and snacks can be found all day long.

The concentration of tourists and foreign students in central Florence cannot be escaped entirely, and, as anyone who has seen or read *A Room with a View* knows, the English presence in Florence goes back a long way. Therefore, do not be put off by English menus and the presence of other Anglophones. Unlike the Romans, who largely treat foreigners as either an annoyance or a cash cow, the clever Florentines treat them like the customers they are. That is not, of course, to say you shouldn't take some precautions in choosing eateries and ordering. The good news is that the monumental center is quite small, and a few minutes' walk in any direction from the Duomo will take you to some semblance of normal Florentine life.

PRACTICAL MATTERS

Florence eats earlier than Rome, meaning that lunch may be well under way by 12:30 and dinner by 7:30. Off-hour meals and other sustenance can be found not only at bars, as everywhere in Italy, but at wine bars.

Much of Florence's small center is pedestrianized. All the restaurants listed here are within walking distance of the Duomo and train station (though not everyone has the same idea of what is an acceptable walking distance). Taxis can be phoned (055/4242; 055/4390; 055/4798; 055/4386), flagged down, or found at numerous taxi stands, such as those at the station, Santa Croce, and Duomo. Florence has no subway; the local bus company, ATAF, offers numerous kinds of tickets and passes. There is an information booth just outside the train station.

The Florence Menu

THE LIST THAT FOLLOWS contains common items on Florence menus. Additional terms are listed in the glossary. The antipasto par excellence in Florence trattorias is a generous plate of *crostini* with some hand-cut prosciutto. The *primo piatto* is likely to be a thick soup or potage, though pasta with a game sauce, or even tomatoes, is also traditional. Fish dishes are not indigenous to Florence, though Tuscany does have a long seacoast with its own cuisine.

Additional information about the dishes may be found in the glossary.

ANTIPASTO

affettate (*prosciutto, finochiello* or *sbriciolona, sopressata* local salamis)

antipasto alla toscana (mixed cold cuts and *crostini*, toast with various pâtés)

crostini

fettunta (toasted bread rubbed with garlic and drizzled with oil)

prosciutto di cinghiale (wild boar prosciutto)
prosciutto toscano (locally made prosciutto)

PRIMO

acquacotta (vegetable soup)
farinata (flour-thickened vegetable soup)
minestra di riso e cavolo (soup of rice and cabbage)
minestra di verdura (vegetable soup)
minestra or *zuppa di farro* (emmer soup)
panzanella (day-old bread crumbled and moistened, mixed
    with chopped tomatoes and onions and dressed with
    olive oil; in summer. *Farro* treated the same way is
    increasingly popular too.)
pappa al pomodoro (mush of day-old bread and tomato
    pulp, especially in summer)
pappardelle con sugo di cinghiale, lepre, or *anatra* (broad
    noodles with hearty meat sauce of boar, hare, or duck)
pasta e fagioli (thick soup of pasta and white beans)
ribollita (classic soup of, mainly, kale, beans, and day-old
    bread; especially in winter)
risolata (a *risotto* with Romaine lettuce)
risotto alla toscana (risotto with ground meat, chicken
    livers, Parmesan, red wine, and vegetables)
strozzapreti (one of many handmade flour-and-water
    pastas, usually served with meat sauce)
zuppa di fagioli (Tuscan bean soup)

SECONDO

arista di maiale (herbed roast loin of pork)
baccalà alla livornese (salt cod cooked in tomato sauce)
bistecca alla fiorentina (large, thick T-bone steak, ideally of
    local cattle breed, served extremely rare)
braciola primavera (thin breaded veal cutlet heaped with
    rucola and tomato salad)
cacciagione (game in various forms)

calamari (or *totani* or *seppie*) *all'inzimino* (squid or cuttlefish in a sauce)

involtini (usually, rolled slices of beef stewed in tomato sauce)

la francesina (lesso rifatto con cipolle) (a beef pot roast with a large quantity of sliced onions stewed into a sweet purée)

lampredotto (tripe)

ossobuco

polpettone (meat loaf)

rosticciana (grilled pork chops or spareribs)

seppie con i piselli (cuttlefish stewed with peas)

stracotto (beef pot roast)

tagliata di manzo (sliced rare beef)

trippa alla fiorentina (tripe with tomato sauce and Parmesan)

CONTORNO

cime di rape (turnip greens, usually sautéed with garlic and hot pepper)

fagioli (cannellini) all'olio (boiled white beans with olive oil)

fagioli al fiasco (white beans stewed with herbs in a glass bottle)

fagioli all'uccelletto (slow-cooked white beans in olive oil, sage, and tomatoes)

fagioli sgranati (fresh beans, in summer)

verdure lesse (plain boiled vegetables, to be dressed with olive oil)

DESSERT

cantucci or *biscottini di Prato con vin santo* (almond *biscotti* to be dunked in sweet wine)

castagnaccio (a flat chestnut-flour cake)

Crème caramel

panna cotta (bland, caloric white custard often served with berry, caramel, or chocolate sauce)

LOCAL WINES

Florence, blessed in so many ways, has the additional good fortune to have its local wine be Chianti, especially Chianti Classico. House wines are invariably Chianti—some rougher, some smoother—and restaurant wine lists dedicate long columns to the multiplicity of producers, vintages, and subdenominations. Tannic Chianti is the wine par excellence to accompany *bistecca alla fiorentina*.

Naturally Tuscany has other wines of distinction too, most based on the same Sangiovese grape: Brunello di Montalcino, Vino Nobile di Montepulciano (and the lesser Rosso di Montepulciano), and Carmignano (and the lesser Barco Reale). The so-called super-Tuscans—unfettered by DOC regulations—can be all Sangiovese or blends of Cabernet Sauvignon or Merlot and Sangiovese.

Tuscan whites can be Chardonnay or Vernaccia, from a native grape. And after dinner, the ubiquitous dessert wine is Vin Santo, a highly variable golden *passito* wine made in special barrels called *caratelli*. It is customary to dunk *cantucci* in it.

Florence Listings

ANGIOLINO

TRATTORIA ANTELLESI

TRATTORIA BALDOVINO

BALDUCCI

LA BARAONDA

BECCOFINO (WINE BAR)

BELLE DONNE

OSTERIA DE' BENCI

OSTERIA DEL CAFFÈ ITALIANO

CANTINETTA ANTINORI

CANTINETTA DEI VERRAZZANO

TRATTORIA LA CASALINGA

CIBRÈO

COQUINARIUS

IL FRANCESCANO

I FRATELLINI

GIACOSA

ENOTECA DE' GIRALDI

IL GUSCIO

DA MARIO

TRATTORIA MARIONE

FIASCHETTERIA DA NUVOLI

TRATTORIA PANDEMONIO

PROCACCI

CAFFÈ I RICCHI

RIVOIRE

DA RUGGERO

Angiolino

✣ ✣ | TRADITIONAL TRATTORIA

Via Santo Spirito, 36 (parallel to Lungarno Guicciardini),
   50125 Firenze
☎ 055 / 2398976
📷 Oltrarno
∅ Monday
Reservations needed
€€ | [MasterCard] [Diners Club] [■] [VISA]

I haven't eaten here—though I've looked through the window—but local friends swear it's the genuine article. It has dark wood, checkered tablecloths, bunches of tomatoes hanging, and such ye olde Tuscan trat décor items as straw-covered bottles, painted tiles, a ceramic lion, and a painted wooden bust of a gentleman in a floppy hat.

Antipasti include the usual *crostini,* and this would be a place to have them. If you want a change, try *fagioli con bottarga,* but pass up the *rucola e gamberetti,* which has been kicking around "alternative" menus for about ten years and not getting any better. *Primi* are the classics—*ribollita, panzanella, spaghetti con pomodoro, pappa al pomodoro*—but also *rigatoni all'amatriciana* and *taglieri freschi con fiori di zucca. Secondi* include the usual variety of grilled meats, as well as tripe, *scaloppine,* and *braciola primavera.*

There is also a menu of *piatti freddi,* such as *carpaccio di manzo con rucola e grana* or the ultratypical *tonno con cipolle e fagioli.* Homemade desserts include cream caramel (sic) and *biscotti* con Vin Santo.

Trattoria Antellesi

❈ ❈ ❈ ❈ | TRATTORIA PLUS | *CUCINA TOSCANA* |
✎

Via Faenza, 9r (Via Nazionale, Via Sant'Antonino),
   50123 Firenze
☎ | 🖷   055/216990
📷   Near train station
Reservations advised
€€ | [MasterCard] [Diners Club] [■■] [VISA]

A five-minute walk from the train station, this gem
   of a well-run little restaurant is a good first stop
in Florence. Although from outside it looks like a simple
trattoria, it is actually a very good restaurant with a rustic
veneer, serving somewhat refined or interpreted (but not
to excess) versions of traditional Tuscan dishes and some
more modern, lighter dishes to vary the diet and satisfy
vegetarians.

The owners are Enrico Verrecchia and his brothers. Janice Verrechia, Enrico's American wife, used to be a constant presence and it is to be hoped that when the *bambini*
who took her away are older, she will be back. A wine
expert, Janice gives wine appreciation classes. The wine
list, which is excellent and emphasizes Tuscany, is a digest
version designed not to frighten the customers—a common practice in Florence—but do ask if you are interested
in something else.

The smaller front room is the livelier of the two rooms,
which are separated by a narrow corridor, like an isthmus.
Among the bottles arrayed behind the bar is one of the
best selections of single-malt whiskeys in Florence. The
customers are both local and foreign, and both kinds seem
to receive the same friendly treatment.

The most typical starter is a particularly good, and generous (share, share), *antipasto toscano,* consisting of *prosciutto di Parma,* Tuscan salamis (including the fennel-flavored *finocchiello*), and *crostini* with liver pâté, though you might have something like a salad of *rucola,* pecorino, and pear. On our last visit, we also tried the *farro* soup, which almost always sounds more interesting than it is. But the house specialty, *spaghetti freschi alla chiantigiana,* lived up to its promise—fresh spaghetti with a superrich sauce of tender Chianina beef stewed with tomatoes and Chianti.

Main courses might include *tagliata di bue con rucola ed arance,* delicious slices of rare local beef on a bed of *rucola* and flavored with orange, a successful rather nouvelle treatment of a simple dish that invites creative variation; or roast lamb stuffed with artichokes; or *ossobuco toscano;* or *straccetti* of pork, very moist tender strips of cooked pork with pieces of artichokes.

For dessert, don't miss the marvelously subtle chestnut pudding.

Trattoria Baldovino

✤ | CASUAL RESTAURANT | PIZZA, SALADS | ➤

Via San Giuseppe, 22r (Santa Croce), 50122 Firenze

☎ 055/241773

◼ Santa Croce

∅ Monday | ⏱ 11:30 A.M. to 2:30 P.M., 7 to 11:30 P.M.

Reservations suggested, not always needed

€ | MasterCard D ▪▪ VISA

*T*his pretty, modern new-old hybrid informal multifunction eatery—part of Glaswegian David Gardner's empire (see Beccofino, page 135)—is everything many people seek in a restaurant but has everything I try to avoid. To judge from its popularity, however, my two recent lunch companions and I belong to a fuddy-duddy minority.

Thus, let us try to be fair. On the pro side, there is a good wine list, fresh ingredients, and a varied menu (including a menu of the month in addition to a few staple items) offering light cuisine, Chianina beef, a variety of main-dish salads, and pizza all day, made in a wood-burning oven by a Neapolitan *pizzaiolo*. On the minus side, the menu offers precious little that is local if you don't want red meat, and the offerings of what you might call normal Italian food are few indeed. Multi-ingredient main-dish salads are not an Italian concept. All of this lightness and novelty may, of course, be just what bored locals and overstuffed tourists want, but then I would quibble with the use of "trattoria" in the name. Across the street is the *enoteca,* under the same management, and as a designation that is enough of a neologism as to constitute fair warning that you may not see *ribollita* and other war horses. But a "trattoria" that does not offer a *panzanella* or a *pappa al pomodoro* on a hot summer day is misrepresenting itself. Also, a trattoria is a place where you eat a meal; Baldovino is probably best considered a place to have a single dish, or the sort of combination of courses only a foreigner could dream up.

Unfortunately, we made the mistake of going for what we hoped would be lunch. We tried oversalted *farfalle* with *fiori di zucca,* and a very tame fillet of *orata* with potatoes and fresh tomatoes, which was pretty good. The antipasto of grilled vegetables had the virtue of being freshly made (too often such dishes sit around for hours before serving), but it arrived completely nude, accompanied by a bottle of excellent oil. A little chopped parsley, garlic, and salt would not have been amiss. As it was, I eventually got up and got the salt myself. Which brings us to service and ambience.

The establishment consists of a large number of small dining rooms with high ceilings and cruel acoustics, exacerbated by the playing of loud music. Conversation? Forget it. The restaurant was nearly full well before one o'clock on a Saturday, and the staff was not equal to the volume of work. I think the word I want is "brusque." The angular wooden tables so loved by the new-generation trattorias were partially covered by the equally favored paper place mats; napkins were that awful cellulose fake cloth that you can't even crumple and shred like an honest paper napkin.

Heads splitting from the din, we could not bear to linger for dessert, though these are reported to be quite good.

The related *enoteca-caffè* across the street at number 18r (tel. 055/2347220) offers drinks and light meals from noon to midnight, seven days a week.

Balducci

❧ | NEW-OLD WINE BAR | LIGHT MEALS | 🥄

Via de' Neri, 2r (between Uffizi and Via de' Benci),
   50122 Firenze
☎   055/216887
📷   Uffizi, Santa Croce
∅   Monday; two weeks in August | Sidewalk tables
€ | ⊟   none

*R*ight next door to and barely distinguishable from Osteria de' Benci (page 137), this inviting little place with a large counter and small tables offers pastas, *bruschetta,* and cold dishes all day long.

La Baraonda

⚜ ⚜ ⚜ ⚜ | CASUAL RESTAURANT

Via Ghibellina, 67r, 50122 Firenze
☎ | 📠 055/2341171
📷 Santa Croce, Casa Buonarroti
Ø Sunday (all day) and Monday lunch
€€€ (less at lunch) | 💳

The name means confusion, chaos, bedlam, mayhem, but don't you believe it. Duccio Magni, an engineer by training, and his wife, Elena, the chef, run a very tight ship. The conceit is trattoria, but very upmarket. About sixty diners in all can be accommodated in the three small, rather dimly lit but pretty dining rooms, one with a marble counter from the butcher shop it once was.

On neither of our two visits did we see a written menu. The offerings were recited on one occasion by Duccio himself with contagious vivacity and on the second by a rather serious young woman. Try to catch Duccio's performance; his enthusiasm carries through the meal.

The food is based in Tuscan tradition but is far more refined than the usual trattoria fare. More vegetarian and lighter dishes are offered at lunchtime. The signature meat loaf (*polpettone*) is made of veal and chicken and served cold at lunch, of just veal and hot (but not heavy) in the evening. Soups predominate by day, pastas after dark. *Polpettone* is always on the menu, but the rest can vary within certain categories: there's always a light soup, a chicken dish, something based on innards, a stew, and a vegetarian main dish. The cold octopus, boiled, cut into chunks, and dressed with olive oil, is superb: it's offered as a main dish but makes a good antipasto too. Soups might include a delicate version of *pasta e fagioli*, made with white beans, and a bit of tomato, with a few *rigatoni*. *Farinata di verdura,* a dark vegetable soup in which kale and beans predominate, thickened with polenta, is thrilling. The *risolata,* a *risotto* made with romaine lettuce, is famous. *Tortelli di patate* with a robust sauce of *cinghiale* (wild boar) is a delicious pasta dish. Main courses might include, besides the *polpettone, trippa alla fiorentina* (tripe in tomato sauce with Parmesan cheese), braised boneless rabbit, sliced and served with *cannellini* beans, *la francesina* (*muscolo di manzo* stewed with onions that dissolve into a creamy sauce), or sirloin of local beef (to be served *al sangue*—rare—or not at all) with cheese on top, and *tomino* (a white cheese) with boiled greens.

The desserts are superb. Don't miss the *torta di mele* (apple tart) unless it's to have the pear cake instead.

The wine list is primarily Tuscan, and, as elsewhere, if you're after something particularly interesting, make your desires known. There is a good house Chianti.

Beccofino (wine bar)

⚜ ⚜ | WINE BAR ANNEXED TO RESTAURANT | DRINKS, LIGHT MEALS |

Piazza degli Scarlatti, 1r (Lungarno Guicciardini), 50124 Firenze
☎ 055/290076
Oltrarno
∅ Sunday | Outdoor tables
€ | MasterCard, Diners Club, Card, VISA

David Gardner, the Glaswegian phenomenon (see Baldovino, page 131), has, a mere six years after moving to Florence, added this spiffy modern complex of wine bar and upscale restaurant to his gastronomic empire. No old Tuscany here—rather, the spacious bright and comfortable premises on the Arno with lots of light wood recalls Scandinavian design.

Stop off for an apéritif, such as a glass of Tuscan *spumante,* or a light lunch. A board lists a few *primi piatti* and desserts each day.

Belle Donne

❧ ❧ | INFORMAL TRATTORIA | *CUCINA TOSCANA*

Via delle Belle Donne, 16r (Via della Spada), 50123 Firenze
☎ 055/2382609
📷 Santa Maria Novella, Via Tornabuoni and shops
∅ Saturday and Sunday
Reservations advised
€ | MasterCard

Should you decide to make a beeline from the train station to Gucci or Ferragamo, you will walk past this popular trattoria, named not for Gucci's customers but for its street. It's adorable to look at—a tiny room with an enormous counter laden with fruit, and a collective table in the middle surrounded by a number of tables for four. Unfortunately, you can't expect any help with the hard-to-see blackboard menu, so try to decipher it before anybody approaches you for your order. This isn't southern Rome, where lunch is for lingering; this is northern, commercial, bourgeois Florence, where somebody is waiting for your seat.

Should you be able to read the menu, which changes daily, you would find a surprising variety and more choice than the size of the restaurant suggests (not so for the wine). On a hot summer day, I noticed a cool selection of *primi*—rice salad, a delicious, typical *panzanella,* as well as one pasta (ravioli) and a soup (vegetable). *Secondi* were more wintry (such as *stracotto* in Chianti, and *ossobuco,* and roast pork), though the *polpettone* came completely covered with sliced raw San Marzano tomatoes, than which nothing is more a symbol of the Italian summer.

Osteria de' Benci

✣ ✣ | NEW-OLD TRATTORIA | *CUCINA TOSCANA* AND CREATIVE FOOD

Via de' Benci 13, 50122 Firenze
☎ 055 / 2344923
📷 Santa Croce, Uffizi
∅ Sunday
€€ | 💳 💳

*T*his is a venerable trattoria restored in youthful key by its owners, Marco Meneghini and Nicola Schioppo. It can be hot (ceiling fans notwithstanding) and crowded and loud, but many people like that, and it's very friendly, with a clientele composed of approximately half tourists, half locals.

There's a daily menu of four courses: *antipasti, primi, secondi,* and *contorni,* as well as a selection of wines by the glass, and not all Italian. The regular menu, printed on brown wrapping paper (to match the place mats) is very user friendly, with prices in euros as well as lire, and helpful descriptions of the dishes, both practices more restaurants would do well to follow. I would not say the same about the paper napkins, however.

The menu, which changes frequently, always has a good Tuscan base, with plenty of Chianina beef in various

ways, soups, *salumi,* and *crostini,* but it also has an eclec-
tic side that might produce an antipasto of a half melon
filled with port, or strawberry *risotto,* not spotted since the
early 1980s, the days of alternative restaurants and buried
experiments.

Osteria del Caffè Italiano

✣ ✣ ✣ | BAR AND RESTAURANT |
LIGHT *CUCINA TOSCANA* | ➤

Via Isola delle Stinche, 11r (Via Ghibellina), 50123 Firenze
☎ 055/289368
📷 Santa Croce, Teatro Verdi
∅ Monday; August and December
🕐 11:30 A.M. to midnight | ♿
Reservations advisable for restaurant
€€ | [MasterCard] [Diners Club] [American Express] [VISA]

*U*mberto Montano, a Florentine only by adoption
(he comes from the Basilicata region in the deep
south), began filling gaps in the Florence restaurant scene
in the mid-1990s with his modern, stylish Alle Muratte;
even then, the restaurant's adjacent bar showed he understood the merits of the multifunction eatery concept,
which has now taken firm hold, and not only in Florence.
Thus, with the acquisition of historic premises on the
ground floor of the fourteenth-century Palazzo Salviati,
near the restaurant, he went a step further and created a
complex that offers a normal coffee bar, excellent wines by
the glass, light meals, and, in a magnificent back room, a
restaurant. Everything Mr. Montano does, he does well,
with attention to the details.

Where Alle Muratte offers an innovative cuisine, a
Lucano-Tuscan fusion you might say, the Osteria proposes

somewhat simpler, lighter, Tuscan-based food and an excellent list of Tuscan wines. The elegant paneled, muraled rooms and beautiful table settings prove that discomfort and rusticity are not a prerequisite to good food in Florence, despite so much evidence to the contrary elsewhere in the city. Only the staff seemed not quite in control of the situation when we had lunch there on a November Sunday. We ate *bollito misto* with green sauce, served in a small portion as a first course; perfectly cooked *farfalle con la verdura,* very light and tasty with peppers, leeks, and zucchini (though that mix involved a little too much fooling around with the calendar); *tagliata al rosmarino,* tender rare slices of beef with fresh rosemary and a salad of *rucola* and cherry tomatoes; and boiled *cannellini* beans with oil and freshly ground pepper—everything superb.

Salamis, cheeses, and the like, are served with wine by the glass in the front-room bar.

Cantinetta Antinori

✣ ✣ ✣ ✣ | RESTAURANT, WINE BAR |
CLASSIC FLORENTINE CUISINE | 🍾

Piazza Antinori, 3, 50123 Firenze
☎ 055/292234, 055/2359827 | 📠 055/2359877
📷 Via Tornabuoni
∅ Saturday and Sunday; August
Reservations a must
€€€€ | MasterCard · Diners Club · [card] · VISA

*B*right yellow walls on three sides and a bottle-lined dark wooden bar on the fourth beneath a loft make this a very attractive little restaurant. It's located on the ground floor of the fifteenth-century Palazzo Antinori, of the Tuscan-based wine-producing empire founded in 1385. But ceilings that seem high enough to contain a Renaissance belfry create an acoustic effect that makes you want to run away screaming. The rather retro-expensive menu made dull reading to boot; all in all, I was ready to write off the evening. But then the food began to arrive. Everything was fresh and delicious, our waiter was kind and professional, and the large noisy party of northern Europeans eventually decamped—and though the acoustics were inherently awful, our party of five ended the evening finally enjoying one another's conversation with a bottle of fine Antinori Chianti and cheese.

The idea behind the Cantinetta is that of a showcase for tasting the Antinori wines together with products from the Antinori estates, led by the two olive oils, produced on the Antinori Chianti Classico estate under the labels Laudemio (used by an association of producers in Central Tuscany) and Péppoli.

On the July evening we dined, the menu included, among many other things, as *antipasti* excellent *crostini*, truffle sandwiches, and *prosciutto di Carpegna; primi* were *panzanella*, superb rich and spicy *pappa al pomodoro*, *spaghetti freddi al pomodoro fresco, crema di zucchine fredda alla menta* (a cold soup), and a couple of normal pastas, *fettuccine* with fresh *funghi porcini* and *fusilli* with tomatoes and basil. *Secondi* were wide-ranging, some hearty and Tuscan, others cool and summery: an excellent seafood salad with fresh *cannellini* beans, superb roast veal with zucchini sautéed in butter (it had sounded so boring on the menu, but it was outstanding), fresh white beans with tuna, cold roast beef.

The dessert choice is small but good; the *torta della nonna* was wonderful.

Only Antinori wines are served, naturally, but the scope is surprising—in addition to the range of Chianti Classico, there are Marchese Antinori Extra Brut *metodo classico* (*champenois*), Solaia (mostly Cabernet Sauvignon), the Castello della Sala wines from near Orvieto (including the superb sweet Muffato della Sala) and Atlas Peak, in the Napa Valley, and many more.

Cantinetta Antinori also has branches in Vienna and Zurich.

Cantinetta dei Verrazzano

❧ ❧ | WINE BAR, COFFEE BAR, BAKERY | ✎

Via de' Tavolini, 18/20 (Via dei Calzaiuoli), 50122 Firenze
☎ 055/268590
📷 Orsanmichele, Bargello, Piazza dell Signoria
Ø Sunday | ⏱ 8 A.M. to 8 P.M.
€ | 📠

*I*t looks more like a gourmet bakery than an outlet of a wine producer, Castello da Verrazzano in Greve; in fact, it is both. Antonietta Bagnoli, the owner, says about half her guests are locals, who come for coffee every day, half tourists, who appreciate the friendly atmosphere, yummy snacks, and convenient location on a side street near the Duomo.

You think you're in bread heaven the moment you walk in the door. The place, all warm lighting and dark wood, is shaped like a U. In one of the long rectangular rooms are the *pasticceria*, coffee bar, and *focaccia* bar. At the front, heaps of sweets, *biscotti*, breads, and cakes are very simply and elegantly presented in a long glass case, with bottles of wine and bags of coffee and chocolate and snacks tastefully displayed on shelves behind the counter. Customers can munch seated on dark wooden benches at tiny tables opposite the counter.

If you manage to penetrate a bit farther in, you come to the clean and elegant coffee bar with the magnificent copper espresso machine (making famously delicious coffee) and pitchers of colorful juices on the marble countertop. Your next stop, at the very back, will be the *focaccia* counter, supplied from a wood-burning oven. The *focaccie* are split horizontally and filled with, say, mozzarella and tomatoes, or *pesto*, olives, and vegetables. Or try the *cecina*, a sort of pizza made from chickpea flour.

If you want to sit down, there's a minuscule dining room to one side of the *focaccia* counter, where salami, prosciutto, and cheeses are served on a plate or in a sandwich, as well as *focaccie*. The menu offers some very toothsome combinations, such as *pecorino senese e cotognata* (quince marmalade) and *pecorino caldo con aceto di mosto cotto*.

The wine bar, in the second long rectangular room, specializing in the estate's wines, is a beauty, adorned with beautiful old maps, old paintings and books, and boxes.

Trattoria La Casalinga

❀ ❀ | TRATTORIA | *CUCINA CASALINGA*

Via dei Michelozzi, 9r (Piazza Santo Spirito), 50125 Firenze
☎ 055 / 218624 | 🖨 055 / 2679143
📷 Oltrarno, Palazzo Pitti, Santo Spirito, Santa Maria del Carmine
∅ Sunday
€€ | 💳 💳

*T*he designation "typical trattoria" can cover a lot of ground, but one requirement has to be local people making noise through the sheer joy of being there to eat, possibly amplified by appalling acoustics. It helps if there are customers who come in every day for lunch or dinner, and if there's an atmosphere of controlled chaos.

The food should be what you would be cooking at home if you lived in the same city and knew how.

Such a place exists a step from Brunelleschi's unfinished masterpiece, the Church of Santo Spirito (for more on that, see I Ricchi, page 156). *La casalinga* means the house-wife, which says it all—nothing cute, nothing ambitious, much less pretentious.

The place consists of two rooms with high brick vaulted ceilings, raising the sound of the happy diners' exuberance well beyond the level of decibels at which con-versation is possible. Walls are adorned with pine wain-scoting. The tables are covered with paper—not those stingy paper place mats favored by the uncomfortable upscale new trattorias, but whole sheets that invite you to roll up your sleeves and make a mess.

The menu changes daily, but the repertoire is what it is. For *primo*, you might have *panzanella* (in summer), or *pasta e fagioli*, or *ribollita*. You will pretend you don't see the offering of *spaghetti alla bolognese, al pesto,* or *alla carbonara,* which, I am informed, are there not for the tourists but for locals who want a change.

Secondi include a standard battery of roasts (beef, chicken, veal) and grilled meats, but also a rotation of other main dishes, such as *lesso rifatto con cipolle* (also known as *la francesina*), *calamari inzimino, trippa alla fiorentina,* or *bollito misto* with excellent fresh *salsa verde.*

Desserts are homemade. Try a Chianti Geografico in place of the (nevertheless acceptable) house Chianti.

Cibrèo

✠ ✠ ✠ ✠ ✠ | RESTAURANT AND TRATTORIA |
IDIOSYNCRATIC TUSCAN | ☞

Via de' Macci, 118 r (Mercato Sant'Ambrogio), 50122 Firenze
☎ 055/2341100 | 👜 055/244966
📷 Sant'Ambrogio market, Santa Croce
∅ Sunday and Monday | ♿
Reservations a must
€€€€ | [MasterCard] [DINERS CLUB] [Amex] [VISA]

VINERIA CIBREINO

Via dei Macci, 122r
☎ 055/2341100
∅ Sunday and Monday
Reservations not accepted
€€

*F*abio Picchi's small empire, founded in 1980 in a roomy, normal corner of central Florence, consists of a gourmet restaurant, a trattoria, and a bar-café. Everything is a little quirky, but of the sort that springs from a great mind. For example, no pasta or grilled meat is served, because it requires too much last-minute attention and the hospitable Mr. Picchi likes to hang out with his guests. This is not everyone's idea of greatness in a chef, but for Cibrèo, it works. No one misses pasta and steaks when they taste his famous soups and stews, all characterized by assertive flavors and thrilling textures. It may be idiosyncratic, but the food may also be the most authentic traditional Tuscan fare served in Florence. It is certainly the most varied.

The restaurant, with its urbane country style, is both elegant and homey.

Antipasti might include tomato and basil gelatin, fava beans with pecorino in oil and vinegar, tripe salad, or pâté "of three livers." *Primi piatti* could include a superb *ribollita*, *minestra "piazzese"* (with sausage and *cavolo nero*), cream of sweet peppers (*passato di pepperoni gialli*), a timbale of potatoes and ricotta with meat sauce, or polenta with butter and sage. For main courses, oxtail with artichokes, sausage with beans, or a succulent pigeon (from a very special breeder in Parma) stuffed with *mostarda*. For *contorni*, you might have *insalata rossa*, a beet salad, or the delicious mashed potato salad.

Many of the same dishes, without the amenities, are served at the adjacent trattoria. This is a tiny establishment with a small glassed-in waiting area (in lieu of reservations) and a single dining room that seats only about twenty-five. Lest the customers get too comfortable and try to linger, some of the seating is on benches. The spare décor (white above the waist, dark wood below, tiled floor) is enlivened by drawings of sailboats, a painting of an elephant, a large blue abstraction over the bar, and many strands of giant hot red peppers strung together like necklaces and hanging from the ceiling.

Service in both establishments is professional but brisk (even the restaurant goes for a quick turnover). If you can hold out till the end of the evening before seeking a table at the trattoria, you might be surprised with some of the gourmet items (like the pigeon) that are normally offered only on the high-rent side of the kitchen.

Cibrèo is a fabled Tuscan dish made of chicken innards and coxcombs. The restaurant will prepare it on advance order, because it takes a good three days to find the poultry. Thus if you want to have this old favorite, you must go to a relatively new restaurant—and one with a branch in Tokyo.

Desserts are still homemade and wonderful (for example, a Bavarian cream with apricot sauce), but Benedetta Vitali, formerly Signora Picchi and Cibrèo's renowned dessert chef, has moved on to found her own restaurant, Zibibbo, in the hills just outside the city (and outside the scope of this book), at via di Terzolina 3r, tel. 055/433383.

Coquinarius

❦ ❦ | WINE BAR, CAFFÈ | 🥄

Via delle Oche, 15r (Via dei Calzaiuoli), 50122 Firenze
☎ 055/2302153
📷 Duomo, Orsanmichele
∅ Sunday
🕐 9 A.M. to late evening (reduced hours in summer) |
   ♿ Wheelchair access but not to bathroom
€ | VISA MasterCard

*T*his is a snappy little refuge at any time of day or evening, in a highly central location. The gastronomic day begins at 9 with breakfast and proceeds through lunch to snacks and light supper from 6 until late. You can have sweets and tea, a tisane, coffee or hot chocolate, or a savory snack, such as Tuscan *crostini*. The menu includes some pastas, such as the highly creative ravioli filled with cheese and pears, and salads based on ethnic stereotyping (the "Scandinavian" salad, for example, contains smoked fish). A wide selection of wines is available by the glass.

Il Francescano

✣ ✣ | TRATTORIA | *CUCINA TOSCANA*

Largo Bargellini, 16 (Santa Croce), 50122 Firenze
☎ 055/241605 | 📠 055/2268340 | www.ilfrancescano.com
📷 Santa Croce
∅ Tuesday
Reservations suggested
€€ | [MasterCard] [Diners Club] [Amex] [VISA]

*T*he name means Franciscan monk, but there is
nothing ascetic about the menu at this friendly
trattoria, recently acquired by David Gardner (see page
131), located just across the street from the Basilica of
Santa Croce. Possibly the wooden tables and chairs and
the brick-vaulted ceiling in one of the several rooms recall
a monastery.

Begin with *fettunta* or *pinzimonio. Primi* include a typical
farinata di cavolo nero, leek and potato soup, *risottino ai
carciofi,* and *taglierini al porcini. Secondi* range from the
fiorentina from the grill, roast pork, *cinghiale in umido,* and
tagliata di manzo su radicchio to something more appropri-
ate for aspiring Franciscans—meatless *melanzane alla
parmigiana, tortino di carciofi,* or *fritto del convento.*

Close with *cantuccini* and, of course, Vin Santo, though
if you're not ready to take the vow, remember what St.
Augustine said: *"Tiramisù,* Lord, but not yet."

I Fratellini

✣ | PANINO AND WINE STAND | 🥄

Via dei Cimatori, 38r (Via dei Calzaiuoli), 50122 Firenze
☎ 055 / 2396096
📷 Orsanmichele, Bargello, Piazza della Signoria
∅ Sunday | Outdoor standing (there is hardly a roof,
   much less tables)
€ | 💳 none

Whenever Franco sees a crowd of people in a small street, he likes to check whether they're eating something. And that is how we discovered this irresistible closet-like purveyor of wine, sandwiches, and *crostini* with, say, prosciutto, salami, or truffle cream. We later learned it's in all the guidebooks and we should have found it years ago.

The drill is you get a glass of "house" wine (we had Toscano *novello*) in one of three sizes (alternatively, there is a range of important bottles) and a sandwich or *crostino*, and hang out in the narrow street. You can rest your glass on the wooden rack hanging on the wall to either side of the stand—just remember the Roman numeral marking the spot where you set it. There might be an impromptu *a cappella* concert in the street for entertainment.

Giacosa

❧ ❧ | CAFÉ, BAR | LIGHT LUNCH, DRINKS

Via Tornabuoni, 83r, 50123 Firenze
☏ 055/2396226
📷 Near fancy shops
∅ Sunday | ⏲ 7:30 A.M. to 8:30 P.M.
€ | MasterCard VISA

*T*his is a beautiful *fin de siècle* bar on the corner of
Via Tornabuoni and Via della Spada, in the prime
shopping zone, and probably Florence's most classic fashionable café. Half the not particularly large establishment
is a fancy coffee and drinks bar, with tables and waiter
service (it's under the same management and ownership
as Rivoire, page 157). The other half has a counter stocked
with very appealing sandwiches, tartines, salads, and some
hot dishes, such as meatballs, for a quick lunch. Lunch is
eaten standing milling with the crowd or at one of the few
small tables.

At cocktail hour, have a Negroni, a cocktail of Campari
and gin (vodka on request) invented here for the count
after which it is named.

Enoteca de' Giraldi

❧ ❧ | WINE BAR

Via dei Giraldi, 4r (Borgo degli Albizi), 50122 Firenze
☏ 055/216518
📷 Bargello
∅ Sunday | ⏲ 11 A.M. to 4 P.M., 6 P.M. to 1 A.M.
€ | MasterCard VISA

*T*his is a new wine bar in an old place, the former stables of Palazzo Borghese. The first of its two rooms features lofty, vaulted ceilings, a multicolored tile floor, light wooden marble-topped tables, paper place mats, white walls, and a plethora of small paintings and collages framed in matching wood hanging beneath shelves of wine bottles, which are the reason you came. Up some steps is the second room with a bar at the back. A strange sculpture hangs from the ceiling.

Wines are offered by the glass along with a small menu of *primi*, salads, *crostini*, salamis, cheeses, and desserts.

Il Guscio

❋ ❋ ❋ | TRATTORIA PLUS |
TRADITIONAL AND CREATIVE

Via dell'Orto, 49 (San Frediano), 50124 Firenze
☎ 055 / 224221
📷 Oltrarno, Santo Spirito, San Frediano
∅ Sunday
€€€ | MasterCard DinersClub ▆▆ VISA

*T*urn your back on Santo Spirito and walk down Via dell'Orto through what seems a blessedly normal neighborhood. Il Guscio is a spiffy but informal and friendly little place that nods to tradition while giving the locals some relief from the food they eat at home, or at least at their parents' house.

The menu changes frequently, but you might find *antipasti* of *sformato di pecorino con salsa di pere, insalata di trippa con pomodoro, cipolla e basilico,* or *salumi misti toscani e crostini,* and *primi piatti* of *zuppa di farro con verdure di stagione, gnocchi di patata con fiori di zucca, melanzane e gamberi,* or *guanciali* (meaning "pillows," nothing to do with bacon) *di ricotta e spinaci ai funghi porcini*. *Secondi* include both meat and seafood, such as *controfiletto di manzo al Vin Santo con pate di fegato, spinaci e purè* (the most elaborate by far on the menu I saw), *straccetti con funghi porcini,* or *braciolina fritta con rucola e pomodorini ciliegini*.

There's a good choice of *contorni* and desserts, including the inevitable cheesecake, *biscottini con Vin Santo,* and *panna cotta*.

Da Mario

❖ ❖ | TYPICAL TRATTORIA | *CUCINA CASALINGA* |

Via della Rosina 2r (Mercato Centrale), 50123 Firenze

☎ 055/218550

📷 Church of San Lorenzo, Capelle Medicee

∅ Sunday; August | 🕐 12 to 3 P.M.

No reservations

€ | 💳 none

*W*ait your turn in line for a free stool at a communal table in the modest rectangle that is the Trattoria Mario, where generations of the Colzi family have nourished generations of thrifty Florentines and impoverished students. This is Tuscan comfort food—a steaming bowl of vegetable soup, heavily laden with bread, or beef stew, held ready and waiting in the kitchen, which is in plain view. You might start with *pappa al pomodoro, ribollita, minestra di farro,* or *tortelli* filled with potatoes. The main dish could be a *bistecca alla fiorentina* (in which case expect to pay more) or a *bollito misto,* including *lampredotto,* the tripe from the cow's fourth stomach, or roast veal or roast beef. On Friday, the menu turns to fish.

To conclude, *cantucci* and Vin Santo are de rigueur. An economical kitchen does not preclude a serious wine, and, as a bonus, if you drink a third of a bottle (a quarter liter) of Brunello, you pay for a third of a bottle.

Trattoria Marione

✤ ✤ ✤ | TRATTORIA | *CUCINA CASALINGA*

Via della Spada, 27r, 50123 Firenze
☎ 055/214756
📷   Via Tornabuoni shopping
Ø Sunday
Reservations not always needed
€ | [MasterCard] [Diners Club] [American Express] [VISA]

*O*n a particularly nice November Saturday, we spent too long fooling around and left choosing a place for lunch until no place would have us. Just as we were gearing up to mutually assign blame for this unhappy state of affairs, we looked up and saw the gilded words "Trattoria Marione" above a wood-framed door and window. Affixed to the window was a promise that here we would find "*ribollita* DOC"; we didn't have to be told twice. While most of the jolly lunchers were in the cozy main dining room at street level, latecomers were accommodated in a basement room with vaulted ceilings.

The superb *ribollita*, with its rich dark flavors of beans and kale, was served in an earthenware dish with bright green olive oil to pour on top. *Pappardelle al sugo di cinghiale,* thick fresh long noodles with a hearty, oily, tasty sauce made from wild boar, was good too on the November day. We followed that with *rosticciana*—pork spareribs roasted dry and falling off the bone—with excellent spinach. Even the saltless bread (called *sciocco,* or "silly," in Tuscany, *sciapo* elsewhere) was superb.

To conclude in autumn, it's hard to resist *castagnaccio,* the traditional flat cake made of chestnut flour.

Fiaschetteria da Nuvoli

⚜ ⚜ | WINE BAR AND TRATTORIA | ✎

Piazza dell'Olio, 15r (Via Cerretani, Via dei Pecori),

50123 Firenze

☎ 055/2396616

📷 Duomo

∅ Sunday; two weeks in August | 🕐 7 A.M. to 8:30 P.M.

€ | [MasterCard] [Diners Club] [card] [VISA]

A fiaschetteria, as this modern wine bar fancies to call itself, is traditionally an establishment for the sale of wine in *fiaschi,* those straw-covered bottles, hence a very informal sort of *osteria. Nuvola* means cloud, but Walter Nuvoli's little establishment, founded in 1987, is located at the other extreme, in tombs belonging to the nearby thirteenth-century church.

At street level is a tiny bar with no place to sit but plenty of photos of both local and famous visitors (including Bill Clinton), paintings, cartoons, and framed cash from around the world. The bar also accommodates a glass case with salads, *supplì,* and *panini.*

The house white wine is fresh, cold, perfectly bubbly, and delicious, but glasses are poured from any number of bottles. A recent inspection found open on the bar: Rosso di Montalcino, Chianti Osteria Nuvoli, Santa Cristina, Clemente VII Chianti Classico. "We have everything," says Mr. Nuvoli.

Downstairs, in the stone-walled, brick-floored tombs, are two more spacious rooms seating more than fifty on wooden stools and benches at four long rectangular dark wooden tables. It's cool and damp in summer (a ceiling fan helps), but one imagines it would be warm and lively in the winter. Old bronze pots hang on the walls amid dusty bottles and vintage black-and-white photographs of Florence.

So what's for lunch? A prix fixe menu offers a *primo, secondo,* and *biscotti* with Vin Santo. *Primi* might include *insalata di farro, panzanella,* or a couple of pastas; *secondi* are split about evenly between hearty meat dishes (*porchetta, arista, milanese*) and such lighter fare as *vitel tonné, caprese, prosciutto e melone,* and salads.

Trattoria Pandemonio

❧ ❧ ❧ | UPSCALE TRATTORIA | VARIED HOME COOKING, INCLUDING FISH | 🖎

Via dei Leoni, 50r (San Frediano), 50124 Firenze
☎ 055/224002 | 📠 055/289712
📷 Oltrarno
∅ Sunday | A few garden tables | Air-conditioned
Reservations needed
€€€ | 💳 💳 💳 💳

*P*andemonium is not what you find, at least not in the kitchen. Giovanna Biagi and family, with a staff of agreeable young people, prepares her own home-style cooking, or such is the modest way in which it is presented. The restaurant itself is most pleasant, with lighting tending toward the romantic. The façade is narrow, but the restaurant goes back some distance from the street, terminating in a charming small garden, the feel of which is carried into the back room.

The house antipasto is superb: roasted peppers and eggplant slices, green beans and zucchini, a *crostino* with tomatoes (warm!), excellent marinated anchovies and herring. But you might try something more unusual, such as *cannellini* beans topped with grated *bottarga,* or the classic Tuscan tuna, beans, and onion, or Tuscan cold cuts (*antipasto toscano*). *Primi* include *tagliatelle con sugo della Mamma* (mother's meat sauce), classic *pappa al pomodoro, bavettine* (thin linguine) *alle vongole veraci* (with a little tomato—delicious). *Secondi* include both meat and fish—*polpo all'olio, inpepata di cozze* (mussels steamed with lots of black pepper in their broth), *pesce spada alla Messinese* (with plenty of tomatoes) for the latter, and for the former, the true *bistecca alla fiorentina, tagliata alla rucola,* classic *trippa alla fiorentina,* and the wonderful *braciola primavera,* a thin, thin breaded slice of veal completely concealed on the plate by a heap of *rucola* and tomato salad.

The desserts are homemade. There is a cheesecake (that's "cheesecake" in Italian), a very good *panna cotta,* and a delicious crème caramel that comes broken into chunks suspended in caramel sauce.

A nice wine list overwhelmingly favors Chiantis, but the house white is from the Marche.

Procacci

✢ ✢ | WINE BAR, GOURMET SHOP | ✎

Via Tornabuoni, 64r, 50123 Firenze

☎ 055/211656

📷 Near fancy shops

∅ Sunday

€ |

*S*tanding in line outside the Uffizi does not make me think of *A Room with a View,* but window shopping on dignified old Via Tornabuoni does. As a gesture just to celebrate being somewhere so nice, and to congratulate the street for maintaining its dignity into the third millennium, stop by this historic shop for a glass of wine and a tiny truffle sandwich. A couple of diminutive tables will accommodate you for a slightly more substantial collation of cheese or cold cuts and a little salad, but most people grab a sandwich (which might also contain smoked salmon, butter, and anchovies or some fanciful combination) and move on.

The Antinori winery, to its credit, bought the shop to save it, so predictably Antinori wines are featured, but not exclusively.

Caffè i Ricchi

❧ | BAR, LIGHT LUNCH ANNEXED TO RESTAURANT

Piazza Santo Spirito, 9r, 50124 Firenze
☎ | 📠 055 / 289712
📷 Oltrarno, Church of Santo Spirito
∅ Sunday | Outdoor tables
€ | 💳 none

*A*nnexed to the fish restaurant of the same name, this is a bar where you can have light lunch (say, a *panzanella* made with *farro* in place of bread) or a sandwich or an ice cream sitting at tables on the pleasant piazza looking at the magnificent church of Santo Spirito. But you'll get another look at the church on the bar's walls and in its back room (which has tables), which contain pictures representing entries in a competition to hypothetically complete Brunelleschi's unfinished façade. Some of the entries are wildly fanciful—Gucci stripes on one, Braille writing on another.

Rivoire

⚜ ⚜ | FANCY CAFÉ

Piazza della Signoria, 5r, 50123 Firenze
☎ 055/214412
📷 Palazzo Vecchio
∅ Monday | 🕐 8 A.M. to midnight
€ (if you just drink) | [MasterCard] [Diners Club] [American Express] [VISA]

It may seem that everyone in this bar is a tourist, but it has been an institution since the nineteenth century, and who can deny tourists the right to sip a world-renowned hot chocolate while looking across Piazza della Signoria at the Palazzo Vecchio? Inside is beautiful too, with marble blue-and-black tiled floors, dark wood paneling, yellow painted walls and high ceilings, and little round tables with pink tablecloths. A former chocolate factory, this is still chocolate heaven, liquid and solid.

Food is served, but you'll probably want to eat elsewhere. The menu includes a wide range of proper bar sandwiches (not your rustic *crostini*), eggs and bacon, cold plates, and pasta, as well as lavish ice cream concoctions and other desserts.

Da Ruggero

✤ ✤ ✤ ✤ | TRATTORIA PLUS | *CUCINA TOSCANA*

Via Senese, 89r (Porta Romana), 50125 Firenze
☎ 055 / 220542
📷 Giardino di Boboli, Palazzo Pitti
∅ Tuesday and Wednesday; August
Reservations a must
€€ | [MasterCard] [Diners Club] [American Express] [VISA]

*W*hen you've had enough paper napkins and earnest young bourgeois—no matter how cheerful their restaurants, how intelligently selected their wine list, how juicy their *tagliata alla rucola*—when you want to roll up your sleeves and relax before the old-style Tuscan meal you've been looking for since you got off the train, look no further.

Ruggero and his family offer a warm welcome, friendly service, and serious home cooking in two crowded (and haphazardly decorated) rooms, one of which contains a communal table for solo diners.

To get the juices flowing—though, believe me, they start gushing as soon as you're in the door—you'll want the *antipasto toscano,* with *crostini* fairly groaning under the weight of the pâtés. *Primi* could be *ribollita* or *pappa al pomodoro,* or *pappardelle con sugo di anatra,* a rich and simple sauce of shredded duck and plenty of olive oil. *Secondi* might be robust, herbed roast *arista di maiale* or rabbit, or *involtini,* or a *bollito misto* with garlic-less green sauce.

For dessert, there are the classic *cantucci di Prato,* large, wonderful almond-studded *biscotti* served with Vin Santo.

Venice

Eating in Venice

WHEN FOOD LOVERS THINK of Venice, they think of spaghetti with juicy *vongole* (clams); little boiled octopuses served and eaten whole; tiny soft-shell crabs; crab salad stuffed into the hard shell of larger crabs; eels from the islands of the lagoon; the most delicate, flavorful scallops; and wild artichokes too, or *risotto* with wild greens. They think of pitchers of fizzy Prosecco or fine Soave or Valpolicella—and they know how good those underrated wines can be.

In fact, one of the stupidest notions propagated by travel guides is that the food in Venice is awful and the city's eateries one big tourist trap. Certainly you can pay dearly for food in Venice. Imagine the logistical difficulty of operating a business where everything has to be brought in by boat; imagine the temptation to cut corners and inflate prices when your main customer base is transient. Furthermore, with a declining local population, tourists (many of them day-trippers) and university students do most of the eating out in Venice, favoring low-end stodge parlors and high-end hotel dining.

You might think that would cut out the interesting middle ground of diligent trattorias catering to average locals and informed visitors, and yet, miraculously, they exist. Venice also has a small population of passionate, patriotic restaurateurs who maintain and cultivate supply lines to obtain the best and the freshest ingredients, which they treat with a light and respectful hand. These superb restaurants are, of course, expensive, but not unreasonably so, given the rarity of their raw materials and complexity of their operations.

The institutions of the *bacaro,* or traditional wine bar, and the *osteria* (see pages 7–10) are completely authentic and an economical substitute for restaurants. In some you will eat finger food and drink small glasses of wine standing at a crowded bar, while in others you'll eat a full meal at wooden tables.

What can you do to protect yourself from tourist traps? Prefer the advice of an independent guidebook to that of a hotel concierge, who is probably getting a fat kickback. In general, avoid places with huge interregional menus, and shun places that solicit your business from the street. Venice has a shocking number of fast-food restaurants, Italian and international, so you can avoid those too. In other words, common sense will go a long way.

Venice is notorious too for having a double price scale, meaning a huge discount for locals in many restaurants. I think this is actually not entirely a bad thing, since tourists like having some local people in the restaurants instead of just other tourists. Nevertheless, in the interest of fair play, a number of Venetian restaurants have formed an association called the Associazione Buona Accoglienza (Good Welcome Association), whose members promise to treat everyone fairly and everyone the same. The association's brochures are available throughout the city.

PRACTICAL MATTERS

Mealtimes tend to be like those of Florence, northern rather than southern. In fact, the gastronomic clock seems never to stop ticking. You can find something to eat or drink at any time of day in Venice, even more than else-where.

You will do a great deal of walking in Venice, a great deal of it around in circles. Don't even think about leaving the hotel without a very detailed map. Vikram Seth's novel *An Equal Music* contains this tip for navigating in Venice, but I don't know whether it is original: "Call one side of the Grand Canal Marco and the other side Polo. Then remember if something's on the Marco side or the Polo side, and you'll know if you have to cross the [Grand] canal to get to it." This is crucial, since there are only three bridges across the Grand Canal. There is also a gondola ferry service, but I have never seen it operating at dinner-time, much less later. An all-day or three-day *vaporetto* ticket not only saves money but simplifies life, since you needn't hesitate to hop aboard for just a stop or two.

The Venice Menu

THE LIST THAT FOLLOWS contains common items on Venice menus. Additional terms are listed in the glossary. As in Rome, the range of choice commonly available on trattoria and restaurant menus does not begin to reflect the spectrum of foods you might have a chance of eating in a private home. In Venice, there seem to be more names for kinds of eateries than there do items on the menu; the repertoire of dishes on which the restaurants draw is much smaller than Rome's or Florence's. Shellfish tends to be boiled and fish to be grilled. Meat choices are usually limited to *fegato alla veneziana* and grilling.

Venetian dialect largely ignores double consonants and the letter l, so don't be surprised by variant spellings.

Further information may be found in the glossary. Note that in Venice the word *baccalà* or *bacalà* indicates air-dried cod (stockfish), not salt cod as in the rest of Italy.

CICHETI (BAR SNACKS)

Cicheti and antipasto offerings tend to overlap. A small portion of anything you see at the bar can be served with a drink.

alici marinate (marinated fresh anchovies)
baccalà mantecato (whipped salt cod served with grilled
   polenta slices)
fondi di carciofo (artichoke bottoms, which look better
   than they taste)
polpettine (meatballs)
salami slice with sweet and sour onion on top
sarde in saor (fresh sardines fried, then marinated)

ANTIPASTO

Cicheti, when available, can be served as antipasto. In
addition, the Venetian antipasto par excellence is a plate
(or platter) of lukewarm boiled seafood dressed only
with olive oil (*insalata tiepida di mare*).

    baccalà mantecato
    canocchie (mantis shrimp)
    caparossoli (clams)
    capesante (scallops)
    cappe lunghe (razor clams)
    folpeto (fist-sized octopus served whole)
    insalata di granseola (crabmeat salad, usually served
       in crab shell)
    moscardini (small octopuses)
    ostriche (oysters)
    sarde fritte (fried sardines)
    sarde or *sogliole in saor* (sardines or small sole, fried
       and marinated)
    schie (tiny brown shrimp), served with slices of
       grilled polenta
    uova di seppie (cuttlefish roe)

PRIMO

bigoli in salsa (thick wholewheat spaghetti with sauce of
   well-cooked anchovies and onions)
linguine con granchio (with a simple crabmeat sauce)
linguine or *tagliatelle nere* (pasta colored black with

cuttlefish ink, usually sauced with cuttlefish or other
 seafood)

risotto con carletti or *bruscandoli* (with selene, an herb, or
 hops)

risotto di gò e bevarasse (with a local small fish)

spaghetti con le vongole (with small clams, in their shells,
 garlic, olive oil, and parsley)

SECONDO

anatra (roast duck)

anguilla (bisato) all'ara (grilled eel)

baccalà alla vicentina (stockfish cooked with onion,
 anchovies, parsley, white wine, and a little milk and
 Parmesan)

branzino (sea bass, often farmed)

coda di rospo alla griglia (grilled monkfish)

fegato alla veneziana (thin pieces of calf's liver sautéed with
 onions)

frittura mista (deep-fried seafood, often with seasonal
 vegetables)

moeche fritte (soft-shell crabs from the Venetian lagoon,
 usually deep fried)

ombrine (croakers)

soaso (rombo) (brill, turbot)

CONTORNO

asparagi (asparagus, in spring)

castraure (wild artichokes, in spring)

fondi di carciofo

radicchio di Chioggia (red chicory; in winter; usually served
 raw)

radicchio di Treviso (long-leafed red chicory; in winter;
 served cooked or raw)

DESSERT

baicoli, zaletti (two of several kinds of local cookies, most
made with cornmeal flour, and usually served with
sweet wine)
pinza (any of a number of sweets made from bread or
flour mixtures, dried and candied fruits, and the like)
sfogliatine (puff pastry cookies)
zabaione caldo (warm zabaglione, served alone or as a
dessert sauce)

LOCAL WINES

The Veneto region produces some of Italy's most celebrated wines. Soave, from near Verona, leads the whites,
and many of Venice's best restaurants use it as a house
wine. Other Veneto whites on Venetian wine lists will
include Bianco di Custoza, Colli Euganei, and Breganze.
But should you some evening have meat instead of fish,
you'll probably drink Bardolino, Valpolicella, or Amarone.
The wine most associated with Venice, however, is light,
fizzy Prosecco—either in a glass with *cicheti* at a *bacaro* or
in a pitcher with dinner at a trattoria. For a local red, drink
ruby Raboso, from the Piave zone right next door. Look
too for the delightful strawberry-flavored *fragolino*.

Venice Listings

AL BACARETO

OSTERIA AL BACCO

BENTIGODI OSTERIA DA ANDREA

ENOTECA BOLDRIN

CA' D'ORO, DETTA ALLA VEDOVA

CANTINA GIÀ SCHIAVI (AL BOTTEGON)

CIP'S CLUB

ENOTECA LA COLOMBINA

TRATTORIA CORTE SCONTA

RISTORANTE VINI AL COVO

ENOTECA DO COLONNE

CANTINA DO MORI

FIASCHETTERIA TOSCANA

OSTERIA DA FIORE

CAFFÈ FLORIAN

HOSTARIA ALLA FONTANA

ANTICA TRATTORIA LA FURATOLA

OSTERIA AL MASCARON

ALLA PATATINA (AL PONTE)

OSTERIA AI QUATRO FERI

TRATTORIA DA REMIGIO

DA SANDRO

VINI DA GIGIO

Al Bacareto

🦁 🦁 | TRATTORIA, OSTERIA

Calle delle Botteghe, San Marco, San Samuele 3447,
   30124 Venezia
☎ | 📠 041/5289336
🚤 San Samuele, Sant'Angelo; *traghetto* San Tomà
📷 Palazzo Grassi Museum, Guggenheim Museum,
   Campo Santo Stefano, Campo Sant'Angelo
∅ Saturday evening and Sunday, holidays; August |
   Outdoor tables
🕐 8 A.M. to 11 P.M.
Reservations suggested for meals
€€ | 💳 VISA 💳

*O*n an attractive quiet street about halfway between
   Campo Santo Stefano and the Grand Canal, this
capacious, friendly bar-restaurant offers Venetians and visitors two menus—one, titled *"piatti tipici veneziani,"*
almost entirely fish (*fegato alla veneziana* being the only
exception), while the other (*"altri piatti"*) offers ichthyophobes a simple, honest menu of pastas with tomato or
meat sauce and main courses of *bistecche, scaloppine, coto-
lette,* and *roasbeef* (sic) or roast rabbit, veal, or chicken.
   Al Bacareto also, like many establishments in Venice,
wears two hats: the sit-down trattoria for complete meals,
and the *osteria,* bar, where you can have a glass of, say,
Prosecco, Tocai, Merlot, or Cabernet and *cicheti* to your
heart's content: batter-fried *baccalà,* fried sardines; *polpettine* of rice, meat, or spinach; or small pizzas and *crostini.*
   Specialties of the Venetian menu include *tagliolini al
pesce, spaghetti con vongole, bigoli in salsa,* and *spaghetti con le
seppie,* but especially *bacalà mantecato* and *bacalà alla vicentina.* There is also a fine *frittura mista* of shrimp, squid, and

small soles, and a good choice of fish to be cooked in the oven, or a *grigliata mista*.

A pitcher of the house Prosecco is just the thing. For dessert, try the assorted Venetian *biscotti* with a glass of sweet Zibibbo wine.

Osteria al Bacco

🐒 🐒 🐒 🐒 | TRATTORIA | FISH

Fondamenta Capuzine, Cannaregio 3054, 30121 Venezia

☎ 041/717493, 041/721415 | www.veneziaweb.com/bacco

🚤 Ponte delle Guglie, S. Alvise

📷 Ghetto

∅ Monday; vacation in January and August | Outdoor tables (garden)

Reservations advised

€€ | [AMEX] [VISA] [MasterCard]

*R*oberto Meneghetti is the hospitable owner (since 1983) of this charming old-fashioned *osteria*-turned-restaurant on a little canal near the iron bridge leading to the Ghetto. If it's open, you'll find it; if it's closed, you won't.

Our most recent meal—there were six of us, some more ichthyophilic than others—began with a gargantuan *antipasto misto* of boiled octopus (in pieces), *folpeti* (whole little octopi), *uova di seppie, sarde in saor, cannochie,* and *baccalà mantecato* (which went over especially well with those who found the octopus daunting), but there really was too much. Everybody loved the *linguine con granchio,* a simple condiment of shredded crabmeat, and the faithful rendition of *bigoli in salsa.* Nobody could face a main course after that, but it could have been grilled monkfish or

Roberto's specialty, *scampi in busara,* cooked with tomato purée, white wine, garlic, and bread crumbs.

Desserts are good (a chocolate mousse got raves from our friends), but *biscotti* and *croccante* with a glass of sweet wine are fine too.

Bacco, of course, means Bacchus, though the wine list we saw was brief and largely regional (we had Soave classico superiore Pieropan 1998).

Al Bacco is primarily a restaurant, not a *bacaro,* but you can stop in during the day for a glass of wine at the bar just the same.

Bentigodi Osteria da Andrea

🦁 🦁 🦁 | WINE BAR, TRATTORIA |
VENETIAN CUISINE, BUT NOT ONLY | ✎

Callesele, Cannaregio 1423, 30124 Venezia
📞 041/716269
🚤 San Marcuola
📷 Ghetto
∅ Sunday | Outdoor tables
🕐 10:30 A.M. to 3 P.M., 6 to 11 P.M.
€€ | 💳 none

*L*ast year, Enrico and Mauro took the reins from Andrea, who is about to open a wine bar in the former wholesale food market near Rialto, an impressive and beautiful complex now being renovated and opened to the public for the first time, while the market has been moved elsewhere.

Meanwhile, at Bentigodi, an old-fashioned *osteria* with a modern spirit, lunch, dinner, and an excellent assortment of wines by the glass and *cicheti* are served both at outdoor tables in the little street and in three rooms, in cleaned-up rustic style. A capacious marble-topped bar dominates the front main room. Seafood dominates the menu.

It can take the form of simple, classic *spaghettini* with *calamaretti,* or simple but gourmet fresh *tagliatelle* with quartered *moeche* (local soft-shell crabs) and sliced artichokes. Main courses likewise range from, say, a perfectly grilled monkfish served with *polenta* to the creative monkfish with *lardo* and potato sauce, to the downright fashionable fresh tuna with puddle of coral-colored sauce, made from sweet peppers, and another sauce of *aceto balsamico* and honey.

Superb *contorni* might include Belgian endive sautéed with walnuts, or carrots cooked very slowly to caramelize in their own sugar, adorned with little raisins (*zibibbi*).

An interesting wine list covers everything from big reds to spumante.

Enoteca Boldrin

🦁 🦁 | *TAVOLA CALDA, ENOTECA* |
REGIONAL VENETO CUISINE | 🍷

Salizzada San Canciano, Cannaregio 5550, 30131 Venezia
☎ 041/5237859
🚤 Fondamenta Nuove Rialto Ca' d'Oro
📷 Rialto, Strada Nova
∅ Sunday; vacation usually in June | ⏱ 9 A.M. to 9 P.M. |
Air-conditioned
€ | ▭ none

*O*pen since 1952, this is a handy place to keep in mind for off-hours or quick meals or snacks. In two rooms with marble-topped tables surrounded by wine bottles lining the walls, it offers a bar plus cafeteria-style meals, as well as a wine shop. Clients include local residents, workers, and visitors. Owner Loredano Sambo says the menu varies frequently, with seasonal specialties, but is likely to include *saor, frittura mista, seppie, lasagne di pesce, lasagne di radicchio,* and for dessert, homemade *tiramisù.*

Ca' d'Oro, detta alla Vedova

🦁 🦁 🦁 | HISTORIC BACARO, TRATTORIA |
CUCINA REGIONALE VENETO; FISH | 🔪

Calle del Pistor, Cannaregio 3912, 30100 Venezia
☎ 041/5285324
🚤 Ca' d'Oro
📷 Ca' d'Oro
∅ Thursday and Sunday lunch; August
🕐 11:30 A.M. to 3 P.M.; 6:30 to 11 P.M.
€ | ⊟ none

*M*irella and Renzo Doni are brother and sister who run what may be Venice's oldest, most beautiful and most authentic *bacaro,* which their family has owned and operated since its foundation 130 years ago. Stand at the bar for *cicheti*—say, a *fondo di carciofo* or a dish of *sarde in saor*—and an *ombreta,* a little glass of Veneto wine. Or sit at the tables for a simple meal of pasta with artichokes or radicchio or a *risotto.* Finish with *biscotti* or apple or pear cake or (inevitably) *tiramisù.*

Cantina già Schiavi
(Al Bottegon)

🐸 | BACARO, WINE SHOP | 🔪

Fondamenta Nani, Dorsoduro 992, 30123 Venezia

☎ 041/5230034

🚤 Accademia

📷 San Trovaso canal

Ø Sunday evening; one week in August

🕐 8 A.M. to 2 P.M., 3:30 to 8:30 P.M.

€ | 💳 none

This classic Venetian *bacaro,* a wine shop with bar, was founded fifty years ago and is still run by the Gastaldi family. Go for wine by the glass (for example, Tocai, Pinot Grigio, Chardonnay, Cabernet, Refosco, or the sweet *fragolino bianco*) and *cicheti* (say, *mortadella, formaggio, salame piccante,* or *crostini con il granchio*) or sandwiches. There are no seats, which encourages the sort of cocktail party atmosphere, since the customers seem all to be habitués, mostly artists in the evening, who know one another.

Cip's Club

🦁 🦁 🦁 🦁 | CASUAL RESTAURANT IN HOTEL |
CLASSIC AND VENETIAN CUISINE; PIZZA | 🍸

Hotel Cipriani, Fondamenta de le Zitelle 10, Giudecca,
  30133 Venezia
☎ 041/2408575 | 📠 041/5203930
🚤 San Marco; then take private Cipriani launch
Wonderful outdoor tables
Reservations a must
€€€€ | [MasterCard] [Diners Club] [Amex] [VISA]

*T*he Cipriani Hotel, a luxurious complex on the
island of Giudecca, is probably one of the best-
run hotels in Italy. A member of the prestigious Relais et
Chateaux group, it has that slick international quality that
provides local color through expensive design and avoids
any local inconveniences like language and plumbing.

I haven't been to the hotel's main restaurant, which is
reputed to be superb; Cip's Club is the supposedly informal eatery of the hotel, only I would not push "informal"
too far. Cip's is installed in a single cheery, clubhouse-like
room that manages to be comfortably spacious and cozy
at the same time (signs of intelligent planning abound). In
warm weather, tables are set out on a deck outdoors with
an absolutely splendid view toward San Marco. Service is
smooth as silk.

Like the hotel itself, Cip's has an international feel. The
local culture is dosed out in quantities that it is believed
the customers can handle, with something for everybody.
Locals can and do come here for excellent Neapolitan-
style pizza made in Venice's only wood-burning pizza
oven. Connoisseurs from abroad can find local ingredients
handled with respect, and wealthy philistines can order
what they think is Italian food, untroubled by the fact that

the restaurant has slipped one over on them: it is very, very good. In other words, the menu is cleverly constructed to offer something for all tastes, for example: sole fillets *in saor;* vegetable soup "from the Rialto market"; *cannelloni* filled with chicken and veal; pumpkin *risotto* with rosemary; fried Adriatic seafood with zucchini and artichoke, with horseradish sauce (which I would bet was added to prevent somebody from asking for tartar sauce); loin of lamb sautéed with herbs and *radicchio di Treviso.*

Do not miss the Cippamisù, a cylindrical individual *tiramisù.* The wine list is brief, good (but predictable), and expensive. On our visit last winter we paid L. 55,000 for the cheapest bottle, Breganze di Breganze Maculan 1998.

Enoteca la Colombina

🦁 🦁 | WINE BAR WITH MUSIC | VENETIAN AND SOUTHERN SNACKS AND MEALS

Campiello del Pergolotto, Cannaregio 1828, 30124 Venezia
☎ 041/2750622 | 📠 041/2756794 | www.lacolombina.it; info@lacolombina.it
🚤 San Marcuola
∅ Sunday
Reservations advised
€€ | [MasterCard] [Diners] [American Express] [VISA]

*T*he cozy dark wood and sardines may be characteristic of Venice's wine bars, but when the fog rolls in and the damp gets into your bones, try this attractive little place for a shot of southern Italian sunshine.

If you drop in at off-hours, you'll be given a little bite of something—bread and sun-dried tomatoes, say—with a glass (a professional ISO tasting glass) of something delicious from the bottles kept open on a rotation basis for the purpose. When the kitchen is open, the fashionable ingredients and dishes on the brief but varied menu include, in addition to sun-dried tomatoes, *carpaccio* of Angus beef, *bottarga,* smoked swordfish, *mozzarella di bufala,* swordfish *involtini,* and *tagliata* of beef.

Trattoria Corte Sconta

🐉 🐉 🐉 | RESTAURANT | VENETIAN AND CREATIVE SEAFOOD

Calle del Pestrin, Castello 3886, 30122 Venezia

☎ 041/5227024 | 📠 041/5227513

🚤 Arsenale

📷 Between San Marco and the Arsenale

∅ Sunday and Monday; January 7 to February 7 and July 15 to August 15 | courtyard tables

Reservations a must

€€€€ | 💳 💳 💳 💳

*S*ince 1980, Claudio Proietto has run one of Venice's most successful restaurants, disguised as a trattoria. The title role (the name means "hidden courtyard") is played by a large rectangular space behind the restaurant's two simple front rooms (with a nice old marble-topped counter), once occupied by a traditional *osteria.* Today the restaurant enjoys international fame, many customers, and mixed reviews.

The trattoria disguise seems to be maintained to justify the lack of a written menu, the mediocre house wine—a Prosecco (there is also a brief wine list), the paper place mats (cloth napkins, however), and inattentive service, but the prices are strictly *ristorante,* and so is the cooking.

The house antipasto costs L. 45,000 per person, which you will never know until the bill comes. It goes on for a long time—plate after plate—but not so long that you don't want to eat anything else. On our recent visit, the friends who came with us swore that when they'd tried the antipasto a few years ago (for the same price), they really didn't want anything afterward. Evidently, instead of raising the price, the restaurant reduced the quantity.

Our antipasto for four consisted of a crab paste with dry toast; marinated salmon with tarragon; small clams with ginger (a signature dish and very good); a platter of shellfish and *folpeti; insalata di granseola* (very good) with Ligurian olive oil; *uova di seppia;* shrimp; marinated anchovies; anchovies (we think) in tomato sauce; *baccalà mantecato* with yellow and white *polenta;* and *sarde in saor.* The pastas were forgettable: *fusilli* with lemon, tuna, artichokes, and no noticeable flavor; *linguine* with *nero di seppia,* an indifferent example of what can be a very tasty dish. The *secondi* were better: red mullets with green peppercorns, and superb deep-fried *moeche,* Venetian small soft-shell crabs.

Panna cotta with strawberry sauce and lemon sorbet were blah, and we had to ask for a piece of *croccante,* which most Venetian restaurants offer automatically at the end of a seafood meal.

Ristorante Vini al Covo

🦁 🦁 🦁 🦁 🦁 | SERIOUS RESTAURANT |
"LA CUCINA VENEZIANA INTERPRETATA";
MOSTLY FISH | ✎

Campiello della Pescaria, Castello 3968 (Riva degli Schiavoni),
   30122 Venezia
☎ | 📠 041/5223812
🚤 Arsenale
∅ Wednesday and Thursday | Outdoor tables | ♿ |
   Nonsmoking room | Air-conditioned
Reservations advised in the evening
€€€€ (less at lunch) | 💳 none (though this may change)

*F*rom San Marco, walk along the Grand Canal
   toward the Castello; turn left when you reach
the Gabrielli Sandwirth hotel. The restaurant, one of my
favorites in all Italy, will be on your left after a few steps.

The finest ingredients money can buy, including the
best seafood from the Venetian lagoon, and the restraint
to do as little to it as possible, characterize Cesare Benelli's
cooking—or so he would modestly have you believe, as
though skill and imagination had nothing to do with it.
Restraint alone cannot account for the exquisite *tagliolini*
with oysters and *scorfano* we tasted last winter, or the
renowned tempura-style *fritto misto,* which will always
include some seasonal vegetables (maybe radicchio or
artichoke wedges), shrimp, *scampi, moscardini,* and some
precious morsel such as a small soft-shell crab (*moeca*) or
canestrelli, the exquisite scallops of the lagoon. Even the
green salad is sublime.

There is always a nonfish choice for each course, such
as a refined *pasta e fagioli* and a local duck. Diane Benelli,
Texas-born, multilingual, and the embodiment of charm
and hospitality, explains the menu, with considerable sen-
sitivity to customers' likes and dislikes. She is also the

dessert chef. We tasted a *semifreddo* (molded ice cream) drenched in *grappa* and covered with *zibibbi*, accompanied by a brittle made of almonds and pine nuts, and a superb *torta di pere e prugne* (pear and plum pie).

There is a very good wine list with very fair prices. Lunch is less formal than dinner, with paper tablecloths and a limited menu based on *cicheti*.

Enoteca Do Colonne

 | BACARO | *CICHETI*

Rio Tera del Cristo, Cannaregio 1814 C, 30121 Venezia
☎ 041/5240453
🚤 San Marcuola
∅ Tuesday in winter and Sunday; two weeks in August |
Sidewalk tables
🕐 7 A.M. to 2 or 3 P.M., 4 to 9 P.M. | ♿
€ | ▭ none

*C*arlo, Patrizia, and Roberta Benjamin, father and two daughters, operate this characteristic bar offering typical *cicheti* and voluptuous sandwiches. Try deviled eggs, marinated anchovies, *nervetti*, *musetto*, or *baccalà mantecato* with a glass of Chardonnay, Cabernet, Merlot, or Tocai. Most of the wines are from the Veneto and Friuli regions, but they also offer Chianti, by popular request.

Locals tend to stand at the large bar inside, while tourists take a load off at the tables outside. Among the curiosities displayed inside is a case with a collection of corkscrews.

Cantina Do Mori

🦁 🦁 | WINE BAR | *CICHETI* | 🔪

Calle dei Do Mori, San Polo 429, 30125 Venezia

☎ 041/5225401

🚤 San Silvestro

📷 Rialto bridge and market

∅ Sunday; August | No seats | 🕐 8:30 A.M. to 8:30 or 9 P.M. | ♿

€ | 💳 none

*T*he management is new (Giovanni Sponza and Rudi Sportelli recently took over from Roberto Biscontin), but this most typical Venetian *bacaro* has been there since 1462. Local wines and serious bottles are poured by the glass and accompanied by an irresistible array of *cicheti*, including *polpette, bacalà mantecato, musetto* sliced and served hot, and artichoke bottoms. The ambience is no less enticing, all wood, copper pots, and happy people.

Fiaschetteria Toscana

🦁 🦁 🦁 🦁 | RISTORANTE | CLASSIC VENETIAN;
FISH AND MEAT | 🍴

Salizada San Giovanni Crisostomo, Cannaregio 5719,
   30131 Venezia
☎ 041/5285281 | 📠 041/5285521 |
   a.busatto@ve.netuno.it;
   fiaschetteria.toscana@ve.netuno.it
🚢 Rialto
Ø Monday lunch and Tuesday; July | Garden tables
Reservations advised
€€€ | 💳 💳 💳 💳

The name refers to an early incarnation of the establishment as a Tuscan wine shop, but since the 1950s, Mariuccia and Albino Busatto have run one of Venice's most respected, and Venetian, restaurants. It is characterized by superb ingredients, splendid service, and a varied menu, which emphasizes seafood but includes plenty of meat. We had some quibbles with some of the cooking on our visit there last winter, but overall it remains an excellent choice when you've had enough rusticity in the wine bars and are ready for something more upscale without going over the top in price or elegance.

The menu varies daily but might include: *insalata di granchio* (this arrived too cold); risotto for two with *carletti* or *gò; gnocchi* with *scampi* and zucchini; grilled monkfish; *fritto misto* (all seafood, including small fish); *frittura la Serenissima* (zucchini strips, artichoke wedges, and shrimp, *scampi,* and *moscardini;* this earns a souvenir *Piatto del Buon Ricordo*).

The wine list, arranged by region, is unusually long for Venice and very good by any standard. Homemade *sfogliatine* (puff pastries), some filled with whipped cream (much loved in Venice), are a delightful conclusion to a meal.

Osteria da Fiore

🦁 🦁 🦁 🦁 🦁 | ELEGANT RESTAURANT
(MICHELIN STAR); GOURMET FISH | ✒

Calle del Scaleter, San Polo 2202 (between *campi* of San Polo
 and San Giacomo dell'Orio), 30125 Venezia
☎ 041/721308 | 📠 041/721343 | www.dafiore.com
 (has reservation form)
🚤 San Silvestro
∅ Sunday and Monday
Reserve well in advance (lunch is easier)
€€€€ | MasterCard 💳 💳 VISA

*L*ong after establishing its reputation among Italy's
 foodies and Michelin stargazers, this quiet but
elegant Venetian fish restaurant was thrust into the international limelight by an article in the *International Herald
Tribune* that declared it one of the world's ten greatest
restaurants. Not even its fans wanted to go that far, but it
certainly became harder to get a reservation. However, we
went back for the first time in several years a few months
ago, and with disclaimers about the impossibility of making a serious ten-best list, we concluded that it really is
right up there.

The façade is that of an old *osteria* (and you can still
drink at the front-room bar), but the restaurant, in two
quiet and smoothly running dining rooms, is elegant,
though in a way that doesn't detract attention from the
food. The menu is exclusively seafood-based, specifically
lagoon-based. Maurizio starts earning that star every day
by managing to stock the kitchen with the best creatures
the Venetian lagoon has to offer in very short supply. His
wife Mara Zanetti's cooking is incredibly skillful: she can
simply fry an eel in butter and make it seem like a plate for a
prince (well, *my* prince), and in her hands old favorites like
bigoli in salsa or *baccalà mantecato* take on new meaning.

But she has imagination too: red mullets rolled around tufts of *radicchio di Treviso* lack nothing in artistic presentation.

The menu changes daily, according to supply, but here are some items from Mara's repertoire: for *antipasti, saor di orate alla Marco Polo, capesante gratinate al timo, granceola e schie olio e limone; primi: vellutata d'asparagi verdi, pennette capesante e broccoli, pappardelle con ostriche e zafferano, risotto di scampi ed asparagi;* and *secondi: frittura mista dell'Adriatico, filetto di branzino all'aceto balsamico, rombo al forno in crosta di patate.*

Dessert could be a *tortino di cioccolato* or an exquisite cake called *pinza* (a traditional Venetian sweet), a sort of firm custard studded with raisins for flavor in a crust, served with cold *zabaglione* as a sauce, or *cremini fritti*, delicious deep-fried cubes of custard.

Caffè Florian

🦁 🦁 🦁 | LANDMARK CAFÉ

Piazza San Marco 56, 30124 Venezia

☎ 041/5285338 | www.caffeflorian.com; info@caffeflorian.com

🚤 San Marco

📷 Saint Mark's, Museo Correr

🕙 10 A.M. to midnight

Reservations not needed

€ for drinks; €€ for meals | [MasterCard] [Diners Club] [American Express] [VISA]

*O*n December 29, 1720, Floriano Francesconi founded a two-room *botega da caffè* (coffee shop) and gave it the patriotic name of Venezia Trionfante, but its habitués—who included the wealthy, the noble, the literary, and the ordinary—called it by its owner's name. And that is how one of the world's most famous and most beautiful cafés got its name. The great Venetian dramatist Carlo Goldoni (1701–93) is said to have observed Venetian mores there from an early age, and, since for a time it was the only café in Venice to serve ladies, Casanova sought female companionship there. The Venice Biennale was conceived in Florian's rooms at the end of the nineteenth century, and as might be expected, Byron, Goethe, Dickens, and Proust are only a few of the illustrious figures who liked to sit at Florian's tables. Since the turn of the twentieth century, however, when the Central European café-concert formula was adopted, conversation has had to compete with music. Florian also organizes art exhibitions and is generally active culturally.

Anecdotes, history, cultural activities, and a tour of the café's magnificent muraled, paneled, and mirrored rooms—whose décor dates to the nineteenth-century expansion of the café—can be found on Florian's interesting website, which merits a visit from anyone planning a trip to Venice. It even includes a page of general links on Venice.

But what do you actually put in your mouth there? In keeping with its origins as a coffee house, coffee (Florian's blend) is available not only in all the usual forms (espresso, *caffelatte,* cappuccino, American, Irish) but in *bicerin* (coffee, chocolate, and cream) and *caffè dell'Imperatore* (coffee, cream, and *zabaglione*). There is excellent hot chocolate, hot *zabaglione* with *baicoli* (*biscotti*), homemade ice creams, and Florian's Prosecco, Mimosa (Prosecco and orange juice), Bellini (Prosecco and peach juice), or Rosso Apéritif (something like Campari). Full-blown afternoon tea is available, with scones and sandwiches.

You can stand at the bar or sit at a table outdoors on the piazza next to the orchestra and pigeons. I think it's better to sit indoors and look at the beautiful rooms. Catch the view of Saint Mark's and the pigeons gratis before or after. If you sit, and the orchestra is playing (even if it's on a brief break), there is a surcharge of L. 7000 per person. Otherwise, a cappuccino costs L. 4500 at the bar and 11,500 at a table.

There is also a line of Florian souvenirs, including cups, book, and comestibles.

Hostaria alla Fontana

🦁 🦁 | OSTERIA | *CUCINA CASALINGA* (FISH)

Fondamenta Cannaregio, Cannaregio 1102, 30121 Venice
🚣 Ponte delle Guglie
📷 Ghetto
☎ 041/715077
∅ Sunday and Monday; August | Outdoor tables
🕐 11 A.M. to 3 P.M., 6 to 11 P.M. or midnight
€€ | 💳 none

*T*he menu is always changing at this cozy *bacaro* cum trattoria, but Bruno Paolin recommends *"pesce, sempre pesce."* Try the calamari, or the linguine with swordfish. The menu depends on what fresh fish they have, though they also offer a *tris di baccalà* (*mantecato, vicentina, livornese*) that is not half bad. This and other prepared dishes (such as marinated fish and an octopus salad) are laid out at the bar to have with wine or as an antipasto or *secondo* with a meal. Linguine with *cappe lunghe* and some fresh tomatoes was quite oily but tasy.

The house wine is a copper-colored Pinot Grigio in carafe, none too cold. Desserts are simple but good, such as *torta di mele*.

La Fontana is located right on a canal, and couldn't be snugger, with low beamed ceiling, copper pots, and a fireplace. Old photos and Sicilian puppets decorate the walls. We observed that the front tables were devoted to exuberant habitués drinking wine, while the outdoor tables, as so often, inadequately sheltered from the noonday sun, were all occupied by taciturn foreigners.

Antica Trattoria la Furatola

🦁 🦁 🦁 🦁 | RISTORANTE | FISH

Calle Lunga San Barnaba, 2870 A, Dorsoduro (between
   San Barnaba and San Sebastiano), 30123 Venezia
☎ 041 / 5208594 | furatola@gpnet.it
🚤 Ca' Rezzonico
📷 Galleria dell'Accademia
∅ Monday lunch and Thursday
Reservations advised
€€€ | ▦ ▣ ▤ 𝗩𝗜𝗦𝗔

*T*he name (accent on the second syllable) means a little shop where the urban poor shopped for bread, soups, and fried small fish, and the little front room continues the conceit. But the dining room, low ceilings and white walls, old photos and copper pots and pans, and an open kitchen, belongs to a serious seafood restaurant.

The excellent seafood antipasto is presented in two tiers. First arrive the delicate flavors. The *bolliti* include octopus, mantis shrimp, ordinary shrimp, the tiny brown shrimp called *schie,* and *uova di seppia.* The more strongly flavored *marinati* include non-Venetian (but good) salmon and sun-dried tomatoes, which can be forgiven, as there are also marinated anchovies, called *sardoni* locally, and *sarde in saor.*

The house specialty is a fish soup that we found a little heavy on the squid, and likewise the *sugo della casa* for spaghetti. I'd try something else the next time, such as spaghetti with mantis shrimp. The pasta portions are huge and intended for two. The main course will, predictably, be fresh fish, such as grilled *coda di rospo.* After the fish, large glasses of *sgroppino,* liquid lemon sherbet, to cleanse the palate, appeared.

We found the assortment of desserts a little dry, except for an excellent *crostata* of mixed fruit. The wine list is limited but adequate.

Osteria al Mascaron

🦁 🦁 🦁 🦁 | TRATTORIA | *CUCINA TRADIZIONALE, REGIONALE*

Calle Lunga Santa Maria Formosa, Castello 5225, 30122 Venezia
☎ 041/5225995
🚤 San Marco, Rialto
∅ Sunday; August
€€ | ▭ none

*L*uigi (Gigi) Vianello's trattoria is generally considered the most archetypal of all Venetian eateries. Venice has dustier and more venerable establishments, but if you want to eat good local food elbow-to-elbow with about fifty local and international foodies, this is your place, especially if you like the paper–place mat ethic.

The menu changes daily, but the repertoire from which it draws is limited. Our spring lunch was typical. We began with a *piatto misto* of tender octopus, *baccalà mantecato* on bread, grilled sardines, and *cicale.* By the time the table next to us ordered theirs, the composition had varied. Pasta was delicious spaghettini with very small *vongole,* spiced up with both *peperoncino* and black peppercorns. For dessert, have *biscottini buranelli con vino dolce.*

So popular is the trattoria that it opened a wine bar,

La Mascareta, down the street, at number 5183 (tel. 041/5230744), evenings only.

Alla Patatina (Al Ponte)

🐾 🐾 | OSTERIA | MEALS AND *CICHETI*

Ponte San Polo, Calle Saoneri, San Polo 274/A, 30125 Venezia

☎ 041/5237238 | 📠 041/710849

🚤 San Silvestro, San Tomà

📷 I Frari

∅ Sunday (though groups may reserve ahead for Sunday); August

🕐 9:30 A.M. to 2:30 P.M., 4:30 to 10 P.M.

€ | [Amex] [Diners Club] [MasterCard] [VISA]

*C*eiling fans, heavy wooden tables, and two columns behind the bar characterize this friendly and unusually roomy establishment, frequented by artists, tourists, and habitués, which specializes in a wide assortment of *cicheti*. The title role is played by large ranch-cut roast potatoes, served incandescent in a generous portion, with a toothpick as weapon of choice. For a late-morning snack, we also tried very good *baccalà mantecato,* marinated anchovies, and *sarde in saor,* as well as a hot dish, *baccalà alla vicentina,* served with grilled white polenta.

There's also an interesting choice of wines by the glass, such as tart Prosecco S. Giovanni *spento,* meaning not fizzy, or Incrocio Manzoni. *Incrocio* means cross, as in hybrid (or intersection, for that matter), and the wine takes its name from a successful agricultural experiment. You might finish with the homemade *tiramisù.*

Osteria ai Quatro Feri

🦁 🦁 🦁 | OSTERIA | TRADITIONAL VENETIAN
CUISINE, WITH LIBERTIES (MEALS AND *CICHETI*)

Calle Lunga San Barnaba, Dorsoduro 2754, 30123 Venezia
☎ | 📠 041/5206978
🚤 Ca' Rezzonico
📷 Galleria dell'Accademia
∅ Sunday; June | 🕐 11:30 A.M. to 2:30 P.M., 6:30 to
   11:30 P.M. | ♿
€€ | ▭ none

*T*here is something irresistible about this snug
little two-year-old *osteria* in neo-rustic style, which
seats more than fifty in its two rooms. Owners Barbara
and Bianca used to work at Mascaron (page 190), so their
antecedents are encouraging. A wooden bar laden with a
particularly welcoming assortment of platters and bottles
greets you as you enter—not only the usual sardines and
baccalà, but also octopus and salads. The food is intended
mostly to be eaten at table in a meal, but you can also stop
in for just a glass of wine and a little dish of something
from the array of appetizers.

For dessert, try the homemade *crema di mascarpone,*
semifreddo, panna cotta, or *budino veneziano.*

Trattoria da Remigio

🦁 🦁 🦁 🦁 | TRATTORIA PLUS |
"CUCINA TIPICAMENTE LOCALE" (FISH) | 🍴

Salizada dei Greci, Castello 3416, 30122 Venezia
☎ 041/5230089 | 📠 041/2417828
🚤 San Zaccaria
📷 San Marco
∅ Monday evening and Tuesday; two weeks in summer and
    December 20 to January 20
Reservations needed
€€ | MasterCard DINERS CLUB Card VISA

*I*n Rome, we never see *coda di rospo* (monkfish)
grilled—it's always cooked with some liquid—
and after encountering several somewhat dry ones in
Venice, I decided this was one call the Venetians got wrong.
But then I tasted a perfect specimen at this large, bustling
restaurant in two rooms, frequented, since its founding in
1954, mostly by Venetians despite its location in prime
tourist territory. The designation "trattoria" is the restaurant's own, but the owner, Fabio Bianchi, is too modest.

Everything is seasonal and presented with a minimum
of manhandling. *Antipasti* include the usual crabs, mantis
shrimp (*canoce*), and periwinkles, but also tart, herbed *sardoni alla greca*. We tried spaghetti with mantis shrimp in
tomato sauce, but it got most of its considerable taste
from the heads, which are left in for an *Aliens* effect. A
huge grilled eel hit the spot across the table, while I
accompanied my splendid monkfish with superb, carefully peeled asparagus. But be warned: like many vegetables, they were overcooked for American taste.

Desserts, which tend toward the voluptuous—such as
tiramisù, or the almond *millefoglie*—are homemade. There

is a good wine list and good wine service, with intelligent suggestions.

Da Sandro

🦁 🦁 🦁 | OSTERIA (MEALS AND *CICHETI*) |

TRADITIONAL VENETIAN CUISINE, BUT NO FISH

Calle Lunga S. Barnaba, Dorsoduro 2753/A, 30123 Venezia

🚤 Ca' Rezzonico

☎ 041/5230531

Ø Sunday and Monday; August | Garden tables |

   ♿ Wheelchair access but not to bathroom facilities

€€ (meals) | 🪪 none

*T*he specialties at this inviting rustic *osteria* (cooking pots hanging from the ceiling, bottles, and lots of wood) are *baccalà* and *bigoli in salsa,* as well as seasonal vegetables and a variety of meat dishes. There is no fish; in Venice, *baccalà* doesn't count as fish.

Sandro is Alessandro di Lena, proprietor for the past three years. The front room is devoted to the bar and wonderful *cicheti.* We tried some *polpettine, baccalà mantecato,* and marinated anchovies. For dessert, try the *zabaglione* or the *dolce di polenta e fichi.*

Vini da Gigio

🦁 🦁 🦁 🦁 | INFORMAL RISTORANTE |
TRADITIONAL VENETIAN FOOD, MEAT AND FISH |
🥄

Fondamenta San Felice, Cannaregio, 3628/A, 30131 Venezia
☎ 041/5285140 | 📠 041/5228597
🚤 Ca' d'Oro
📷 Ca' D'Oro
Ø Monday; three weeks between August and September
and between January and February | ♿ Wheelchair
access but not to bathroom | No-smoking room
Reservations essential
€€ | 💳 💳 💳 💳

*P*aolo, Laura, and Nicoletta Lazzari are at the
helm in this respected, charming rustic-style
restaurant, complete with beamed ceilings, perhaps offering the best value in all of Venice. The superb and reasonably priced wine list offers more than four hundred Italian
wines, most of which come from the Veneto, but Friuli
and Toscana are also well represented. There is no wine by
the glass, but you can order a quarter or half liter of a
wine that changes weekly. You can also go and just have
antipasto or *cicheti*, but at a table.

The menu is divided into a meat side and a seafood
side. It includes: *caparossoli alla marinara, sarde in saor, baccalà mantecato con polenta, penne con granceola, tagliolini con
scampi e pesto di basilico, seppie alla griglia,* and *fritto misto
di mare.* From the land side: fried taleggio cheese with
polenta, *salumi, tagliolini* with tomato sauce, *penne al
Gorgonzola e pistacchi, tagliolini con ragù di anatra, vitello
in salsa di tonno, ossobuco,* and *fegato alla veneziana con*

polenta. A digest of wine suggestions is appended to the menu.

The desserts, which are exquisite, are all made by Laura. Look for *torte, bavarese con gianduia, crostate,* and *panna cotta.*

Trattorias Open Sundays and Mondays

SUNDAY AND MONDAY are the two most difficult days of the week for finding open eating places in Italy. This lists the places that are open for at least part of those days; see the main listings for details. Restaurants are open for lunch and dinner unless otherwise noted.

ROME

Open on Sunday

Ristorante vegetariano
　　Arancia Blu (evening)
La Buca di Ripetta (lunch)
Da Bucatino
Ristorante la Campana
Da Cesare
Osteria Checco er
　　Carettiere (lunch)
Ristorante Il Ciak (evening)
Colline Emiliane
Cul de Sac 1

Ditirambo
La Dolce Vita
Antica Enoteca di Via
　　della Croce
Palazzo del Freddo Fassi
Ferrara (except in summer)
Frontoni (evening)
Il Gelato di San Crispino
Osteria la Gensola
Giggetto al Portico
　　d'Ottavia

Giolitti
Hostaria Romanesca
Trattoria da Lucia
Pizzeria ai Marmi
   (evening)
Trattoria Monti
Ristorante Paris (lunch
   only)

Ricci (Est! Est! Est!)
   (evening)
Osteria della Suburra
   (Da Silvio)
Taverna dei Quaranta
Tram Tram
Zi' Fenizia

Open on Monday

Ristorante Agata e Romeo
Agustarello a Testaccio
Osteria dell'Angelo
Ristorante vegetariano
   Arancia Blu (evening)
Trattoria Armando al
   Pantheon
Augusto
Fiaschetteria Beltrame-
   Cesaretti
La Bottega del Vino di
   Anacleto Bleve
Ristorante Pizzeria al
   Callarello
Cantina Cantarini
Enoteca Cavour 313
Le Colline Emiliane
Enoteca Corsi (lunch)
Cul de Sac 1 (evening)
Ditirambo (evening)
Osteria il Dito e la Luna
   (evening)
Enoteca al Parlamento
   (Achilli)
Antica Enoteca di Via
   della Croce
Ferrara

Dar Filettaro Santa Barbara
Frontoni
Il Gelato di San Crispino
Osteria la Gensola
Pizzeria Leonina
Trattoria Lilli
Pizzeria ai Marmi (evening)
Trattoria Monti
Antica Trattoria al Moro
Hostaria da Nerone
Nino
Trattoria Otello alla
   Concordia
Ristorante la Piazzetta
Ristorante la Pigna
Al Ponte della Ranocchia
Il Quadrifoglio
Il Sanpietrino
Sora Lella
Sora Margherita (lunch)
Trattoria St. Teodoro
Taverna dei Quaranta
Trimani il Wine Bar
Ristorante Vecchia
   Locanda
Volpetti Più
Zi' Fenizia

FLORENCE

Open on Sunday

Angiolino	Osteria del Caffè Italiano
Trattoria Antellesi	Il Francescano
Trattoria Baldovino	Rivoire
Balducci	Da Ruggero

Open on Monday

Trattoria Antellesi	Giacosa
La Baraonda (evening)	Enoteca de' Giraldi
Beccofino	Il Guscio (evenings;
Belle Donne	in summer)
Osteria de' Benci	Da Mario
Cantinetta Antinori	Trattoria Marione
Cantinetta dei Verrazzano	Fiaschetteria da Nuvoli
Trattoria la Casalinga	Trattoria Pandemonio
Coquinarius	Procacci
Il Francescano	Caffè i Ricchi
I Fratellini	Da Riuggero

VENICE

Open on Sunday

Osteria al Bacco	Ristorante Vini al Covo
Ca' d'Oro, detta alla	Fiaschetteria Toscana
Vedova (evening)	Caffè Florian
Cantina già Schiavi	Antica Trattoria la
(Al Bottegon)	Furatola
(lunchtime)	Trattoria da Remigio
Cip's Club	Vini da Gigio

Open on Monday

Al Bacareto	Enoteca Boldrin
Bentigodi Osteria da	Ca' d'Oro, detta alla
Andrea	Vedova

Cantina già Schiavi
   (Al Bottegon)
Cip's Club
Enoteca la Colombina
Al Covo
Enoteca Do Colonne
Cantina Do Mori
Fiaschetteria Toscana
   (evening)

Caffè Florian
La Furatola (evening)
Osteria al Mascaron
Alla Patatina (Al Ponte)
Osteria ai Quatro Feri
Trattoria da Remigio
   (lunch)

Glossary

THE GLOSSARY LIST that follows is based on Howard Isaacs and my *Dictionary of Italian Cuisine* (see Bibliography), to which the reader is referred for expanded definitions, pronunciation and grammar, variant spellings, geographical attributions, botanical and zoological names, and all sorts of other useful and entertaining information. Words are given in singular or plural according to the form in which they are most commonly used, or both, if both are found with about equal frequency. Note that many terms have multiple meanings, but only those common in Rome, Florence, and Venice are given here. See also the lists of common menu items and discussions of wine at the beginning of each city section. Words in small capitals are defined elsewhere in the glossary.

In Italian pronunciation, stress is normally on the penult (next to last syllable). Exceptions to this rule are indicated in the list by underlining of the stressed vowel or vowel cluster. Accent marks over a vowel are part of the spelling of the word.

An equals sign (=) sends the reader from a variant to the standard form of the word. It is not used in the case of parallel terms with the same meaning.

abbacchio milk-fed lamb; lamb in general

abbastanza enough

abbinamento matching

abboccato between semi-sweet (AMABILE) and medium-dry

acciuga; pl. acciughe anchovy; anchovies

acerbo sour; unripe; harsh

aceto balsamico balsamic vinegar; the best quality is called
  aceto balsamico tradizionale

acido sour, acidic; sharp-tasting

acqua water; *acqua minerale,* mineral water

acquacotta vegetable soup, usually spiced with peppers and
  thickened with bread, sometimes containing egg and cheese

affettati cold cuts, sliced meats

affumicato smoked

aglio garlic; *aglio e olio,* literally, garlic and (olive) oil, a quick
  sauce for spaghetti of olive oil and sautéed garlic, sometimes with PEPERONCINO and/or parsley

agnello lamb

agnolotti ravioli-like pasta, usually filled with meat

agosto August

agretti in Rome, a green vegetable that looks like grass (or
  chives), customarily boiled and served with lemon and
  olive oil

agro, all' with olive oil and lemon

agrumi citrus fruits

aio, ajo = AGLIO

ala wing

alcol, alcool alcohol; *alcolici,* alcoholic beverages

Aleatico di Gradoli sweet red wine from Lazio

alici anchovies, often served fresh

alimentari, prodotti groceries

alloro, foglia di bay leaf

alzavola teal (a duck)

amabile semisweet (of wine)

amarena morello cherry, sour cherry

amaretto almond cookie; *amaretto di Saronno,* an almond-flavored liqueur

amaro bitter; unsweetened; herbal liqueur

amatriciana, all' (for pasta) with tomatoes, PECORINO, and GUANCIALE

American bar bar primarily for the service of alcohol rather than coffee

ammazzacaffè literally, coffee killer; an alcoholic beverage served after coffee

analcolico nonalcoholic or soft drink, especially bitter non-alcoholic *aperitivi*

ananas pineapple

anara col pien Venetian stuffed duck

anatra, anitra duck; *anatra di Barberia,* Barbary duck

anatroccolo duckling

anciò = ACCIUGA (Veneto)

anello ring; ring-shaped mold; anything ring-shaped

anguilla eel

anguria watermelon

anice anise

animelle sweetbreads

annata vintage, vintage year

anno year

antico ancient, old; antique

antipasto, antipastino appetizer, appetizer course; *antipasto all'italiana,* prosciutto, salami, and a few pickled vegetables

aperitivo apéritif

aperto open

aprile April

arachidi peanuts

aragosta clawless lobster; rock lobster; spiny lobster (*langouste*)

arancia orange (the fruit)

aranciata orange drink, orange soda

arancino (di riso) fried ball of rice bound with meat sauce (served in pizzerias)

aringa herring

arista (di maiale) roast pork loin flavored with garlic and herbs

arlecchino harlequin; mix of different colored pastas; potentially anything multicolored

armelìn apricot

armleti type of dumplings

aromatico aromatic

aromi aromatic herbs

arrosticini skewers of roast sheep meat

arrosto roast, roasted; *arrosto morto,* pot roast

articioco artichoke

artigianale artisanal, not industrial; homemade; made on the premises

arzilla skate (ray)

ascè chopped steak; steak tartare (phonetic transliteration of French *haché*)

asciugamano towel

asciutto dry; used for pasta served on its own as opposed to in soup

asino, asina donkey

asparagi asparagus; *asparagi selvatici,* wild asparagus

aspretto fruit vinegar

asprigno somewhat tart or sour

aspro sour (like a lemon)

assaggio a taste; *assaggi,* little tastes or small portions

assortito assorted

astice clawed lobster

autunno, autunnale autumn

avanzi leftovers; remains

avena oats

azienda estate; farm; company

azzimo, azimo unleavened

azzurro, pesce "blue fish," including many of the stronger-tasting, darker-fleshed fish, such as TONNO, SGOMBRO, ARINGA, PESCE SPADA, ACCIUGA

babà Neapolitan pastry like a French baba

bacaro Venetian wine shop or wine bar, serving an OMBRETA and CICHETI

baccalà mantecato Venetian specialty of boiled STOC-CAFISSO beaten with olive oil into a thick cream

baccalà, bacalà salt cod, except in the northeast, where it is air-dried stockfish (STOCCAFISSO) and salt cod is known as BERTAGNIN. Both cods are used in a wide variety of regional recipes—for example, *alla fiorentina* has tomatoes, potatoes, garlic, and rosemary; *alla vicentina* (made with STOCCAFISSO) has onion, anchovies, parsley, white wine, and a little milk and Parmesan; *alla livornese,* tomato sauce; *in guazzetto* is fried, then cooked in tomato sauce flavored with anchovies, pine nuts, and raisins.

baccello, baccelli bean pod; immature fava beans

baccellone in Toscana, a soft sheep's and cow's milk cheese to eat with fava beans; various mild cheeses suited for eating with beans

bagigi peanuts; groundnuts (Veneto)

baicoli a type of Venetian *biscotti, biscotti di Chioggia*

banco counter; *servizio al banco,* counter service, as opposed to table

bar bar; coffee bar; snack bar

barbabietola beets

barman bartender

basilico basil

basso low; short; for coffee, = RISTRETTO

bauletti literally, little trunks—hence potentially any food stuffed and tied or rolled (usually meat)

bavette, bavettine pasta similar to LINGUINE

bazzoffia a spring vegetable soup of Lazio

beccaccia woodcock

beccaccino snipe

beccafico fig-pecker, warbler (small birds); *sarde a beccafico*, various Sicilian preparations for sardines—nothing to do with birds

belga Belgian; *insalata belga*, Belgian endive

ben cotto well-done

bere to drink; *uovo da bere*, literally, egg to drink, extremely fresh egg

bertagnín salt cod

besciamella béchamel; white sauce

bettola tavern; low-grade OSTERIA

bevande beverages, drinks

bianchin glass of white wine taken as an APERITIVO

bianco white; *in bianco*, without tomatoes; usually denotes not the presence of anything white but the absence of anything red

biancomangiare blancmange

bibita, pl. bibite beverage, drinks

bicchiere drinking glass; *bicchierino*, paper cup for ice cream

bietola Swiss chard

bignè cream puffs; buns usually made of choux pastry; in Rome, also used for the common ROSETTA roll

bigoli fat fresh spaghetti, traditionally made by extruding the dough through a special device

biondo blond

biroldo a type of Tuscan sausage with raisins and pine nuts

birra beer; *birra* ROSSA or SCURA, dark beer; *birra chiara,* light beer

birreria beer hall; pub

bis encore: *fare il bis,* have a second helping

bisat, bisato eel; *bisat in tecia,* eel sautéed with onion, wine, and tomato; *bisat sull'ara* ("on the altar"), eel cooked with bay leaves

biscotti generic term for cookies

biscottini di Prato see CANTUCCI

bisi, risi e see RISI E BISI

Bismarck, (bistecca) alla (steak) topped with a fried egg

bisse S-shaped lemon cookies of Venice

bistecca steak, usually beef or veal, but may be any meat cut to be grilled (see also FIORENTINA)

boccale pitcher, jug; beer mug, tankard

bocconcino any bite-sized food, as the word simply means little mouthful; most often used for stewed veal; little fried rolls or balls of veal, ham, and cheese; small oval FIOR DI LATTE cheeses

bollicine bubbles, *perlage*

bollito misto an assortment of boiled meats, usually served (in restaurants) from a special trolley that keeps the meats warm in their individual broths and accompanied by condiments, typically including SALSA VERDE or MOSTARDA. *Bollito misto* is somewhat more likely to be found in the northern regions (famously, Piemonte, Emilia-Romagna, and Lombardia) and is subject to regional variation.

bolognese, alla outside Bologna, and especially outside Italy, the term designates a substantial meat sauce for pasta containing almost no tomato; in Bologna the sauce is known simply as RAGÙ

bombolotti a short cylindrical pasta shape

bordatino Tuscan soup with corn flour, beans, vegtables, and (possibly) fish

borlotti, fagioli cranberry beans; pinto beans, used in Rome in PASTA E FAGIOLI

borragine borage

boscaiola, alla generally indicates the presence of mushrooms (from *boscaiolo,* woodsman)

bosco woods; wild; *misto di bosco,* mixed berries

bottarga dried, pressed roe of mullet (MUGGINE), gray mullet (CEFALO), sea bass (SPIGOLA), or tuna (TONNO). Highly prized and very expensive, *bottarga* comes mostly from Sicily and Sardinia but is sold and eaten throughout Italy.

botte barrel, cask

bottega shop

bottiglia bottle

bottiglieria wine shop; a place where wine can be drunk by the bottle or glass and where bottles can be bought

bovino cattle, of cattle

bovoleto snail

brace embers; *alla brace,* roasted over wood or charcoal embers

braciola chop or cutlet, usually pork but also lamb, beef, or game (and even fish)

branzino sea bass, striped bass; SPIGOLA

brasato braised beef or pot roast, often *al Barolo,* with red wine

bresaola cured lean beef, usually served sliced thin like prosciutto and dressed with lemon and olive oil

brioche not usually the French brioche, but generically breakfast pastries; pronounced as in French

brocca pitcher

broccoletti broccoli rabe

broccoli siciliani broccoli

broccolo romanesco broccoflower—it looks like a pale green cauliflower but the florets come to a point; used in PASTA E BROCCOLI IN BRODO DI ARZILLA

brodettato, abbacchio lamb pieces cooked in white wine and then enriched with egg yolks and lemon

brodetto Adriatic fish soup, in numerous variations

brodo broth

bruscandoli wild hops, often boiled for use in soup or RISOTTO

bruschetta toasted bread rubbed with garlic and drizzled with olive oil, sometimes with the addition of tomatoes or other toppings

brustolini, bruscolini toasted ZUCCA (squash) seeds

brutti ma buoni literally, ugly but good, drop cookies containing hazelnuts

bucatini long thick spaghetti with a small hole, almost always served *all'*AMATRICIANA or *alla* GRICIA

buccia peel (of fruit or vegetable); crust; rind

budino pudding; custard

bue beef

bufalo, bufala water buffalo, the meat of which is eaten in some southern areas and whose milk is used for MOZZARELLA

buffet buffet; also cafeteria, TAVOLA CALDA

buongustaio gourmet

buono good; coupon, chit

buontalenti custard-flavored ice cream

buratelli, buratéli eels, elvers

burro butter; pasta *al burro* has only sweet butter and Parmesan cheese

busara, alla Veneto mode of preparing shrimp or prawns, octopus, or crab in a sauce of olive oil, garlic, white wine, possibly tomato or paprika, parsley, and bread crumbs

cacao cocoa

cacciagione game

cacciatora, alla various diverse methods of stewing chicken, lamb, veal, and rabbit. In the north, the ingredients usually include tomatoes, while in central and southern Italy, rosemary, garlic, and vinegar are the predominant flavors.

cacciucco   most commonly, a robust and peppery fish soup from Livorno

cachi   kaki, a kind of persimmon

cacio e pepe (pasta)   (usually tonnarelli or other long pasta) dressed with grated *pecorino romano* and black pepper

cacio   cheese

caciotta   various fresh or hard white cheeses or soft, yellow buttery cheese

caffè   generically coffee, but in a bar, the word used alone means ESPRESSO

caffelatte, caffè latte, caffellatte   roughly equal parts of hot milk and coffee, poured from separate pitchers

caffetteria   coffee service

calamari   squid

caldo   hot

calice   wineglass

calzone   stuffed half-moon pizza, in many regional variations

cameriere   waiter, steward; *cameriera*, maid, waitress

camicia   literally, shirt; *in camicia*, unskinned, as a baked potato; *uova in camicia*, poached egg

camino   fireplace

camomilla   chamomile, chamomile tea

campagna   the country, countryside

campagnola, alla   country-style; eggs with vegetables and cheese

campo   field; countryside; *di campo*, of the country, i.e., wild, not cultivated

canarini   small artichokes (Venice)

canditi   candied fruit

cannaiola   young ANGUILLA (Toscana)

cannella cinnamon

cannellini elongated white beans; very pale light white wine of the CASTELLI ROMANI

cannelloni tubular stuffed pasta or crêpes (literally, big tubes) filled with meat or RICOTTA, usually topped with a sauce or sauces and cheese and baked

cannolicchio, cannolicchi razor clam; a tubular pasta

canocchia = PANNOCCHIA

cantalupo melon, cantaloupe

canterello chanterelle mushroom

cantina cellar, hence also wine cellar; wine shop; winery

cantucci, cantuccini Tuscan almond cookies that look like slices from a larger cake, traditionally dunked in VIN SANTO

caparossolo, caparozzolo clam

capitone large female eel cooked in vinegar and traditionally eaten on Christmas Eve

capo head

capocollo meat, usually cured pork, from the top of the neck

caponata a relish usually made with eggplant, onions, and other vegetables

cappalunga razor clam

cappelletti TORTELLINI

capperi capers

cappesante, capasante scallops

cappone capon; *pesce cappone,* sea-hen, gurnard, gurnet

cappuccino ESPRESSO with steam-frothed milk

capra goat

caprese, insalata mozzarella and tomato salad with basil

capretto kid

capricciosa, pizza pizza topped with various ingredients, supposedly chosen at whim but which are usually artichoke hearts, hard-cooked eggs, prosciutto, and mushrooms

caprino any of various goat cheeses

capriolo roe deer; venison

carabaccia Florentine onion soup, Tuscan onion soup

caraffa decanter, carafe

caramei Veneto sweet: skewers of nuts and dried fruits coated in hard caramel and arranged in the shape of a fan

caramella caramel; toffee; almost any kind of small (usually) nonchocolate candy

carciofini small artichokes or artichoke hearts, often marinated in olive oil

carciofo artichoke; *alla giudia* (Jewish-style), fried whole in olive oil with resulting crisp leaves and soft heart; *alla romana,* slow-cooked with olive oil, garlic, MENTUCCIA, and/or parsley; *alla matticella,* crushed flat between two bricks and cooked on an open fire

cardi cardoons

carne meat, flesh (of anything); *carne macinata,* ground meat

carote carrots

carpaccio originally thin-sliced raw beef with mayonnaise dressing, invented and named at Harry's Bar in Venice; now used for thin-sliced raw (or sometimes smoked) fish or other meats

carpione a kind of trout; *in carpione* describes food (usually fish) fried and then marinated in vinegar, herbs, and spices

carrè roast loin (usually veal or pork) or saddle

carrello cart; trolley

carrettiera, alla a hearty sauce for pasta subject to much local variation but usually containing some form of tomatoes and garlic

carrozza, mozzarella in mozzarella between slices of bread, floured, dipped in egg, and fried

carruba carob

carta menu; *carta dei vini,* wine list

cartoccio improvised paper (*carta*) cone for carrying food; *al cartoccio, en papillote* indicate cooking in parchment, or, now more usually, aluminum foil

casa house; *della casa,* of the house; *fatto in casa,* homemade

casalingo home-style; *casalinga,* housewife

casareccio, casereccio homemade or home-style; *pane casareccio,* the basic loaf of chewy, good-quality bread

casher kosher

cassa cash register, hence cashier, signs in bars will advise you to get a receipt (*scontrino*) at the *cassa* before ordering.

cassata mold of mixed ice creams; *cassata siciliana,* PAN DI SPAGNA with almond paste, chocolate, candied fruit, and RICOTTA cream

castagnaccio flat cake made of chestnut flour and decorated with pine nuts

castagne chestnuts

Castelli Romani the hill towns around the volcanic lakes Albano and Nemi, southeast of Rome, including Castel Gandolfo (site of the Pope's summer residence) as well as Frascati and Marino and other towns producing the wine that is collectively known in Rome as *vino dei Castelli*

castrato mutton; older lamb that will never be a ram

castraure small wild artichokes, most notably of the islands of the Venetian lagoon, available in spring

cavatappo corkscrew; *cavatappi* (plural), corkscrew pasta

cavatelli southern handmade short pasta

caviale caviar

cavolfiore usually cauliflower

cavoli, cavolini, cavoletti di Bruxelles or Brusselle Brussels sprouts

cavolo cabbage; *cavolo rapa,* kohlrabi; *cavolo riccio,* similar to kale. *Cavolo nero* is a dark green cabbage, typical of Toscana, closely related to curly kale; *cavolo palmizio, cavolo Toscano,* and *cavolo a penna* are other names for *cavolo nero. Cavolo verza* and *cavolo verzotto* belong to the family of Savoy cabbages.

cecamariti literally, husband-blinders; see STRANGOLAPRETI

ceci chickpeas (garbanzo beans)

cecina = FARINATA

cedioli elvers

cedro citron

cée young ANGUILLA (Toscana)

cefalo gray mullet (many people don't like it on grounds that it's a bottom-crawling scavenger fish, but it was much admired by the late Greek poet Oppian for its gentle vegetarian lifestyle)

cena supper, dinner

cenci literally, rags; fried pastry ribbons; = FRAPPE or CHIACCHIERE

ceneri ashes

centerbe an herbal liqueur

centrifugato fresh vegetable or fruit juice made with a juicer

cerfoglio chervil

cernia grouper

cervella brains

cervo stag, venison

cesta basket, any number of basket-like objects; *cestino,* bag lunch, often sold at railroad stations or prepared by hotels on request; wastebasket; various small baskets

cetriolini very small cucumbers, usually pickled (SOT-TACETO)

cetriolo cucumber; often used for cucumber pickles (SOTTACETO); *cetriolo di mare,* sea cucumber

champignon cultivated button mushroom

charlotte a common ice cream cake

checca, alla (spaghetti) (spaghetti) with raw tomatoes

chiacchiere strips of fried or baked pastry dusted with powdered sugar, traditional during Carnevale, known by various names

Chianina prized breed of Tuscan and Umbrian beef, the source of choice for the classic BISTECCA ALLA FIORENTINA

Chianti a celebrated Tuscan DOCG red wine from near Florence, first recorded in 1398. In this century, it was once considered the "typical" Italian wine, not for its taste but for its characteristic straw-covered FIASCO; since the 1970s, it has been taken seriously as a dry, tannic wine to drink young. Chianti Classico, from a restricted zone within the Chianti region, ages better.

chiaro light (in color); clear

chilo, pl. chili kilo, kilogram (2.2 pounds), abbreviated kg

chiocciola snail; *chiocciola di mare* (sea snail), periwinkle

chiodini small nail-shaped mushrooms

chitarra literally, guitar; a wire apparatus for cutting sheets of fresh pasta to make square-cut MACCHERONI or SPAGHETTI

chiuso closed

chizze fried pastry squares

ciabatta a flat bread

cialda a delicate wafer, often served with ice cream

ciambella any ring-shaped sweet

ciambotta vegetable stew with potatoes, tomatoes, eggplant, onion, and peppers

cianfotta mixed cooked summer vegetables

cibo food

cibreo classic Tuscan dish made from chicken livers, coxcombs, and giblets, with egg yolks and lemon

cicala di mare = PANNOCCHIA

cicerchie a chickpea-like legume

cicheti small tastes of things, put out as bar food or appetizers in Venetian BACARI

cicoria chicory or endive, in many varieties; *cicoria di Brux-elles,* Belgian endive; see also RADICCHIO

ciliege cherries

cima veal breast, which can be roasted or stuffed *alla Genovese,* with eggs, nuts, herbs, chopped meats, spinach, and peas

cime di rapa turnip greens

cinghiale wild boar

cioccolata, cioccolato chocolate; a chocolate drink

cioccolatino piece of chocolate candy; praline

ciociara, alla in the style of the Ciociaria, a mountainous area of Lazio's hinterland, southeast of Rome, whose cooking has much in common with that of Abruzzo

ciotola bowl, basin; cup

cipolla onion

cipolline; sing. cipollina generically, small/young onions or specifically pearl onions; *cipolline verdi,* scallions; *cipolline in agrodolce,* sweet-and-sour pearl onions

ciriola a small eel; a type of bread shaped like a small football; a kind of handmade pasta

clementina clementine (small citrus fruit)

coccio earthenware, clay; *al coccio,* cooked in earthenware; a red-skinned, white-fleshed fish (red gurnard)

cocco, noce di coconut

cocomero watermelon

cocuzza = ZUCCA (squash)

coda tail of anything (hence its meaning as a fancy ending to a piece of music, and also a line, especially at toll booths); *coda di bue,* oxtail; *coda di rospo,* the tail of the RANA PESCATRICE (monkfish); *coda alla vaccinara* is braised oxtail in tomato sauce, a classic Roman dish of the QUINTO QUARTO

colazione sometimes lunch but usually breakfast, which is correctly *prima colazione*

colle, pl. colli hill(s)

collina hill, slope

collo neck

colomba wood pigeon; dove-shaped Easter cake with orange peel and almonds

colombo dove, pigeon

colore color

coltello knife

commestibile edible

completo complete; as a noun, it can mean a set. Ordering breakfast at a hotel, you may be asked if you want your coffee or tea *completo,* i.e., with rolls and jam; when a restaurant is *completo,* you won't get a reservation—it's fully booked.

compreso included

con with

conchiglie shells; pasta shells; shellfish

condimento condiment, dressing, sauce—the word is much more general than the English *condiment*

condito seasoned; pickled; treated with one or more CONDIMENTI, or flavorings; dressed, in the case of a salad

confetti sugar-coated, or Jordan, almonds, traditionally presented to guests at weddings

confettura jam; sweetmeat

confezionato prepackaged, industrial; as opposed to ARTIGIANALE, or homemade

confezione package; anything ready-made

congelato frozen; by law, Italian menus must indicate frozen products

coniglio rabbit

cono (ice cream) cone

consumo, al according to consumption—indicating, say, that you'll be charged for wine by how much disappears from the bottle or how much you take from the antipasto table

contadina, alla   country-style, peasant-style

contadino, contadina   peasant; small farmer; foods whose names or labels invoke the *contadino* are boasting tradition, authenticity, or the like

contorno   side dish; vegetable or salad

controfiletto   = LOMBATA; regional variations

copata   almond brittle

coperto   place setting; cover charge

coppa, coppetta   cup, bowl; Champagne glass; dish for ice cream; head cheese (pork head meat boiled, pressed, and sliced)

coque, uova alla   coddled eggs

corallina   a type of salami eaten in Lazio at Easter; an alga, eaten raw; small pasta for soup

corallo, fagioli a   see FAGIOLI A CORALLO

coratella   pluck (i.e., heart, liver, and lungs), usually of lamb, possibly also of pork, classically cooked chopped up with artichokes

coregone   a delicate white-fleshed lake fish

coriandolo   coriander, both leaves (cilantro) and seeds; usually in the plural, confetti (in the English sense; cf. CONFETTI).

cornetto   croissant, roll; though crescent-shaped like the croissant, the dough is not necessarily the French-style flaky pastry; an industrial ice cream cone

corpo   body; *di corpo,* full-bodied; *corposo,* full-bodied, thick

corretto   "corrected" with a drop of alcohol; usually for coffee

corta, pasta   short pasta shape(s). RIGATONI, PENNE, and similar are thus placed in a different category from long pastas, such as SPAGHETTI or FETTUCCINE, or stuffed pastas, such as RAVIOLI.

cortile   courtyard; barnyard; yard. *Animali da cortile,* literally, courtyard animals, is a generic term covering poultry and rabbits.

coscia thigh, haunch, or, by extension, the whole leg; a variety of pear

costa rib; sirloin; a rib of anything, e.g., celery

costarelle chops, baby lamb chops (ABBACCHIO)

costata beef rib steak from the LOMBATA; see FIORENTINA

costicine spareribs

costine rib tips; small chops

costola rib; in beef, goats, and sheep, the *costole* are the thirteen bones that make up the rib cage. Sliced apart, some of these are used to make COSTATE.

costoletta cutlet from the rib; *costoletta* (or *cotoletta*) *alla milanese* is pounded till it covers a dinner plate, then breaded several times and sautéed in butter; veal (but not beef), lamb, mutton, pork, or game sliced from the LOMBATA

cotechino a large-diameter pork sausage of Emilian origin, served boiled and sliced, usually with lentils

cotenna pork rind

cotiche pork rinds; *fagioli con le cotiche,* beans cooked with tomatoes and pork rinds

cotogna quince; *cotognata,* quince marmalade, quince cheese

cotoletta cutlet (veal unless otherwise specified), usually breaded and fried, though geographic attributions indicate a variety of preparations. See also COSTOLETTA.

cotto cooked

coturnice pheasant-like bird

coulis sauce (French)

cozze mussels

crema anything creamy or very smooth, with or without actual dairy cream; the basic white ice cream; *crema di latte,* dairy cream (see PANNA); *crema cotta,* cream and milk thickened with gelatin and usually flavored; *crema inglese,* custard sauce. *Crema pasticciera* (often called simply *crema*) is custard or custard sauce; chunks of firm custard can be breaded and fried as *crema fritta*.

cremini cocoa-colored cultivated mushrooms; deep-fried pieces of CREMA PASTICCIERA (syn. CREMA FRITTA)

cremoso creamy or thick, as opposed to liquid or runny

crescenti fried dough squares, usually served with cheese or salami

crescenza a soft, buttery white cheese

crescione cress; *crescione inglese,* garden or pepper cress

cresciuta, pasta yeast-raised dough; a yeasty pizza

crespelle crêpes

creste di gallo coxcombs; pasta in that shape

creta clay; *alla creta,* cooked sealed in clay or in a clay pot

cristallizzato crystallized

croccante crunchy; nut brittle

croccantino potentially anything crunchy and yummy; ice cream with crunchy bits

crocchette croquettes; croquettes of mashed potatoes are staples of the pizzeria menu

crosta crust; cheese rind; pastry crust

crostata fruit tart, often made with jam

crostini toasts with toppings; croutons

crostoli strips of fried or baked pastry dough dusted with powdered sugar

crostoni crouton; fried bread; piece of dry bread to put in a soup bowl

crudo raw, rare; for salami and fish, often means cured

crusca bran

cucchiaio tablespoon, dessert spoon; *cucchiaino,* teaspoon, coffee spoon

cucina creativa creative cuisine; the term is usually glossed as the Italian equivalent of the French *nouvelle cuisine,* but it is not so much a specific cooking style or movement as a nontraditional approach. Creative chefs usually follow the time-honored practices (as those of eating pasta or rice before meat or fish) with a lighter hand and like daring combinations of ingredients.

cucina kitchen; stove, range; cuisine, style of cooking

cuoco cook, chef

cuore heart; *cuore edule,* cockle, heart shell (mollusks)

cuscinetti di vitello "cushions" of braised veal stuffed with cheese and ham

DOC, D.O.C. *Denominazione d'Origine Controllata:* limited geographic zone of distinction, registered designation of origin; governmental designations for wines produced from specific grapes, grown in limited areas, and vinified according to certain standards; some ham, cheeses, and olive oils are also D.O.C. *D.O.C.G.* or *DOCG, Denominazione d'Origine Controllata e Garantita:* the same plus "guaranteed."

d.o.p. *denominazione d'origine protetta:* a legal designation that assures that a product name is used only for foods produced in a specific geographical area

dadini small dice

dadolata diced food used as a garnish

daino fallow deer

dattero di mare date shell (mollusk). Their sale and consumption is illegal; to catch them, pneumatic hammers are used to break up the rocks where they live. It takes ten years for one of them to reach a length of two inches and 20 to grow to three inches.

decaffeinato decaffeinated, caffeine-free

decalitro decaliter (10 cc, about 3 ounces)

degustazione tasting, sampling; *menù degustazione,* tasting menu

delizie delicacies

delizioso delicious

denominazione name, designation; *denominazione commerciale,* trade name, trade description; *denominazione d'origine,* designation of origin; *denominazione dei prodotti,* list of products; *denominazione d'origine protetta,* protected designation of origin (often applied to cheeses)

dente di leone dandelion

dente, al (of pasta) resistant to the bite, not overcooked

dentice dentex, dog's teeth, a white-fleshed saltwater fish

desco table; dining table

diavoletto, diavolicchio, diavolillo hot red pepper

dicembre December

digestivo a liqueur consumed after eating in the belief that it will aid the digestion

dindo turkey

disossato boned

disponibile available

distillati distillates, hard liquors

distributore automatico vending machine

ditalini short pasta tubes

diverso different

dolce, pl. dolci sweet, mild; dessert; *acqua dolce,* freshwater

dolcificante sweetener, artificial sweetener

dolciumi sweets, confectionery

domani tomorrow

domenica Sunday

dopo after, sometimes used informally as a noun to mean SECONDO PIATTO

doppio double

dorato lightly browned; *fritto dorato,* dredged in flour and dipped in egg, then deep-fried

dorso back

dragoncello tarragon

drogheria originally a spice (*droga*) shop, now a small grocery store, like the French *épicerie*

due two

duro hard

e, ed and

ebraico Jewish; *all'ebraica,* Jewish-style

emmental Emmenthaler cheese, Swiss cheese

enogastronomico relating to food and wine

enologia oenology

enoteca wine store; restaurant with wine cellar; wine bar serving snacks

equino equine: horse, donkey, or mule; *carne equina,* horse meat

erba cipollina chive or other thin grass with mild onion flavor

erbe aromatiche herbs

erbetta in Rome, usually parsley

erborinato said of cheeses that develop a mold, such as GORGONZOLA, Roquefort, and other blue cheeses

espresso concentrated coffee made in a special machine by infusing the coffee with steam. Stove-top Italian coffee, however dark and nasty, is not properly called *espresso* but rather CAFFÈ.

essenza extract, essence; juice; broth

estate, estivo summer

estero foreign; imported

etto; pl. etti hectogram, 100 grams (3.5 ounces); the basic unit of food purchases, the practical equivalent of the quarter pound

facoltativo optional

fagianello young pheasant

fagiano pheasant

fagioli a corallo runner beans (broad green beans), usually cooked with tomatoes and onions

fagiolini string beans, green beans; haricots verts

fagiolo, pl. fagioli beans

fagottini literally, little bundles; hence, dough or meat stuffed and/or wrapped

fame hunger, appetite

faraona guinea fowl, guinea hen

farcito stuffed

farfalle bow-tie pasta; *a farfalla,* butterflied

faricella a soup made of FARRO

farina flour; *farina gialla,* cornmeal (cf. POLENTA)

farinata FOCACCIA-like crust made of chickpea flour; a Tuscan variant is made from cornmeal with vegetables and legumes; cornmeal mush, porridge; *farinata d'avena,* cooked oatmeal; INFARINATA

farro emmer, a relative of wheat used to make soups, porridges, pasta, and other cereal products. The same word is used for spelt, on which the Roman army marched.

farsi, da (on a menu) made to order

fasolaro a type of clam

fatto made, ready

fattoria farm

fattura manufacture; invoice

fava, pl. fave broad bean, pigeon bean, fava bean. *Fave* can be eaten dried all year round, but in spring are eaten fresh—e.g., stewed with GUANCIALE—or, if young and tender, eaten raw with fresh PECORINO cheese

fave dei morti literally, beans of the dead—almond cookies for All Souls' Day (November 2), also called, more pleasantly, *fave dolci* (sweet beans)

favollo large GRANCHIO of the Venetian lagoon

febbraio February

fedelini a very thin spaghetti-like pasta

fegatelli small livers (always plural), usually of pork but sometimes of chicken, often cooked wrapped in caul fat (see RETE)

fegatini livers of fowl or small animals, such as chicken or rabbits

fegato liver, usually calf's, most famous served *alla veneziana,* sautéed with onions; *fegato grasso,* foie gras

Felino, salame di a salami named for the town of Felino, near Parma (nothing to do with cats)

feriàda = SARAGO

ferie holidays, vacation; *feriale,* any nonholiday weekday (including Saturday); *giorni feriali,* weekdays

fermentare to ferment (both transitive and intransitive)

fermentazione fermentation

fermenti lattici vivi active milk cultures (as in yogurt)

Fernet-Branca a very strong-tasting, quasi-medicinal DIGESTIVO

ferri, ai grilled, broiled

festivo festive; *giorni festivi* are Sundays and holidays

fetta, pl. fette slice; *fette biscottate,* slices of bread dried in the oven, often served for breakfast in hotels

fettina, pl. fettine thin or small slice; if otherwise un-qualified in a list of second courses, it most likely means a large but thin slice of veal to be grilled simply

fettuccine the basic flat egg noodles; *alla papalina,* with pro-sciutto, eggs, and Parmesan; *alla romana,* with tomatoes and dried mushrooms; *al triplo burro,* the correct name for "fettuccine Alfredo," with a sauce of butter, cream, and Parmesan

fettunta, fett'unta bread slices rubbed with garlic, then grilled and brushed with olive oil, or fried therein

fiamma, alla flambé

fiammiferi matches; julienne

fiaschetteria traditionally, an establishment for the sale of wine in FIASCHI, hence, a very informal OSTERIA

fiasco, pl. fiaschi flask, bottle; glass bottle, traditionally cov-ered with straw, for Chianti

fichi d'India prickly pears

fico, pl. fichi fig (both the tree and the fruit)

fieno literally, hay; homemade TAGLIATELLE

figà liver; *figà garbo e dolce,* liver breaded and fried, with a touch of vinegar and sugar; *figà col radeselo,* liver cut up, wrapped in caul fat along with sage leaves, and fried in butter (Venice)

filetto tenderloin, filet mignon

finferli chanterelle mushrooms

finocchiella fresh wild fennel

finocchio fennel; *finocchio selvatico,* wild fennel

finocchiona Tuscan SALAME flavored with fennel seeds.

finochietto herbal fennel variety, sometimes called "wild fennel"

fior di latte mozzarella-like cheese made from cow's milk

fiore, pl. fiori flower; *fiori di zucca* are squash or zucchini blossoms, which may be used in RISOTTO or stuffed and/or batter-dipped and then sautéed or fried

fiorentina, la the famous Florentine beefsteak, a thick T-bone from the LOMBATA, ideally from CHIANINA beef, grilled very rare over coals

fioretto fresh cheese of the Veneto, also called *grasso monte*

fischione species of duck

fitto thick

fiume river; as adjective, freshwater

fluviale from a river

focaccia basically a flatbread, usually flavored with oil and herbs, but subject to huge variation in flavoring, fillings/toppings, and thickness of dough; can also refer to bread-like cakes, such as a home-style PANETTONE. The word has become widespread in the United States, but note that in Italy it still has only three syllables: fo-ca-ccia.

focolare hearth, fireplace

foglia, pl. foglie leaf (of a plant); very thin slice

folpeto, folpo = POLPO

fondente flourless cake; baking chocolate, bittersweet chocolate; French *fondant*

fondo bottom

fonduta fondue, usually of cheese

fongadina stew from pluck (heart, liver, and lungs) of veal and/or lamb or kid, mushrooms, and spices

fontana fountain

fonte spring (water); source

foralattina can opener

forchetta fork

formaggio cheese

fornara, vitello alla veal breast cooked with herbs and potatoes (Rome)

forno oven; bakery

fragole strawberries; *fragoline di bosco,* tiny wild strawberries. Both are served with sugar and lemon juice or with CREMA gelato, or, much more rarely, with balsamic vinegar.

fragolino red sea bream

francese French

francesina, la in Florence, a beef stew with onions

francolino grouse

frantoiana, zuppa soup from Toscana with BORLOTTI beans and olive oil

frantoio olive press

frappe strips of fried dough with powdered sugar; = CHIAC-CHIERE, CENCI

frattaglie innards, offal

freddo cold

fresco cool, fresh; *al fresco,* outdoors

fricassea any of various meat dishes enriched with egg yolks and lemon juice; fricassee

friggitoria literally, fry shop; a shop where foods are deep-fried and sold to take out

frigo "fridge" (short for *frigorifero*)

frigobar minibar

frisciolata = FARINATA

frittata an omelet that has been turned over, not folded in half

frittella fritter; pancake

fritto deep-fried; *fritto misto,* a mix of batter-fried meats and, sometimes, other ingredients (vegetables, eggs, cheese, custard); *fritti,* catchall term for deep-fried foods

frittura any deep-fried dish

frizzante effervescent

frollini shortbread cookies

frullato blender drink made from milk and fresh fruit

frumento wheat

frutta fruit

frutti di mare shellfish

fruttosio fructose

fumo smoke

funghetto, al see TRIFOLATO

fungo, pl. funghi mushroom; the word applies to all mushrooms, but is especially used in contradistinction to CHAMPIGNONS.

fuoco fire

fuori stagione out of season

fuori out, out of, outside

fusaie in Rome, *lupini* (a legume), soaked in salted water and eaten as a snack

fusilli short spiral pasta

fuso melted

galani = CHIACCHIERE

galantina galantine; poultry pâté

galitola = CANTARELLO

galletto young cock; = CANTARELLO

gallina stewing hen

gallinaccio turkey (popular); = CANTARELLO; a wild carrot

gallinella, gallenella chanterelle mushroom; sea-hen, gurnard, gurnet; type of mullet; lamb's lettuce (corn salad); = VALERIANELLA; pullet; *gallinella d'acqua,* water-hen, moorhen

gallo cock, rooster

gambcro shrimp; *gambero di fiume,* crayfish

gambo stem, stalk

garganelli a handmade short pasta

garofano clove (spice); *chiodi di garofano,* cloves

garofolato beef pot roast with red wine and cloves

garusolo − MURICE SPINOSO

gassato, gasato carbonated

gassosa, gazzosa the name of a particular lemon-flavored fizzy drink

gastronomia gastronomy in all its aspects, but the word is also seen in shops and bars, to signal the sale of prepared foods, usually more snacks than meals

gattopardo = GATTUCCIO (Toscana)

gattuccio dogfish (small shark)

gelateria ice cream shop

gelatina aspic; gelatin

gelato iced, frozen; ice cream

gelso mulberry

gennaio January

germano reale wild duck, mallard

germogli di soia bean sprouts

ghiacciato frozen; iced

ghiaccio ice

ghiottone gourmand, glutton

ghiozzo goby

gialletti cookies containing cornmeal (northeast Italy)

giallo yellow

giambonetto roast veal shank; stuffed chicken or turkey thigh

gianduia, gianduja a combination of chocolate and hazelnuts

ginepro juniper

giorno day

giovedì Thursday

girarrosto rotisserie; *al girarrosto,* spit-roasted

girello eye of round

giudia, alla Jewish-style; most famously refers to artichokes (see CARCIOFI)

giugno June

glassato glazed, frosted

gnocchi essentially dumplings of any kind, but usually small potato-and-flour dumplings, served in place of pasta

gnocchi alla romana semolina patties, usually with scalloped edges, baked in a cream, cheese, or tomato sauce and served as a pasta course

gnudi see IGNUDI

gò de mar see GHIOZZO

gobbi cardoons

goccia, goccio drop

golosità literally, gluttony; tasty tidbits

golosone epicure; glutton

Gorgonzola blue-veined cheese of Lombardia and Piemonte

grana padano Parmesan-like cheese from the Po Valley, DENOMINAZIONE DI ORIGINE

grana any number of hard, sharp grating cheeses, including PARMIGIANO-REGGIANO, GRANA PADANO, and PECORINO ROMANO

granatina, pl. granatine grenadine (pomegranate syrup); usually in plural, small balls, as of meat or rice

grancevola = GRANSEOLA

granchiessa = GRANCHIO (Toscana)

granchio crab

granciporro large oval-bodied crab

grande large

granelli veal testicles; meatballs

granita frozen and crushed coffee or fruit juice

grano saraceno buckwheat

grano grain; wheat

granoturco sweet corn

granseola large round-bodied crab with small front claws

granso = GRANCHIO (Veneto)

grappa grape distillate, eau-de-vie

grasso fat; rich

gratè, al pseudo-phonetic spelling of *au gratin*

gratinato au gratin; with bread crumb and/or cheese crust

grattachecca crushed ice with flavored syrup, a specialty of Rome, traditionally sold at street stands

grattata (una) (a) grating; a unit of measurement for truffles, for example

grattugiato grated

greca, alla *à la grecque*

grezzo unrefined; coarse

gricia, alla ALL'AMATRICIANA without the tomatoes; pasta sauce made with pork jowl and PECORINO cheese

grigette small snails

grigio gray

griglia grill; *alla griglia,* grilled or broiled

grigliata mixed grill

grissini breadsticks

grongo, gronco conger eel

groppa = SELLA

grosso big

grotta cave; grotto; wine cellar

groviera Gruyère cheese

guanciale cured pork jowl (resembles PANCETTA)

guasto broken; gone bad

guato de mar = GHIOZZO

guazzetto, in cooked in a light tomato sauce

gustare to taste; to enjoy

gusto flavor (e.g., of ice cream); taste; pleasure

gustoso tasty, but literally, in the sense of being full of taste

Hag brand of decaf coffee

hamburger the same, but note where the accent falls

IGP *Indicazione Geografica Protetta;* literally, protected geographical indication (similar to D.O.P.), a legal designation that assures that a product name is used only for wines or foods produced in a specific geographical area

IGT *Indicazioni Geografiche Tipiche,* Typical Geographic Indications; new European Union designation roughly equivalent to the French *vin du pays*

ignudi "naked" RAVIOLI, i.e., a spinach-ricotta-egg "filling" without the pasta

imbottito stuffed

impanato breaded

impasto dough; mixture

impepata shellfish (usually COZZE), served in their own juices with plenty of pepper (PEPE), parsley, and lemon

importo amount; the bottom line; *importo da pagare,* what you owe

inchiostro ink, in pen or squid

indiavolato deviled, i.e., spicy

indivia endive, frisée; chicory; *indivia belga,* Belgian endive; *indivia riccia,* curly endive; *indivia scarola,* escarole; *indivia selvatica* wild endive

indiviola a wild endive

infarinata hearty vegetable-bean soup thickened with corn-meal

infiammato flambé

infuso infusion, a beverage made by means of infusion (*infusione*)

ingresso entrance

insalata salad; lettuce; raw greens in general; *insalata mista,* greens plus at least tomatoes

insalata caprese sliced tomatoes and mozzarella with fresh basil

insalata di mare an appetizer of tepid (ideally) boiled or steamed seafood, including at least some squid or octopus (cut in chunks) and mussels or clams, dressed with oil or lemon and chopped celery

insalata russa cooked vegetables bound with hard-cooked egg or mayonnaise, sometimes encased in gelatin

insieme together; set, whole, ensemble

integrale whole, complete; whole wheat, whole-grain

interiora offal

intero whole, entire

intingolo sauce, dip; flavorful meat or fish sauce for dipping bread; gravy; stew; any particularly tasty dish

intruglia = INFARINATA

invecchiato aged, seasoned

inverno, invernale winter

involtino virtually any food rolled into a cylinder, usually thin slices of meat, but eggplant and swordfish are also used (notably in Sicily)

inzimino, all' see ZIMINO

inzuppare to dunk; to drench, to imbue

iper- hyper- (prefix), high

ipo- hypo- (prefix), low

ittico- prefix denoting something to do with fish (from the Greek *ichthus*)

kaki = CACHI

kasher kosher

lacustre from a lake

lagane = LASAGNE

laganelle narrow LASAGNE noodles

lago lake

lamponi raspberries

lampreda lamprey

lampredotto the tripe from the cow's fourth stomach, a Tuscan specialty served with vegetables; young lamprey eel

lardo cured pork fat; fatty bacon, fatback; *lardo rosa di Colonnata,* a particularly prized type

lardone salt pork or bacon

lasagna, pl. lasagne broad ribbon-shaped pasta, usually in plural; *lasagne al forno,* sheets of pasta layered with fillings and cheese and baked

lasagnette narrow LASAGNE

latte fritto fried custard dessert

latte milk; *da latte,* milk-fed, baby

latteria dairy; name for various fresh cheeses; place to buy milk products and/or a bar that serves dairy products and coffee

latticini fresh cheeses; milk products

lattina can, especially for beer or soft drinks; see also SCATOLA

lattuga certain types of lettuce; in Rome, refers almost exclusively to romaine lettuce, elsewhere called *lattuga romana; lattuga a cappuccio,* Bibb lettuce

lattughella, lattughino lamb's lettuce (corn salad)

lauro, foglio di bay leaf

lavandino sink, washbasin

lavarello = COREGONE

lecca-lecca lollipop

leccornia some specially prized tidbit

leggero light

legno wood; *forno a legna,* wood-burning oven

legumi legumes

lenticchie lentils

lepre hare; *leprotto,* leveret, a young hare

lesso boiled

lievito yeast; *lieviti,* pastries

limonata lemon soda, lemonade; see also ARANCIATA, SPREMUTA

limoncello lemon liqueur, once associated with seaside resorts and sun-kissed islands, now ubiquitous

limone lemon

lingue di gatto light, delicate cookies

linguine thin, flat, spaghetti-like pasta

liquido liquid; see also PANNA

liquirizia licorice

lista list; menu

listino a little list (of prices)

litro liter

livornese, alla Livorno-style. TRIGLIE (mullet) *alla livornese* are sautéed with garlic and tomato and sprinkled with parsley; BACCALÀ *alla livornese* is stewed with oil, onion, tomato, and a little sweet wine; and CECHE (eels) *alla livornese* are sautéed with garlic and sage.

locanda inn

lollo very curly bright red or green lettuce (LATTUGA), named in honor of "La Lollo," Gina Lollobrigida

lombata loin

lombatina COSTOLETTA of veal or pork

lonza usually, cured pork loin

lucioperca pike-perch

luganega a mild pork sausage

luglio July

lumache snails, usually quite small and cooked in tomato sauce

lunedì Monday

lungo long; *caffè lungo,* ESPRESSO diluted with about double the usual amount of water

lupo di mare lobster

luppoli hops; the sprouts are used in RISOTTO and FRITTATA

lutto, in in mourning, i.e., in black—usually indicates the presence of squid ink

maccarello mackerel

maccheroni PASTASCIUTTA in general

macchiato, caffè coffee with a "spot" of milk, hot, cold, or foamed; *latte macchiato,* hot milk with a shot of ESPRESSO

macedonia fruit cocktail, a dessert

maciarella young GO DE MAR (Venice)

macinapepe pepper mill

macinato ground; minced

maggio May

maggiorana marjoram

magro thin; lean; meatless

maiale pork; *maialino da latte,* suckling pig; cf. PORCHETTA

maionese mayonnaise

mais corn, sweet corn; *fiocchi di mais,* cornflakes

Malaga ice cream flavored with Malaga raisins

malfatti a type of GNOCCHI

maltagliati different pasta shapes mixed together, or irregular triangles or diamonds, usually in soup

mandarancio cross between MANDARINO and orange; temple orange

mandarino mandarin orange, tangerine, satsuma

mandorle almonds; *mandorla amara,* bitter almond

mandorlato almond cake; almond paste; nougat

maniera, alla, di in the style of

mantecato creamed; ice cream

manzo beef

maracuja passion fruit

mare e monti SEE MONTI E MARI

mare sea

margarina margarine

Margherita, pizza pizza with MOZZARELLA or FIOR DI LATTE, tomato sauce, and (ideally but rarely) basil

marinara, pizza alla pizza with tomato sauce, olive oil, oregano, and garlic

marinato marinated

maritozzo BRIOCHE filled with whipped cream, eaten for breakfast or as a snack

marmellata marmalade; any type of CONFETTURA

marmora a bream

marrone a prized type of large chestnut, marron; *marroni glassati, marrons glacés*

martedì Tuesday

maruzele small sea snails (Veneto)

marzo March

mascarpone a rich, fresh, very soft white cheese, traditionally made in winter

matriciana, alla common phonetic misspelling of ALL'AMATRICIANA

mattarello rolling pin; its invocation indicates the pasta dough is handmade

mazoro a la valesana wild duck cooked in a terra-cotta pot with herbs, sardines, and capers

mazzancolla large Mediterranean shrimp

medaglione medallion, small round; also, small slices of meat or sandwiches on small round rolls

mela apple

melacotogna, mela cotogna quince

melagrana, melograno pomegranate

melanzane eggplant

melone melon

menta mint

mentuccia pennyroyal, a mint-like herb used in Rome to flavor CARCIOFI ALLA ROMANA

menù menu; *menù degustazione,* tasting menu

mercato market

mercoledì Wednesday

merenda snack, usually for children—a grown-up's snack is a SPUNTINO; also, picnic

meringa, pl. meringhe meringue

merluzzo fresh cod (as opposed to BACCALÀ)

mescita wine (as opposed to food) service (prounounced MESH-)

mestolone a wild duck

metà half

mezze maniche a short tubular pasta similar to RIGATONI

mezzo half; *piatto di mezzo,* a course between the first and the main courses, such as a fish course served before the meat, though nowadays it often serves as a main course

midollo bone marrow; pulp

miele honey

migliaccio black pudding, blood pudding; chestnut cake

miglio millet

milanese, alla see COSTOLETTA

millefogli = OMASO

millefoglie mille-feuille, napoleon (pastry)

millesimo vintage (year of production)

milza spleen; milt

minestra the PRIMO PIATTO, whether soup or pasta or rice; soup; cf. ZUPPA

minestrina light or clear soup

minestrone hearty mixed vegetable soup, subject to enormous local variation

mirtillo bilberry, whortleberry, a relative of the blueberry

miscela blend (usually of coffee)

misticanza a tasty salad of bitter wild greens that grow around Rome, where it is not a synonym for *insalata mista*, though this is a common error; elsewhere, may mean mesclun

misto mixed

moda, alla, di in the style of

moka a common type of stove-top coffee maker

moleche, moeche soft-shell crabs from the Venetian lagoon, usually deep-fried

molle soft; weak

mollusco mollusk

molto very; much; many

montata, panna whipped cream

monte e mare "mountain and sea," the Italian version of "surf 'n' turf" (seafood and meat) when referring to a second course; for pasta, it usually indicates seafood and mushrooms

montebianco mont blanc (a dessert)

montone mutton

morbido soft; tender

more blackberries

morellini purple artichokes, but potentially anything small and dark

morello morel mushroom

mormora a bream

mortadella the genuine bologna sausage from Bologna

moscardino a kind of octopus, usually tiny

moscato muscat, a fragrant grape used in a variety of sweet wines, ranging from the delightful light Moscato d'Asti to the deep golden Moscato di Pantelleria, and in dry wines as well

moscato, noce nutmeg

mostarda mustard; any of a variety of chutney-like fruit-based condiments

mozzarella soft, fresh white cheese, properly from water buffalo's milk, but often from cow's milk

muffa mold, fungus

muggine gray mullet

mugnaia, alla literally, miller's style; exactly the French *meunière,* i.e., breaded and sautéed with butter; with butter, lemon, and parsley

murena moray eel; serpentine fish

murice spinoso murex, various gastropods with helical shell

muschiata, anatra Barbary duck

muscolo various cuts of meat from the upper leg; mussel

musetto a pork sausage similar to COTECHINO

muta, anatra see MUSCHIATA

nasello cod, hake, whiting, sea pike

nastro ribbon, band; Nastro Azzurro ("blue ribbon") is a domestic beer

Natale Christmas: *natalizio,* of Christmas

naturale plain; unsweetened; uncarbonated; natural

navone nape, rutabaga, parsnip

nazionale domestic; Italian

necci crêpes or waffles made from chestnut flour

Negroni cocktail of Campari and gin

nero black; dark; squid or cuttlefish ink

nervetti (insalata di) (salad of) boiled calf's shank and knee cartilage, cut in strips and usually dressed with oil, onions, and capers

nespole medlars; loquats

nettarina nectarine, also called *pesca noce*

neutro neutral

nido nest, literally and figuratively; long egg pastas (such as FETTUCCINE) are often packaged in little bunches called *nidi*

nini = ACCIUGA (Veneto)

nocciola hazelnut

noccioline americane peanuts; groundnuts

noci nuts; walnuts; *noce di cocco,* coconut; *noce moscato,* nutmeg

nocino AMARO-like liqueur made from green walnuts and spices

nodino loin chop, noisette

nonna grandmother; *torta della nonna,* a plain yellow cake with some CREMA PASTICCIERA inside and pine nuts on top

norcineria pork butchery, pork products, from Norcia, a town in Umbria famous for its tradition of both, as well as of surgery. *Alla norcina* refers to pork, specifically a sauce for pasta of sausage and cream; *alla nursina* refers to the town of Norcia and indicates the presence of black truffles, for which Norcia is also famous.

Norma, pasta alla Sicilian pasta dish with fried eggplant, rich tomato sauce, RICOTTA SALATA, and basil, loved and prepared throughout Italy

nostrano homegrown; domestic; regional

novello new; VINO *novello* is Italian *vin nouveau*

novembre November

oca goose

occhio, pl. occhi eye, or anything that looks like an eye; FAGIOLI *all'occhio* are black-eyed peas, cow peas

occhio di bue literally, bull's eye; potentially, anything that looks remotely like a large eye, including a round, flat cookie with a jam center; *all'occhio di bue* indicates fried eggs sunny side up

odori herbs

ogio = OLIO (Veneto)

olandese Hollandaise, or simply Dutch

oligominerale, acqua spring water with a low concentration of minerals

olio oil; usually olive oil

oliva olive; *olive ascolane, olive all'ascolana* meat-stuffed green olives, breaded and fried; common in pizzerias, but a poor imitation of the original from Ascoli Piceno, in the Marche region

omaso pocket tripe

ombra, ombreta, ombretta small glass of wine; *andar all'ombra* is a Veneto expression meaning "to go out for a glass of wine" or, more broadly, to go on a kind of a pub crawl for wine and small plates of food

ombrina corb, croaker (fish)

omento caul fat

orata gilt-head bream

ordinazione, su by (prior) request

orecchiette literally, little ears; a handmade pasta typical of Puglia but found elsewhere

orecchio, orecchia ear

origano oregano

ortaggi vegetables; greens; literally, what comes from the kitchen garden (ORTO)

ortica nettles

orto (kitchen) garden (the Latin *hortus*), as opposed to a flower or decorative garden, which would be *giardino*

ortolano "from the garden" or "from the market"—generally indicates the presence of vegetables

orzo barley; a small barley-shaped pasta used in soup

osei small game birds (generic)

osso, pl. ossa bone, of animal (a fish bone is called SPINA or *lisca*); stone or pit, of fruit

ossobuco, osso buco braised shin or knuckle of veal prepared in many regional variations.

osteria inn; tavern; traditionally, a place for a glass of wine
and simple food. Most *osterie* today are indistinguishable
from TRATTORIE and RISTORANTI (one of Italy's finest,
most expensive restaurants calls itself an *osteria*).

ostriche oysters; anything oyster-sized and squishy

ottobre October

ovini sheep and goat meats

ovolo *Amanita caesarea,* an expensive mushroom with an
orange cap, ovoid shape, and delicate flavor

Pachino, pomodoro di properly, the small, fragrant winter
tomatoes from a limited area in the province of Trapani
(Sicily), but the designation is widely applied to cherry
tomatoes

padella frying pan, skillet

paese country; village; region

pagello red sea bream, any of several species of the genus
Pagellus

paglia e fieno literally, hay and straw; mixed green and yellow pasta strands

pagliata see PAIATA

paglierino light straw colored

pagnotta loaf of bread

pagro sea bream

paiata, pajata the small intestine of a milk-fed calf, with its
milky contents, a Roman specialty usually cooked in
tomato sauce and served over RIGATONI, but also served
on its own

paillard steak, pounded thin and grilled; the restaurant
name for what is called FETTINA at home

palla ball; *le palle del nonno,* literally grandfather's balls, a
delicious dessert of fried RICOTTA balls

palombaccio wood pigeon

palombo ringdove; dogfish, smooth dogfish, smooth hound

pan di ramerino a Tuscan cake flavored with rosemary

pan di Spagna, pandispagna sponge cake, used as the basis of countless confections

pan molle see PANZANELLA

pan, pane bread, loaf; various types of spicy fruitcakes

panato breaded

pancarrè, pancarré sliced packaged bread that was baked in a loaf pan

pancetta salt-cured fatty pork belly

pandoro type of pound cake. Industrial *pandoro* is widely sold at Christmastime, along with PANETTONE; it is not quite as dry and boring as it looks.

pane in cassetta = PANCARRÈ

pane integrale whole wheat bread

panettone sort of an Italian coffee cake, traditionally served at Christmas

panforte (di Siena) (Sienese) cake with almonds and dried fruit

pangrattato dried bread crumbs

panino roll; generically, a sandwich; *panino imbottito,* filled roll, i.e., sandwich

paninoteca neologism for a place that sells PANINI

panna dairy cream; *panna cotta,* a ubiquitous gelatin-thickened, molded cream dessert

pannocchia ear of corn (maize), corn on the cob; mantis shrimp, squill; syn. CANOCCHIA

panpepato gingerbread

panunta, panunto = FETTUNTA, BRUSCHETTA

panzanella salad made of moistened dry bread, tomatoes, and onions, among other ingredients; in western Toscana, can sometimes mean fried strips of dough

papardele, paparele = PAPPARDELLE; homemade TAGLIE-

RINE, cooked in broth, possibly with the addition of sautéed chicken giblets; *paparele e bisi* are thin noodles with pea sauce or in broth with peas (Veneto)

papavero, semi di poppy seeds

papazoi bean soup with barley and corn

papero, papera goose

pappa mush; baby food; soup thickened with bread; *pappa al* (or *col*) POMODORO a very thick soup of fresh tomatoes and stale bread, usually associated with Toscana but also found in other parts of central Italy

pappardelle broad, flat noodles; like TAGLIATELLE but much wider

paranza, fritto da mixed fry of fresh fish—*paranza* is a fishing boat

parmigiana, alla Parma-style, but not necessarily with Parmesan cheese

Parmigiano-Reggiano possibly the best cheese in the world, a hard GRANA-type cheese, aged two years, used for both grating and eating. The designation refers to cheese produced under specific conditions in a legally limited geographical area in the Emilia-Romagna region.

parte, a apart; on the side

parzemolo = PREZZEMOLO (Veneto)

Pasqua Easter; *pasquale,* of Easter; *torta pasqualina,* a pie with flaky crust filled with greens, cheese, and hard-cooked eggs

passera flounder, fluke

passero sparrow; *lingue di passero,* a LINGUINE-like pasta

passito a type of dessert wine, usually sweet or semisweet, made with *uva passa,* partially dried grapes, usually with aromatic varieties such as MOSCATO and Malvasia. The hot climate of Sicily and the smaller islands of the Sicily region (famously Pantelleria) are suitable for outdoor drying of the grapes; indoor *passito* wines of the chillier regions include VIN SANTO, Vino Santo, Amarone, and RECIOTO.

pasta di . . . paste of (something); *pasta d'acciughe,* anchovy paste; *pasta di mandorle,* almond paste, marzipan

pasta e . . . pasta and (something); usually means the pasta and the other ingredient are used together in a very thick soup in approximately equal amounts; *pasta e* FAGIOLI, LENTICCHIE, CECI, or PATATE are common; *pasta e broccoli in brodo di arzilla,* skate broth with broken spaghetti and broccoflower

pasta fredda cold pasta. Don't expect the imaginative pasta salads of New York gourmet shops. Cold pasta is offered only as a grudging concession to modernity (viz. the *pronunciamenti* of Marcella Hazan on the topic) and inevitably is based on mozzarella, raw tomatoes, olive oil, and basil; obviously, the quality of the ingredients can range from tasteless to sublime. Note that it is considered a *primo piatto,* not a salad.

pasta generically, dough, pastry, paste (as in anchovy paste), equivalent to the French *pâte;* short for *pasta alimentare,* meaning pasta

pastafrolla, pasta frolla short pastry dough, piecrust

pastasciutta, pasta asciutta "dry" pasta; *pasta asciutta* is properly not "dried" pasta (as opposed to fresh), but pasta that is drained after being boiled (as opposed to being served in broth)

pastella batter

pasticceria pastry, collectively as a food group; pastry shop. *Piccola pasticceria* means an assortment of small cakes and cookies (petits fours).

pasticciere as noun, pastry cook; as adjective, pertaining to pastry

pastiera (napoletana) characteristic (Neapolitan) cheesecake with slow-cooked whole kernels of wheat, orange water, candied fruit, and ricotta in a pastry crust; traditional for Easter

pastina small pasta for soup, as in *pastina in brodo*

pastinaca parsnip

pastizzada horse or donkey meat or beef, marinated in red wine and slowly braised; *pastizzada alla feltrina,* done with beef, calls for the addition of vinegar, cinnamon, and cloves (Veneto)

pasto meal

pastorizzato pasteurized

patanabò Jerusalem artichoke

patate potatoes

patatine potato chips; small potatoes or potatoes cut into pieces

pattona a kind of POLENTA; CATAGNACCIO (Toscana)

pavese, zuppa alla broth with bread, egg, and cheese (something like French onion soup with egg instead of onion)

pearà, salsa sauce of bread crumbs with butter, cheese, beef marrow, and broth, to go with boiled meats

pecorino sheep's milk cheese (the name comes from *pecora,* sheep); the family is large and varied, but most often its members are on the hard and sharp side. *Pecorino romano,* a hard, sharp cheese, is one of the major *pecorino* cheeses; it is produced in a geographically limited zone, which includes Lazio and Sardinia, as well as parts of Tuscany.

pedocchio COZZA

pelati, pomodori canned peeled tomatoes

pelle skin

penne pasta "quills," slim, tubular pasta cut on a slant; *penne all'arrabbiata,* with tomatoes, garlic, and PEPERONCINO

pentola (cooking) pot

peoci mussels

pepato peppered or spiced; *pan pepato,* gingerbread

pepe verde green peppercorns

pepe black pepper

peperonata stew of sweet peppers, onions, and tomatoes

peperoncino hot red peppers

peperone, pl. peperoni sweet bell pepper; *peperoni arrostiti,* sweet bell peppers, roasted and peeled (the word has nothing to do with the American pizza sausage called pepperoni)

pepolino = TIMO

peposo slow-cooked beef or veal stew from northern Toscana

pera pear; *pera cotogna,* quince; *pera cotta,* pear cooked in wine

pernice partridge

persa marjoram

persego = PESCE PERSICO

persichina = CEDRINA

persico trota black bass, large-mouthed bass, *Microptereus salmoides;* the American species, introduced into Italian lakes

persico, pesce perch

pesca noce nectarine

pesca, pl. pesche peach

pescatrice, rana see RANA PESCATRICE

pesce limone syn. PESCE SERRA

pesce serra bluefish, mackerel

pesce spada, pescespada swordfish

pesce, pl. pesci fish

pesche see PESCA

pescheria fish market; mix of very small fish for frying

pesciolini (pl.) small fish, usually fried

peso weight; *peso lordo,* gross weight; *peso netto,* net weight

pesto anything that has been *pestato,* pounded in a mortar, but usually meaning *pesto alla genovese,* the Ligurian sauce for pasta of basil and nuts; *pesto alla siciliana* (or *trapanese*) adds tomatoes. In Parma, the word *pesto* used alone means horse burger.

petto breast

pexe = PESCE (Veneto)

pezzo, pl. pezzi piece

piacere, a literally, at pleasure; meaning any way you like it, as much as you like

piastra plate or slab; in the kitchen, the term is applied to practically any hot flat surface where food is cooked. It can be an oven pan, a stove-top burner, a hotplate, a griddle, or a cast-iron grill pan. *Alla piastra* means cooked on the (steel) griddle.

piattino saucer, small plate

piatto plate; dish; course; *piatto fondo,* soup (or pasta) plate; *piatto piano,* dinner plate; *piatto unico,* one-dish meal. Eggs *al piatto* are fried. See also RISTORANTE DEL BUON RICORDO.

piccante piquant; spicy

piccata slices of boneless veal, sautéed, e.g., in butter with parsley and lemon (*al limone*) or with Marsala wine or done in many other versions

picchiante veal or beef lungs and spleen with herbs and tomatoes; the ingredients are first pounded (*picchiato*), hence the name (Toscana)

picchiapò NERVETTI with beans

piccione pigeon

piccola pasticceria *petite patisserie,* petits fours

piccolo little, small

pici handmade pasta similar to SPAGHETTI

piè di pellicano literally, pelican's foot; = MURICE SPINOSO

piedino trotter, foot

pieno full

pietanza meat or main dish; second course

pinoli, pignoli pine nuts

Pinot Bianco white grape used in many wines of northeastern Italy

Pinot Grigio dry white wine from northeastern Italy

Pinot Nero red grape and DOC wine of northeastern Italy

pinza several kinds of sweets made from bread or flour mixtures, dried and candied fruits, and the like (Veneto)

pinzimonio seasoned olive oil used for dipping crudités

pinzin fried strips of pasta made from flour, yeast, and broth (Veneto)

piselli peas; *piselli alla fiorentina,* peas cooked with onion and PROSCIUTTO CRUDO

pistacchio pistachio. Note pronunciation: pee-STAK-yo.

piunca = GATTUCCIO

pizza can be applied to virtually any sort of bread or pie, but is usually used for what is universally recognized as pizza. Some classic pizzas are *Margherita* (tomato and mozzarella), *quattro stagione* ("four seasons," with quadrants devoted to various ingredients, including mushrooms, artichokes, anchovies, prosciutto, and olives), and *napoletana* (in Rome: mozzarella, tomato, and anchovies).

pizza al taglio ready-made rectangular pizza cut in slices and sold by weight

pizza bianca in Rome, a plain PIZZA AL TAGLIO cooked without a topping, from which portion-sized slices are cut; these may be split horizontally and filled

pizzaiola, alla in tomato and olive oil sauce with oregano, usually used for a slice of beef

pizzetta, pl. pizzette tiny pizzas used as canapés or bar snack food

pizzicagnolo, pizzicaiolo = SALUMIERE

pizzoccheri buckwheat noodles, traditionally served with potatoes, cabbage, and cheese, a specialty of Valtellina in Lombardia

platessa see PASSERA

pocio, bigoli col BIGOLI with a hearty meat sauce

poenta = POLENTA

polenta porridge, pottage; best known as a thick cornmeal mush preparation something like grits, though other grains (and even potatoes) can be used; served as a pasta substitute, but can also be left to cool, then sliced and grilled

pollame poultry

pollanca young turkey

pollo chicken; *pollo alla diavola,* a chicken, split, flattened under a weight, brushed with oil, and grilled

polmone lung; *polmoncino,* the lung of something small

polpa lean, boneless meat; pulp or flesh of a fruit, or potentially anything else; *polpa di granchio,* crabmeat; *polpa di pomodoro,* peeled and seeded tomatoes

polpette, polpettine meatballs, patties, including meatless "meatballs" of other ingredients

polpettone meat loaf, often cooked in a pot rather than baked

polpo, polipo octopus

pomidoro variant spelling of POMODORO

pomodorino, pl. pomodorini diminutive of POMODORO; any small tomato; sun-dried tomato

pomodoro tomato; *pomodoro col riso,* tomato with rice, a large tomato filled with rice and baked, with potatoes on the side, eaten, usually in summer, as a PRIMO PIATTO

pompelmo grapefruit

porchetta herb-roasted hog, usually sold in slices at special stands with chewy bread; *in porchetta* refers to herb-roasting of other foods

porchetto roast suckling pig; diminutive of PORCO

porcini, funghi boletus mushrooms, cèpes

porco pig

porro leek

portata course (of a meal)

porzione serving; portion

posate flatware

potabile potable, drinkable

pralina praline; filled candy

pranzo lunch; dinner

prataioli field mushrooms; CHAMPIGNONS

precotto precooked

prenotazione reservation; *fare una prenotazione,* to make a reservation

prete, pesce = NASELLO

prezzemolo parsley

prezzo price

primavera, primaverile spring

primizie first fruits or vegetables of the season

primo first; early; *primo piatto,* the first course of the meal (not counting the antipasto), consisting of pasta, rice, or soup (often shortened to *primo*)

prodotto product; produced

produzione production; *produzione propria,* homemade; "own production," i.e., homemade, but sometimes in the same way a paint-by-numbers kit produces a piece of original art

pronto ready; ready-made

proposta bill of fare; suggestions

proprio (one's) own

prosciutto generically, ham; *prosciutto crudo,* "raw ham," what is called prosciutto in the U.S. and Parma ham in Britain; *prosciutto cotto* (cooked), boiled or baked ham

prosciutto di montagna general term for nonspecific artisanal PROSCIUTTO, which tends to be saltier than Parma and San Daniele and other prized hams, and is often sliced by hand; delicious on the saltless breads of central Italy

prosciutto di Parma a prized type of very sweet PROSCIUTTO CRUDO from a limited geographical area in Emilia-Romagna

Prosecco white wine grape and the DOC wine made from it, which is famously, but not always, sparkling

provatura a soft, fresh white cheese from cow's or buffalo's milk, similar to MOZZARELLA

provola fresh buffalo's milk cheese similar to SCAMORZA

provolone smooth, mellow, light-colored cheese in many versions

prugna plum; prune

pulcino young chicken

punta, pl. punte point, tip; tine (of a fork); *punta di vitello,* veal breast (see CIMA)

puntarelle the Roman name for *cicoria catalogna,* a bitter crunchy green vegetable, available only in the cooler months and customarily served *con la salsa,* a dressing of anchovies and garlic, mashed together in a mortar with olive oil and sometimes vinegar

purè, purea puréed, mashed; used by itself, it is nearly always shorthand for PURÈ DI PATATE, mashed potatoes

puttanesca, alla literally, whore's-style; a quick-cooked tomato sauce for spaghetti that contains black olives, capers, anchovies, and red pepper

quadretti, quadrucci small square egg pasta, usually used in broth

quaglie quails; a food the approximate size and shape of a very small quail

quaresimale Lenten; MARITOZZO

quartino quarter-liter carafe

quattro stagioni, pizza alle see PIZZA

quinto quarto "fifth quarter," the innards, tail, and other less-prized parts left over after an animal has been quartered

rabarbaro rhubarb

radicchio any of several species of chicory, red or green; *radicchio di Chioggia,* round-headed red chicory usually eaten raw; *radicchio di Treviso,* family of prized red chicories from the province of Treviso, usually cooked

ragù generically, a hearty sauce, usually meat sauce, and subject to great regional variation; cf. BOLOGNESE

rame copper, copper-colored

ramerino = ROSMARINO

rana frog; *ranocchio,* green frog

rana pescatrice monkfish, angler, anglerfish, frog-fish

rapa turnip

raperonzolo rampion, small wild turnip-like root

raviolo, pl. ravioli the basic small stuffed pasta, savory or sweet, in innumerable variations, but the most traditional filling is RICOTTA, with or without greens; cf. AGNOLOTTI

razza skate (ray)

Recioto a dessert wine from the Veneto

reginelle pasta strips with curly edges

regionale regional; from the region

rehaminà, indivia curly endive soup (a Roman Jewish dish)

renga = ARINGA (Veneto)

resto remainder; change (for money)

rete caul; net; mesh; *rete di maiale,* pork caul fat, is used with pork liver

reticolo honeycomb tripe

rhum rum

ribes red or black currants

ribollita bread-thickened kale soup (Toscana)

ricciarelli Sienese almond cookies, usually covered with powdered sugar

riccio literally, curl, as adjective, curly; *ricci di mare* are sea urchins (which are eaten raw or lightly cooked with oil, garlic, and white wine and then tossed with pasta)

ricciola amberjack, yellowtail; also called SERIOLA

richiesta (a) (by) request

ricotta a soft, very fresh cow's or sheep's cheese; *ricotta salata,* ricotta dried to a consistency for grating

rifatto literally, redone, remade; name given to a dish that might, e.g., include meat that is fried and then braised

rigaglie giblets

rigatoni short, hollow pasta tubes with a large hole; the name comes from the ridges around the sides

ripassato (in padella) sautéed after cooking; in the case of green vegetables, sautéed after boiling in olive oil with garlic and PEPERONCINO

ripieno stuffed, filled; as a noun, stuffing, filling. *Zucchine ripiene* are large zucchini hollowed out, filled with ground meat, and cooked in tomato sauce.

riposo settimanale a restaurant's weekly closing day

risi e bisi rice and peas in thick soup, a typical Venetian dish

riso rice; *insalata di riso,* rice salad, a standard summer dish usually containing small pickled vegetables, as well as small pieces of meat or fish

risolata RISOTTO with Romaine lettuce

risotto rice slow-cooked in broth to a creamy consistency, usually enriched with meat, vegetables, cheese, and other flavorings. Note that not all cooked rice is *risotto.*

ristorante can be generically restaurant, in the sense of any public eating place, but usually a degree of formality and service over and above the generic meaning is implied. Its range begins just above TRATTORIA and encompasses everything from modest to extremely elegant. See page 6.

Ristorante del Buon Ricordo member restaurant of the international Associazione del Buon Ricordo, which awards a souvenir plate to diners who order a particular dish, the Piatto del Buon Ricordo. The restaurants in the group tend to be well above average in quality and pretty upmarket, though not all are fancy.

ristretto concentrated; consommé; *caffè ristretto* is made with less water than usual

ritagli scraps; odd bits; trimmings

ritto literally, upright; *carciofi ritti* are Tuscan artichokes stuffed with parsley, garlic, and PANCETTA and braised in water and oil

robiola creamy, rich white cheese

rognone kidney; when the animal is small, the diminutive, *rognoncino,* is used

rollè roll; rolled roast

romanesco Roman; the adjective for anything Rome-grown, from the fresh vegetables to the accent

rombo brill, turbot; various flatfish (with both eyes on one side)

rosa, salsa pink sauce; dressing for shrimp cocktail or hard-cooked eggs, but also a tomato-and-cream sauce for pasta, popular in the 1970s

rosato pink; rosé

rosbif roast beef

rosetta anything rosette-shaped, but especially a kind of roll

rosmarino rosemary

rosso red; *rosso d'uovo,* egg yolk; *rosso siena,* a mild cheese from blended sheep's and cow's milk

rosticceria storefront eating place purveying, among other ready-to-eat foods, roasted meats, often only spit-roasted chicken; usually indistinguishable from a TAVOLA CALDA

rosticciana, rostisciada grilled pork chops (Toscana)

rotini wheel-shaped pasta

rubinetto, acqua del tap water

rubino ruby

rucola, rughetta, ruchetta rocket, arugula

rumine flat or smooth tripe

ruota wheel; in plural, *ruote,* wheel-shaped pasta

ruspante free-range

rustico rustic; country-style; standard adjective used in describing restaurant décor ranging from true country-style to total absence of any attempt at décor; various

savory snack foods, such as small pizzas; see also TORTA
RUSTICA

s.g. *secondo grandezza*—that is, by size

s.q. *secondo quantità,* according to quantity; appears on
menus in lieu of price for variable-quantity items, such as
antipasto from the buffet

sabato Saturday

saccarina saccharine

sacchetto (small) bag, sack

sagne stubby strips of pasta from chickpea or emmer flour;
LASAGNE

sagra festival

salame, pl. salami salami

salamoia brine; pickle

salatini salted crackers

salato salted; savory (as opposed to sweet)

sale salt

salmerino salmon trout, char

salmì game marinade; stew; *in salmì,* marinated in wine

salmistrato pickled

salmonata, trota salmon trout

salmone salmon—very popular but not Italian

salsa generically, sauce, condiment, also dip; *salsa verde,*
green sauce for BOLLITO MISTO of minced herbs, anchovies, and capers in a mild vinaigrette

salsamenteria store where cured meats and cheeses are
sold

salsiccia, pl. salsicce sausage, usually fresh

salsina an uncomplicated quick sauce or dressing

saltaleone = RICCIOLA (Toscana)

saltato literally, to jump or skip; *saltare in* PADELLA means
to sauté

saltimbocca alla romana literally, jump in the mouth; SCALOPPINE with PROSCIUTTO and a sage leaf attached with a toothpick

salumeria shop where SALUMI are sold

salumi (pl.) the entire category of cured, ready-to-eat pork products, including PROSCIUTTO, SALAME, and many others

salumiere vendor of SALUMI

salvia sage (herb)

sambuca anise-flavored liqueur, customarily served *con le mosche* ("with flies"), meaning with three coffee beans floating in it

sambuco elderberry

sampiero = PESCE SAN PIETRO (Veneto)

San Jacopo, conchiglia di = CAPASANTA

San Pietro, pesce John Dory, or St. Peter's fish

Sangiovese principal red grape of Italy

sangue blood; *al sangue*, rare

sanguinaccio blood pudding, black pudding, blood sausage; sweet pudding made of pig's blood with chocolate

sanpiero = PESCE SAN PIETRO

santoreggia summer savory

saor sweet vinegar and onion marinade for fish, *sarde in saor* (Venice)

sapere to know; *sapere di (qualcosa)*, to taste like (something), to have the flavor of; *il vino sa di tappo*, the wine is corked

sapiotto = LAMPREDA

sarago white bream

sarda sardine

sardela = ACCIUGA (Veneto, Marche)

sardella = SARDINA

sardôn = ACCIUGA (Veneto)

sargo white bream

sauté, sautè used as a noun, clams or mussels cooked over high heat with a little tomato and served with their broth

sbirraglia, risi in a rice soup with chicken RIGAGLIE

sbriciolona a crumbly Tuscan sausage (from *briciola,* crumb)

sbucciato peeled

scaglie scales; flakes; shavings; *scaglie di* PARMIGIANO, made with quick short strokes of the cheese slicer, are modish (but good) on various salads and pastas

scalogna, scalogno shallot

scaloppine thin-sliced, pounded veal scallops; scallops of other meats, such as turkey or pork

scamorza a pear-shaped white cheese that can be melted on the grill and served as a main course

scampo, pl. scampi Dublin Bay prawn; langoustine; Norway lobster. Note that in Italy *scampi* is the name of the animal, not the prepared dish, and that *scampi* are not shrimp.

scampolo = SCAMPO

scarola escarole

scatola, in canned; *scatolame,* canned goods

scelta choice; *a scelta* means as you choose, however you like; *di prima scelta,* as a modifier, means first choice

schiacciato crushed; flattened

schie, schile tiny brown shrimp of the Venetian lagoon

schienale, pl. schienali on a menu, spinal marrow, though the word can have various meanings having to do with backs

schiuma foam; mousse; *schiuma di mare,* very small anchovies

sciapo, sciocco without salt; *pane sciapo* or *sciocco,* bread made without salt in the dough

scontrino cash-register slip, cash-register receipt; under the complicated Italian fiscal laws, this is to be distinguished from a *ricevuta,* or proper receipt you can deduct from your taxes

scopeton = ARINGA; herring fillets in oil with herbs, sometimes served over POLENTA (Veneto)

scorfano Mediterranean scorpionfish (*rascasse*)

scottadito, abbacchio a literally, finger scorchers; plain grilled lamb chops, usually pounded before cooking

scottiglia Tuscan dish consisting of several varieties of chopped meats stewed with wine, tomato, and herbs; sometimes referred to as a meat CACCIUCCO

scuro dark; the opposite is CHIARO, as in chiaroscuro

secchiello ice bucket, wine cooler

secco dry, used for wine, the air, the desert, dehydrated foods; it can also mean thin (for a person); cf. ASCIUTTO

secoe, secole bits of meat from beef backbone, used in a classic Venetian RISOTTO

secondo second, often used alone, short for *secondo piatto,* to mean the second, or main, course; as preposition, according to; *secondo mercato,* depending on what is available in the market; *secondo quantità* (abbr. S.Q.), according to how much you consume

sedanini short tubular pasta

sedano celery; *sedani,* a pasta shape similar to rigatoni; *sedano rapa, sedano di Verona,* celeriac

sedia chair

segale rye

seggiolone high chair for the *bambino*

sella saddle of lamb, veal, venison, or rabbit, or potentially anything with hind legs

seltz soda water

selvaggina any game animal; *selvaggina da piuma* is feathered game, *da pelo,* furred

selvaggio, selvatico undomesticated; wild (plant or animal)

semifreddo literally, half-cold; generic term for ice cream–based desserts; type of soft ice cream made with meringue and whipped cream

semolino ground durum wheat flour, called semolina in English

senape mustard; cf. MOSTARDA

senza without

seppia cuttlefish; *seppioline,* very small cuttlefish; *uova di seppia,* cuttlefish roe, which is white, mild-flavored, and somewhat scallop-like in form

servizio service; service charge

settembre September

sfiziosità anything that catches the fancy; something tasty, usually savory rather than sweet

sfogio = SOGLIOLA

sfoglia rolled sheet pasta; mille-feuille; phyllo pastry; = SOGLIOLA

sfogliatine Venetian puff pastry cookies

sformato flan or savory pudding made in a mold (*forma*) and turned out

sfuso (in) bulk; i.e., not packaged; *vino sfuso* is bulk wine

sgombro mackerel

sgranato husked; shelled; *fagioli sgranati* are fresh beans, just removed from their pods, as opposed to reconstituted from a dehydrated state, which are just called *fagioli*

sgroppino liquidy sorbet containing alcohol

sguazzetto alla bechera stewed innards

sgusciato shelled

sidro cider

sofisticazione adulteration

sogliola sole

soncino lamb's lettuce (corn salad); = VALERIANELLA

sopressa a Veneto sausage

sorbetto sherbet, sorbet

sorgente spring; source (of mineral water)

sotè = SAUTÉ

sottaceti pickled vegetables

sottile thin

sottoli, sott'oli vegetables conserved in oil

souté = SAUTÉ

spada, pesce swordfish

spadon = PESCE SPADA

spaghetti classic long thin pasta of hard-wheat flour and water, usually made industrially by extrusion

spalla shoulder

spannocchio = GAMBERO

sparaglione close relative of the SARAGO

specialità specialty, specialties

speck a type of smoked PROSCIUTTO

spezie spices

spezzatino a rather dry stew

spiedini skewers; brochettes; shish kebab

spiedo, allo spit-roasted

spigola sea bass, striped bass; = BRANZINO

spina, birra alla draft beer

spina, pl. spine bone (of a fish)

spina, uva gooseberry

spinaci (pl.) spinach

sporco dirty

spremuta fresh-squeezed juice

spuma foam, froth

spuntature spareribs, usually served with POLENTA; often used to make sauce; can also be applied to other regional cuts of meat

spuntino snack

squisito exquisite (one of the standard exclamations for something delicious)

stagionale of the season

stagionato aged; seasoned

stagione season

stampo mold; form

starna gray partridge

stinco veal or pork shank, often roasted, also braised

stoccafisso, stocco stockfish, air-dried cod; dried (unsalted) cod (cf. BACCALÀ)

storione sturgeon

stra- prefix meaning "extra," as, for example, *stravecchio,* extra old

stracchino a soft, fresh white cheese

stracci, straccetti literally, rags, small pieces of beef cooked in oil, often with RUGHETTA or CARCIOFI; irregularly shaped pasta pieces

stracciatella alla romana egg-drop broth, in which the egg drops are supposed to resemble rags (*stracci*); *stracciatella,* an ice cream, sort of like chocolate chip, in which the chocolate supposedly resembles the eggs in *stracciatella alla romana*

stracotto long-cooked beef pot roast

strangolapreti, strozzapreti literally, priest-chokers; one of many homemade flour-and-water pastas with fanciful names

strangozzi short hollow eggless fettuccine

strapazzate, uova scrambled eggs

strapponi broad noodles

strascinato describes vegetables that are first boiled or steamed and then sautéed with oil, hot pepper, and garlic; RIPASSATO

stravecchio very old; aged for a long time

struzzo ostrich

stufato, stufatino stew or pot roast cooked slowly for a long time over a low flame

stuzzicadente toothpick

stuzzichino *amuse-gueule* or *-bouche,* the pre-appetizer offered gratis by some restaurants

su on

succo juice. Individual bottles of *succo di frutta,* fruit juice, are a staple of the bar menu; to specify fresh, ask for a SPREMUTA.

sud south

sugo sauce; juice

suino pork

sultanina a variety of green grape used for raisins

superalcolici hard liquor

supplemento extra charge

supplì al telefono rice croquettes, made and sold in pizzerias, containing a glob of mozzarella, which forms long strings when melted—like telephone cords

surgelato frozen

suro horse mackerel, jack mackerel; a PESCE AZZURRO similar to SGOMBRO

susina verde greengage plum

susine plums; *susine secche,* prunes

tacchino, tacchina turkey; hen turkey

taccole broad bean; sugar snap pea; snow peas (pea pods)

tagliare to cut

tagliata thinly sliced beef, usually served rare with a condiment

tagliatelle flat noodles, often made with egg; essentially the same as FETTUCCINE

tagliere cutting board; bread board; a board brought to the table with an assortment of foods for tasting, such as salamis

taglierini narrow flat strands of fresh pasta

taglio cut; *al taglio,* by the piece, often used in reference to pizza

tagliolini narrow flat strands of pasta

taleggio rich, very slightly sharp cow's milk cheese from Lombardia, closely related to STRACCHINO; of protected origin

talleri thin pasta disks

tarocchi prized red oranges from Sicily

tartara tartare; chopped raw meat

tartina, pl. tartine canapés, little bread hors d'oeuvres with varied toppings; French *tartine*

tartufo truffle; *tartufo (di mare),* a kind of clam; *tartufato,* with a truffle flavor; an ice cream "truffle" whose industrial version is popular in pizzerias

taverna tavern; pub; OSTERIA

tavola table; *tavola, da:* for wine, table wine; for cheese, table cheese, eating cheese; *tavola calda,* an eatery offering (mostly) hot food, (mostly) ready to serve, a steam table, shopfront or part of a bar; a *tavola fredda* provides the same service for cold foods

tazza cup, teacup; an ESPRESSO cup is a *tazzina;* cf. BICCHIERE

tè, thè tea

tegame pan; frying pan; *in tegame,* fried, braised, pan-roasted

tegamino small frying pan; shallow dish or frying pan

tellina a tiny clam with a triangular shell

tenerumi soft gristle, cartilage; often part of a BOLLITO MISTO

tenuta farm; estate

Terni, pane tipo bread made without salt

terrina terrine, pâté

testina (di vitello) (calf's) head cut up and dressed to look like an innocent antipasto dish

testoni young eels

tiepido tepid, lukewarm; room-temperature

timballo timbale; traditionally, a pie or varied ingredients baked in a mold

timo thyme; thymus gland

tinca tench (fish)

tipico typical; characteristic

tipo type

tiramisù literally, pick me up; ubiquitous rich, layered dessert of sponge cake with brandy and ESPRESSO, MASCARPONE with egg, and chocolate

tisana tisane, herb tea

toast *un toast,* a grilled cheese and ham sandwich, available at nearly any bar in Italy; toasted bread is *pane tostato,* but see BRUSCHETTA

tonica, acqua tonic water

tonnarelli squared strands of pasta

tonno tuna

topinambur, topinambolo Jerusalem artichoke

torchio a press, as for grapes, duck, or olives; a special instrument for making certain pastas (e.g., BIGOLI)

Torcolato a dessert wine from the Veneto

tordelli = TORTELLI; Tuscan half-moon–shaped pasta with a filling of veal brains and meat, eggs, and herbs, dressed with a veal RAGÙ

tordo thrush

torrefazione the roasting of coffee or seeds; the place where the freshly roasted product is sold

torrone nougat candy made of honey, nuts, and egg whites

torta cake; tart; pastry; pie; *torta fritta,* a type of CRESCENTE; *torta rustica,* a savory pie

tortelli a stuffed pasta

tortellini small filled pasta with meat, properly served in BRODO

tortino a small flan

toscanello sharp sheep's milk cheese, aged at least six months

totano squid

totariello little squid

tovaglia tablecloth

tovagliolo napkin

tozzetti hazelnut BISCOTTI resembling CANTUCCI

tradizionale traditional

tramezzino sandwich. Sold ready-made in bars, these are characterized by their triangular shape and industrial bread.

trancia, trancio slice

trattoria a catchall term for any informal restaurant, especially small family-run ones specializing in local home-style cooking. Unlike even more informal eating places, at the trattoria, tables are set and customers are served. See page 6.

Trebbiano ubiquitous white grape of central Italy

trenette linguine

trevisano, trevigiano of Treviso

trifolato literally, truffled; usually used for vegetables or kidneys, ROGNONI, meaning sliced very thin and sautéed with garlic and parsley

triglia, pl. triglie red mullet

triplo triple. The proper name of the dish known to the world as "fettuccine Alfredo" is FETTUCCINE *al triplo* BURRO—with triple butter.

trippa tripe; *trippa alla romana,* with tomato sauce, grated PECORINO, and mint; *trippa alla fiorentina,* with tomato sauce and Parmesan cheese

tris three-pasta sampler plate

tritato minced; ground

trittico literally, triptych; = TRIS

trofie, troffie   GNOCCHI-like pasta from Genoa

trota   trout; *trota iridea,* rainbow trout; *trota salmonata,* a pink-fleshed trout

trotella   small TROTA

tuorlo   egg yolk

ubriaco   drunken

uccelletti   small birds; *all'uccelletto,* literally like little birds, usually means cooked with sage or bay leaves; *fagioli all'uccelletto,* slow-cooked white beans in olive oil, sage, and tomatoes

umido   wet, damp; humid; *in umido,* in liquid, i.e., stewed, moist-cooked; *sugo d'umido* is the stew's sauce, which can be served separately over pasta

unto   oily, greasy

uovo, pl. uova   egg(s); *uovo sodo,* hard-cooked egg

uva spina   gooseberry

uva   grape, grapes; *uva passa,* semi-dried grapes (see PAS-SITO); *uva secca,* raisins

uvetta   raisins

vaccinara, coda alla   oxtail braised slowly with tomato sauce and celery, from the Roman tradition of the QUINTO QUARTO

valeriana, valerianella   lamb's lettuce (corn salad)

vaniglia   vanilla

vapore, al   steamed

vassoio   tray, platter

vegetale   vegetable (as opposed to animal or mineral)

vegetariano   vegetarian

vellutato   creamy, smooth; *vellutata,* a smooth soup

venerdì   Friday

Venexiana   Veneziana

ventresca   the preserved belly of the tuna; potentially, anything involving belly meat, e.g., a Tuscan dish based on pork belly

ventriglio gizzard

verace true, real; most often applied to a type of small clams (VONGOLE VERACI)

verde green; young; unripe

verdura greens, the category of vegetables (including those of other colors)

vermicelli thin spaghetti

vermut vermouth. Note that the pronunciation is regular for Italian: VER-moot.

verza Savoy cabbage

vetro glass; bottle

vigna, vigneto vineyard

vignarola springtime Roman dish of braised fresh peas, fava beans, and artichokes, with the possible addition of GUANCIALE

Vin Santo Tuscan aromatic dessert wine, traditionally served with CANTUCCI

vino wine; *vino della casa,* house wine; *vino da arrosto,* wine for roasts, i.e., big reds; *vino da pasto,* table wine, now replaced by VINO DA TAVOLA as a legal designation; *vino novello,* see NOVELLO

visciole a type of AMARENA; CROSTATA *di visciole,* a traditional Roman dessert

vitella, vitello veal

vitello tonnato, vitel tonné a cold sliced pot-roasted veal masked in a sauce of mayonnaise, tuna, and capers

volatile poultry, fowl

volpina large MUGGINE (Veneto)

vongole clams; *vongole veraci,* small clams with a pair of tiny "horns" on the meat

wurstel frankfurter

zabaglione a dessert of egg yolks, sugar, and Marsala, or an ice cream of the same flavor; sweetened egg custard with Marsala; often spelled *zabaione*

zafferano saffron

zaletti crisp cornmeal cookies (Veneto)

zamarugolo = MURICE SPINOSO

zampa, zampetto leg, foot, trotter

zampone boned pig's foot stuffed with chopped pork, rind, ears, snout, and sinew, a prized element of a classic BOL-LITO MISTO

zarzegna duck, teal

zenzero ginger; red pepper

zimino sauce of tomato, olive oil, and parsley, also usually spinach or chard and hot pepper; fish stew; *calamari in zimino,* stewed squid or cuttlefish

zolletta (sugar) cube

zucca pumpkin; squash, winter squash; see also FIORE.

zucchero sugar

zucchine, zucchini summer squash, zucchini

zuccotto a type of SEMIFREDDO made in a hemispherical mold

zuppa soup; various items of different degrees of soupiness, e.g., *zuppa inglese,* literally, "English soup," because it supposedly resembles English trifle. Though it is subject to wide variation, the usual ingredients include PAN DI SPAGNA layered with CREMA PASTICCIERA and soaked in liqueurs.

Selected Bibliography

THE FOLLOWING WORKS were of particular use in preparation of this book.

Ashley, Maureen. *Italian Wines*. London: J. Sainsbury, 1990.

Cesari Sartoni, Monica. *Dizionario del Ghiottone Viaggiatore, Italia*. Bologna: Fuori Thema/Tempi Stretti, 1994.

Claridge, Amanda. *Rome: An Oxford Archaeological Guide*. Oxford and New York: Oxford University Press, 1998.

Davidson, Alan. *Mediterranean Seafood*. 2nd ed. Baton Rouge: Louisiana State University Press, 1981.

De Vita, Oretta Zanini. *The Food of Rome and Lazio: History, Folklore, and Recipes*. Rome: Alphabyte Books, 1994.

Fant, Maureen B. *Eat Like the Romans*. Rome: Alphabyte Books, 1992.

———, and Howard M. Isaacs. *Dictionary of Italian Cuisine*. Hopewell, NJ: Ecco Press, 1998.

Muscatine, Doria. *A Cook's Tour of Rome*. New York: Charles Scribner's Sons, 1964.

Osterie d'Italia 2000. Bra: Slow Food Arcigola Editore, 1999.

Roma 2000. Rome: Gambero Rosso Editore, 1999.

Time Out Guide Florence and Tuscany. London: Time Out Guides, 1999.

Time Out Guide Venice. London: Time Out Guides, 1999.

Willinger, Faith Heller. *Eating in Italy.* Rev. ed. New York: William Morrow, 1998.

Zardo, Manuela, and Jakob Brandis. *Bàcari a Venezia: Mangiare e Bere a Venezia.* Bolzano: Frasnelli-Keitsch, 1994.

Index